Westward into Kentucky

Westward into Kentucky

The Narrative of
DANIEL TRABUE

Edited by
Chester Raymond Young

With a New Foreword by
Daniel Blake Smith

THE UNIVERSITY PRESS OF KENTUCKY

Publication of this volume was made possible in part
by a grant from the National Endowment for the Humanities.

Copyright © 1981 by The University Press of Kentucky
Paperback edition 2004

Scholarly publisher for the Commonwealth,
serving Bellarmine University, Berea College, Centre
College of Kentucky, Eastern Kentucky University,
The Filson Historical Society, Georgetown College,
Kentucky Historical Society, Kentucky State University,
Morehead State University, Murray State University,
Northern Kentucky University, Transylvania University,
University of Kentucky, University of Louisville,
and Western Kentucky University.
All rights reserved.

Editorial and Sales Offices: The University Press of Kentucky
663 South Limestone Street, Lexington, Kentucky 40508-4008
www.kentuckypress.com

Library of Congress Cataloging-in-Publication Data
Trabue, Daniel, 1760-1840.
   Westward into Kentucky : the narrative of Daniel Trabue / edited by Chester
Raymond Young ; with a new foreword by Daniel Blake Smith.
     p. cm.
   Originally published: 1981.
   Includes bibliographical references and index.
   ISBN 0-8131-9119-X (pbk. : alk. paper)
   1. Trabue, Daniel, 1760-1840. 2. Pioneers—Kentucky—Biography. 3. Pioneers
—Virginia—Biography. 4. Frontier and pioneer life—Kentucky. 5. Frontier and
pioneer life—Virginia. 6. Kentucky—Description and travel. 7. Virginia—Description and travel. 8. Virginia—History—Revolution, 1775-1783. 9. Kentucky—Biography. 10. Virginia—Biography.   I. Young, Chester Raymond, 1920-   .
II. Title.
F454.T728 2004
976.9'02'092—dc22
[B]   2004014888
ISBN-13: 978-0-8131-9119-5 (pbk. : alk. paper)

This book is printed on acid-free paper meeting
the requirements of the American National Standard
for Permanence in Paper for Printed Library Materials.

Manufactured in the United States of America.

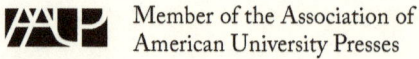

Member of the Association of
American University Presses

Contents

Foreword vii

Preface xi

Introduction 1

THE NARRATIVE OF DANIEL TRABUE

1. The Huguenot Heritage 37
2. A Martial Introduction to the Kentucky Wilderness 44
3. Disruptive Indian Incursions 51
4. The "Big Siege" of Boonesborough 57
5. The "Hard Winter" of 1779–1780 69
6. The Captivity and Escape of Two Trabue Brothers 79
7. Militia Service in Old Virginia 95
8. Wartime Stress on Civilian Life 106
9. Yorktown and War's End 114
10. The Separate Baptists of Revolutionary Virginia 128
11. Postwar Conditions in Trans-Appalachia 134
12. Violence on the Kentucky Frontier 146

Notes 155

Bibliographical Essay 200

Index 209

To Tossie
with love

Foreword
Daniel Blake Smith

Kentucky began as a dream. For some, it promised an edenic paradise across the mountains; for others, it was hope for a second chance, a place to start over. One of the many virtues of Daniel Trabue's colorful *Westward into Kentucky* lies in the evocative way that it captures the seductive sense of wonder and hope that beckoned borderers. Just as memorably, it suggests the gritty and bitter reality of dashed dreams in early Kentucky.

As a young adolescent in revolutionary Virginia, Daniel Trabue's interest in Kentucky was stimulated initially with the stories told by his older brother James. James Trabue, a lieutenant serving under Governor Dunsmore, regaled Daniel with tales about Kentucky, the promised land, "a new Decovered wonderfull country" (42). But Kentucky was more than just a story to the Trabue family; it was a "great calculation." Four years later, when Trabue was eighteen, he joined his brother James in a venture into the wilds of Kentucky. "We entered the wilderness in high spirits," Trabue noted. "I was truly Delighted in seeing the mountains, Rivers, hills, etc. . . . Every thing looked new to me" (44). Later, while tracking Indians past the Cumberland Gap and down the mountain, he observed how bewildering and disorienting this new land was to him, "It looked like I was going out of the world" (45). And upon encountering Indian devastations and abandoned cabins, Trabue "began to feel strange" (44).

Trabue's narrative offers up more than a "wonderfull country"; it showcases a powerful, transforming experience that both required and revealed an odd mixture of bravado and fear, individual determination and family devotion. Life on the borderlands tested Trabue's manhood and militia training, and like other long hunters and settlers who left behind memoirs, Trabue was eager to focus on acts of courage—especially his own. At one point, a small company of young men traveling with Trabue confided to him that they were afraid of pushing on not only because of the danger of Indian attacks but also because of the fear of getting lost in the wilderness and running short of food. Trabue clearly enjoyed contrasting his own confidence and courage against their fears: "As to finding the way I was not uneasy about that as I knew about steering in the woods. I could find the way as I had been their" (71). Having considerable skills in the woods gave Trabue confidence that many others lacked. Trabue relished the story of his timid friends out in the Kentucky woods who, while feasting on a "large fat Rackoon," began to whine and worry about their fate: "We are in a wilderness without any path, nothing to eat but a koon for 6 or 7 Men without Bread or Salt, liable every moment to be Masscreed by the Indians." They were all ready to scamper back to the safety of the fort. "One of them," Trabue recalled, "said he would return to Old Virginia as quick as he could and them that liked Kentucky might enjoy it but he would not stay in such a country" (71).

If competence in the woods was helpful to settlers, courage was downright necessary. And for young men like Trabue cowardice was simply unacceptable. A young man in the militia who tried to parlay his sickness into an excuse to avoid combat received universal disdain. His commanding officer swore "he would cut of[f] his head as he was a Coward." Trabue's opinion was no less harsh: "I make no Doubt but this young man was sick, but it was fear that was the cause of it and Major Boyse cured him" (102).

And yet despite all the bravado that pervades Trabue's account, even a cursory reading of this memoir reveals the fear that lurked beneath every Indian attack, every harsh winter, and every moment spent lost in the woods. From Trabue's perspective, Indians were clearly dangerous and "cuning" enemies—oftentimes "waching the roads, killing Men, or steeling our horses, or killing our cattle" (51). Trabue confessed that his "heart would go piti pat," any time he sensed the presence of Indians. Early on, in a truly remarkable passage, he gave voice to his deep-seated fears about being "defeeted," which could come not only at the hands of angry Indians but also from within, by simply giving in to weakness: "I for my part began to feel chikinhearted. I was afraid I should be killed in this Drary howling Wilderness but I never mentioned it to any one. I thought if we come in contact with the indians I would keep behind or in the reare, but I thought that would not Do as I might be called a coward" (45).

Maintaining one's dignity was nearly as important as simply staying alive. And according to Trabue and other early pioneers, that was no easy task. Much of Trabue's account consists of descriptions of numerous hunting expeditions to find food. There was a massive amount of buffalo and turkey killed in the wilds of Kentucky that thinned out the meat supply all too quickly. In the especially hard winter of 1779–80, Trabue reported that nearly all of the game and livestock were gone, with very little corn in the fields. Trabue's observations are terse but evocative: "The people was in great Distress. Many in the wilderness frosbit. Some Dead. Some eat of the dead cattle and horses" (75). Sometimes hunters found themselves caught between hunger and fear—as when Trabue remembers wanting to retrieve some meat that his company of hunters had left hanging up only to realize that their meat supply was now being watched by Indians as well.

Such moments of frustration must have been frequent and painful—and they sometimes prompted both regret for having ever entered Kentucky and fantasies about the lives they had left behind. Trabue and his friend Jeffrey Davis headed for the deer licks one day looking to hunt, but they could find nothing to kill. "When we was lying and waching the lick," Trabue remembered, "Mr. Davis said, 'If we was only now in Old Virginia. At this very time their is preaching at Dupuy's Meeting house. So many prerty Girles their. If I was their I could go with some of them and eat a good Dinur, have something good to Drink. But hear we are. Nothing to eat in this Dreary Wilderness, and we Don't know when we shall if ever get anything to eat'" (76).

Besides sheer survival instinct, what sustained men like Trabue while they were out on the margins of society as they knew it were their family memories and connections. Despite a frontier ethos that prized individualism and personal courage, the truth about early settlers is that they rarely came alone or operated by themselves. Removal to the West was nearly always a family decision; for the Trabues, it involved several brothers who helped one another settle in Kentucky.[1] Daniel's relations and former neighbors came to see him frequently, and he also visited them in Virginia. During one memorable visit the whole family—which included one of Trabue's cousins, who was also named Daniel Trabue—took to calling the author "Kentucky Daniel" and calling his cousin "River Daniel," as he lived on the James River (67).

Whatever survival issues loomed on the frontier, family clearly weighed heavily in the minds and hearts of the Trabue boys. Despite Daniel's desperate request to be trusted to go alone on a dangerous errand, his brother James refused. The risk was simply too high for their mother to bear. "If any thing would happin to you," James told him, "how could I Ever see our Mother? She would say, 'James, how come you to lit Daniel go on such an errand?'" (55). Daniel frequently worried about his mother in Virginia, especially with his brother James fighting the Indians and another brother serving in the Revolutionary militia. What would happen, he wondered, to his mother who "had no son of any size [at home], only a parsil of children and many Nigros that was not easy to manage" (81).

Of course, long hunters and woodsmen who spent extended stretches away from home, including years of captivity with the Indians, ran the risk of losing their families. Historians are well aware of "Boone's Surprise," when Daniel Boone returned after years in Kentucky to find that his wife had conceived a child with another man—his own brother.[2] Trabue tells a similar story—one with less permanent impact—of a veteran woodsman and hunter who after several years of Indian captivity escaped and returned to his home in Bedford County, Virginia. There, to his chagrin, he found that neither his father, his mother, nor even his wife recognized him. Other settlers that he knew, Trabue claimed, returned home only to discover that their spouses, thinking them dead, had married other people.

Despite all of the hope and wonder, Kentucky could dash dreams more quickly than it could fulfill them. Nowhere is this conveyed with greater sadness than in Trabue's own overwhelming sorrow when his world of family and westward ambition exploded. While Trabue made his way back to Kentucky from Virginia in 1780, he learned that his beloved brother John, who had also explored Kentucky in the mid 1770s, had died. Meanwhile, his brother James had been captured during the Revolution and was "now with the Indians or british and uncertain whether we ever would see one another again. My land warrants gone and the land located by others. My great calculation in Kentucky seemed to be blasted" (89).

Trabue recovered his "calculation," but his legacy, like so much else in early Kentucky, turned out different than he had imagined. What Trabue has left behind is a remarkable memoir of this formative moment in Kentucky's past. Historians continue to mine the pages of *Westward into Kentucky*, to find revealing insights into a wide range of issues concerning life on the borderlands. From Boone's court-martial to settler's perceptions of ethnicity and environment and to cultural attitudes toward Native Americans, Trabue's narrative continues to fascinate.[3] And for general readers, one cannot easily find a more engrossing guide than Daniel Trabue's indelible portrait of a young man's hopes and fears on the Kentucky frontier.

Daniel Blake Smith
University of Kentucky

Notes

1. See Stephen Aron, *How the West Was Lost: The Transformation of Kentucky from Daniel Boone to Henry Clay* (Baltimore: Johns Hopkins University Press, 1996).

2. See John Mack Faragher, *Daniel Boone: The Life and Legend of an American Pioneer* (New York: Henry Holt & Company, Inc., 1993).

3. In addition to the works of Aron and Faragher cited above, see also Craig Thompson Friend, ed., *"The Buzzel About Kentuck": Settling the Promised Land* (Lexington: University Press of Kentucky, 1998) and Elizabeth A. Perkins, *Border Life: Experience and Memory in the Revolutionary Ohio Valley* (Chapel Hill: University of North Carolina Press, 1998).

Preface

During my high-school years at Columbia, Kentucky, I first heard about Daniel Trabue. While working on a project under the National Youth Administration in 1937—to produce a typescript of the historical articles of Judges Herschel C. Baker and Rollin M. Hurt, which had appeared two decades earlier in the weekly newspaper of the town, *The Adair County News*—I discovered that Trabue had written in Columbia a narrative which had survived as part of the Draper Collection of Manuscripts at Madison, Wisconsin.

Also I hold pleasant childhood memories concerning one of Trabue's grandnieces, Matilda Jane Trabue. Even yet I can see Miss Tilly, as she was affectionately called, parking her horse-drawn buggy in front of the Columbia Baptist Church, at which she was a faithful worshipper. She had a deep interest in the work of the Baptist Young People's Union and annually welcomed that group to a picnic at her rural estate just beyond the county seat of the Old Greensburg Road.

Only a few years ago did I learn that one of the town druggists of my youthful days at Columbia—the late Thomas C. Brown—was a great-great-grandson of Daniel Trabue. I appreciated him, the earliest descendant of Daniel I have known, for his concern about the editing of his forebear's narrative and for his assistance to me in this endeavor.

The manuscript of Daniel Trabue's work is owned by the State Historical Society of Wisconsin. Through its acting director, Richard A. Erney, the organization has permitted this publication of the narrative. For its cooperation I am very grateful. Miss Josephine L. Harper, the reference archivist of the society, has extended to me uniformly prompt and courteous service over a number of years. Also thanks are due Robert Michael Duncan, Inez, Kentucky, for his provision of photocopies of Trabue's manuscript.

Three Columbia women—Mrs. Allie Garnett Cundiff, Mrs. Ruth Paull Burdette, and Mrs. Nancy Montgomery Berley—have been just as enthusiastic about this edition as they would have been about one dealing with the writing of one of their early ancestors in Adair County. To these dear friends, who have actively gone far out of their way to enhearten and aid me in my work, I owe an unpayable debt.

By many a librarian and many an archivist I have been befriended in countless ways. Especially do I appreciate the urbane help shown me by the staffs of the Virginia State Library in Richmond, the Norma Jeanne Perkins Hagan Memorial Library at Cumberland College, and the clerks' offices of the Adair Circuit and Adair County courts.

Numerous historians and other persons have generously shared their knowledge with me. Patient encouragement from Professor Douglas Edward Leach of Vanderbilt University has been a refreshing boon during barren seasons. For their help in numerous ways over an extended period, I am indebted to a number of colleagues at Cumberland College, including Professors John E. Lancaster, Jeannette M. Palmer, Rayford Watts, Charles M. Dupier, Jr., and Richard W. Foley.

A group of student researchers at this institution, who worked as my assistants, rendered yeoman's service when I carried the regular duties of teaching. These young men were David Eugene Shinkle, Eddie Joe Wilburn, Arthur Boebinger, Richard Bryan Stokes, Philip James Davis, William Frank Thompson, Donald Morrow Black, Russell Wayne Steele, Daniel Lee VanOver, and Warren Dale Waddell. My typists, Mrs. Maxine Martin and Mrs. Glenda Helton Tarvin, did their duty with wonted skill and dispatch. To David Kent Humphreys, my son-in-law, I express a word of thanks for the well-executed drawings in this book. To Peter Michael DiMuro, Jr., I make known my gratitude for his efficient work as proofreader and indexer.

Through the kindness of President James M. Boswell, Cumberland College subsidized the publication of this volume. I am doubly grateful to him for this support.

To the director and editors of the University Press of Kentucky goes my appreciation for their interest and encouragement in the production of this work.

Since Daniel Trabue penned his narrative 154 years have come and gone. Were he aware that at long last all the words of his story are to appear in print for the first time, I feel that he would give his hearty consent.

Introduction

When Daniel Trabue came home from Yorktown in the fateful autumn of 1781—home to his widowed mother's farm on Tomahawk Creek in upper Chesterfield County, Virginia—his head was full of unforgettable memories and his pockets were full of jingling specie, the coin of several kings' realms. The memories he would use as the stock-in-trade of the raconteur, not that of the historian or the philosopher. The coin he would use in pursuing business enterprises. Daniel was destined to tell and retell the things he himself had experienced and the happenings friends had recounted to him. Calling back his yesterdays, he would simply repeat these accounts, not interpret them as the scholar would do years later with the perspective that the passage of time brings.

In the decades ahead Trabue must have told these stories over and over countless times to his children and grandchildren. All who had a mind to listen probably became his audience—boys and girls in the neighborhood, farmers who took their turn at his grist mill, customers at his frontier store, travelers who warmed themselves before his tavern fireplace, anxious men who came to his house to make a deposition or to swear to the contents of a legal document, idle whittlers gathered at the courthouse on the town square, or church representatives who waited under the shade of great trees for the summer sessions of the Baptist association to begin. These listeners would repeat his tales too and change them by their retelling in the way that storytellers had done for ages.

In one respect, however, Daniel was to be different from most narrators: he proposed to commit his stories to paper. And he did just that in 1827 in the little village of Columbia in southern Kentucky, where he had finally settled down. There amid his financial woes, his burdens as a public servant, and his difficulties in building an iron bloomery he put on paper—148 pages of it have survived, thanks to the gathering hand of Lyman Copeland Draper—the things he had so often talked about.

Striking the mystic chords of memory, he dwells on traditions of his French ancestors, on childhood events, on the adventures of three epical years on the Kentucky frontier, on what he did and observed as a soldier and sutler in Virginia during the closing year of the Revolutionary War, and on his experiences as a settler in the Bluegrass country. Trabue does not carry the story forward into the next century, and history is accordingly poorer. Perhaps he never found time after 1827. He kept busy, and there were many things to worry him.

The story that Daniel Trabue relates is significant for its poignant account of the fear that seized him as a teenager during his first brush with Indians on the Wilderness Road, its singular recording of Daniel Boone's court-martial following his valiant defense of Boonesborough in 1778, its picture of the rapid depletion of the buffalo herds in Kentucky, its description of suffering and deprivation in the backcountry during the "Hard Winter" of 1779-1780, its vivid depiction of the siege of Yorktown, its rare testimony of Trabue's religious conversion, and its insight into attitudes of white people toward Indians.

Trabue's work, like all narratives and memoirs, is encumbered by the likelihood of his unreliability. If it is true that memory plays tricks upon a man, especially is it so in the case of an aged man. Trabue had lived sixty-seven years, and it is natural that he made mistakes in his writing, given his methodology. For this reason one must use his work with caution and keep in mind the lengthy time between occurrences and their narration. To this problem I have given over much of the annotation of his narrative. It should be noted, however, that Trabue could have produced more accurate writing only with source materials unavailable to him. The narrator has a noticeable bias—his tendency to picture his own actions in the most favorable light possible, especially to place himself in the forefront during an emergency. In spite of an old man's inclinations, his occasional errors, and his lapses of memory, historical knowledge is all the richer because Daniel Trabue opened his brown ink and took up his pen.

The style Trabue employs marks him as a storyteller of considerable skill. He had apparently perfected his anecdotes through repetition; accordingly, once written down, they received little revision. Their oral quality comes out quite strongly in his attempt to reconstruct conversations. At worst, this practice represents a degree of fabrication; at best, it is what the mind conjures up of some past event.

His writing is occasionally spiced with dry humor. A mountain home which provided no food but corn he calls a "poor man's hominy house." At a time of starvation on the frontier, people were said to have been "keeping a fast Day for the want of something to eat." One of Daniel's brothers who had seen a woman captive tomahawked by an Indian who was cavorting at her back recalled that he often looked around "to see if they was cuting capers behind him." When a certain band of travelers had to subsist on wild turkey, a black slave remarked, "If we have a plenty of Turkeys we will never Die; but if we have bread and bacon too, we would live a heap longer."

Sarcasm, akin to humor, also found its way into his narrative.

INTRODUCTION 3

Usually the British king or a royal officer is the object of ironical taunting. George III is described as "his Gracious Majesty." The chief English cavalryman in North America is called "the mighty Tarleton." When a group of Kentucky-bound Virginians was accosted by the agents of a justice of the peace for traveling on Sunday, a slave attached to the party exclaimed with obvious ridicule, "I spose you is sich good fokes hear you will let us all stay hear and find us and won't charge any thing for it."

The resulting narrative represents fairly closely the vernacular of Virginians and Kentuckians of the Revolutionary Era and the first quarter of the nineteenth century. One of the chief values of Trabue's work is its utility as a linguistic record covering half a century. Spelling words as they were pronounced, it preserves the informal, colloquial speech of that period. Trabue uses several proverbs, such as "Hunger is the best of sause" and "Many hands make light work." Also in the narrative are to be found the Indian words hominy, moccasin, powwow, raccoon, squaw, tomahawk, and wampum. Here is seen the influence of the wilderness upon the speech of frontiersmen.

A trace of national bias—perhaps related to modern-day racial prejudice—is found in Trabue's recording of the dialectal speech of persons from Germany and Ireland. Even though the narrator was of French ancestry, he was identified by his speech with the English majority. German and Irish people were of the minority.

Even what the storyteller omits is instructive. Only vaguely does he hint at the causes of the Revolutionary War. The Declaration of Independence is mentioned but indirectly—by way of a celebration of July the Fourth. Perhaps the average Virginian comprehended the Revolution only so far as its changes impinged on his daily activities; accordingly, Trabue apparently understood the expansion of religious freedom which coincided with the outbreak of hostilities better than he understood the meaning of political theories about separation from the British Empire.

Trabue had planned for a long time to write his memoirs. It is easy to imagine that when at last he finished the task his literary manuscript became quite a conversation piece within his family. The aged patriarch bequeathed this treasured heritage to his sixteen-year-old grandson Robert Paxton Trabue, eldest son of Daniel, Jr.[1] In time this promising lad would study law in Columbia under Judge Zachariah Wheat, be admitted to the bar there, become a captain in the Mexican War, and serve as a colonel in the Confederate military.

A "few years" before 1844 Trabue's narrative was lent by the father of its youthful owner to Dr. John Croghan, who lived at Locust Grove near Louisville. In June of that year young Robert requested his Uncle James Trabue, a thriving merchant of the Falls City, to repossess it for him. Shortly thereafter, however, the uncle promised Lyman Draper, who was then cutting a wide swath across the Ohio Valley as a collector of historical papers, that he could examine the narrative upon his proposed visit to Kentucky.[2] The following November found Draper at Locust Grove, where he first saw the Trabue manuscript. From it he filled seventy-nine pages of his Note Book L with excerpts and paraphrases.[3]

It is not known under what circumstances Trabue's work passed permanently into the hands of Draper. The administrators of the State Historical Society of Wisconsin, the custodian of this valuable document as part of the Draper Collection of Manuscripts, have traditionally conjectured that it was included with the papers of George Rogers Clark which had been gathered by Croghan, a nephew of the famed general, and delivered to Draper soon after July 1846.[4]

Another, and more likely, theory as to Draper's possession of the Trabue material was advanced probably around 1880 by a sister of the second owner. She contended that her father, while living in Saint Louis during 1849-1863, had lent the manuscript to the author of *Field's Scrap Book on the History of the Great West.* Daniel Trabue, Jr., "always said it was stolen or run away with after his lending it under undue persuasion."[5] The mystery surrounding Draper's acquisition of the Trabue paper cannot now be unraveled. One thing is sure—historical scholarship has been well served for over a century because it has been lovingly preserved by the society at Madison, Wisconsin, the heir of Draper's imposing collection.

The earliest publication of part of Trabue's narrative was in the *Richmond* (Va.) *Standard* on May 10, 17, 1879. Its initial six pages—except for the last six lines—had been edited by Draper and supplied to Robert A. Brock, corresponding secretary of the Virginia Historical Society, who inserted them in the weekly newspaper.

A substantial edition of the narrative did not appear until 1916, when Lillie DuPuy VanCulin Harper, a great-grandniece of Daniel Trabue, published it in Philadephia as the opening portion of a work entitled *Colonial Men and Times,* primarily a genealogy of the Trabue, Dupuy, and related families. Her edition leaves much to be desired. She corrected Trabue's spelling, eliminated his grammatical flaws, and in places attempted to improve his literary style. Her greatest sin as editor was to omit 379 sentences of the text, including intimate and revealing materials. Most of these deletions probably violated her sense of propriety. Numerous words were mistranscribed and some mistakes were made in the footnotes. Her edition contains no corrections of textual errors. It is impossible to determine, however, whether the responsibility for many of these editorial faults lies with her, with Alvah L. Terry (a Louisville cousin who supplied her with the transcription she used), or with an unknown copyist.

5 INTRODUCTION

In preparing this present transcription I have been guided by the goal to allow the narrator to have his say. To this end all his words have been used. In order to maintain the original charm and quality of Trabue's manuscript and to give clues to contemporary pronunciation, his spelling of words has been retained. His capitalization and punctuation have also been kept, but with the following exceptions: the first word of a sentence has always been capitalized and the proper mark of punctuation has been placed at the end, regardless of what Trabue does.

Abbreviations which are not presently in common usage have been expanded. Superior letters are normalized. Omitted letters in the middle of a word are supplied without indication that this has been done. If final letters are missing, they are provided and enclosed in brackets.

The ampersand is transcribed *and*; the symbol &c is rendered *etc.*; the tailed *p* is expanded to *per*. Quotation marks are furnished to indicate conversations which Trabue has tried to recall. The apostrophe is inserted where a contraction or the possessive case is intended.

Interlineations have been put into the line of text at the proper places. Cancellations have been placed in the annotation, except in one instance where retention is required to complete the textual meaning.

To make Trabue's work more meaningful I have devised a full system of editorial annotation. The resultant notes serve several purposes: to identify persons, places, and events; to interpret the significance of concepts, movements, and occurrences; to remove errors; to correct misspelled words which might not be readily recognized; to expand data; to explain occasional garbles; and to cite bibliography.

Daniel Trabue, a fourth-generation Huguenot in British North America, was born on March 31, 1760, in the Virginia Piedmont. His grandfather Trabue and his mother's grandfather Dupuy had settled on the James River at the turn of the eighteenth century with other pioneers in a social experiment which a benevolent king had sponsored at Manakin Town. From these French forebears young Trabue inherited the noble traditions which instilled in him an ardent familial pride. Abhorrence of despotism, love for the untrammeled life, and zeal for the evangelical faith, all were part and parcel of the patrimony he received.

The eighth of fifteen children in John James Trabue's burgeoning family, Daniel grew up in a revolutionary age when the common man of the Old Dominion was already meaningfully participating in the governmental process and when this developing democracy was about to open the door for political separation from Great Britain. As a lad he acquired the benefits of a brief English education, learned the obligation of compulsory militia service, and imbibed the folk wisdom of his generation.

After a tour of nearly three rigorous years on the Kentucky frontier, where he served as a military commissary, Daniel returned home to

Chesterfield County and early in 1781 plunged excitedly into the eventful stream which would issue in American victory at Yorktown. During much of that closing year of the Revolutionary War, Trabue, now a promising youth of twenty-one years, tried his hand at buying liquor and retailing it to servicemen at a profit. He did well at this venture because his Kentucky experience had prepared him to transact common business matters, to handle money, to keep accounts, and to make reports. In time Daniel could reflect on the war and see its final year as the beginning of a lifelong attempt to succeed as an entrepreneur.

The month after Yorktown, Daniel purchased his father's old farm home and the land immediately surrounding it from his brother James, still in the Kentucky wilderness. In 1775 John James Trabue had willed this two hundred-acre tract to his five-year-old son, Samuel, who died two years later. Under Virginia's law of primogeniture, title had passed automatically to the boy's eldest brother, James. Daniel paid James £30,000 in depreciated paper money for this land on Tomahawk Creek in Chesterfield County.

Marrying in 1782 on July the Fourth, Daniel brought his bride, Mary Haskins, to this plantation and to the weatherboarded and plastered house where his mother still lived. Affectionately called Polly, Mary was a daughter of Robert Haskins, a former colonel of the Chesterfield militia. Three brothers of Daniel would later marry three of her sisters.

In August, Daniel added to his farm thirty adjacent acres which he bought for £45 current money from his neighbor Edward Moseley, the militia captain who had treated him like a son during the weeks of active duty a year earlier. Profits from his wartime business enterprise enabled young Trabue to set himself up as the proprietor of his childhood home.

But Daniel, not satisfied with this situation for long, decided to try his luck at the miller's craft. In February 1783 he acquired a grist mill on a six-acre plot in adjoining Powhatan County at a cost of £100 current money and soon moved there with Mary. Shortly thereafter he paid £300 for two hundred additional acres once part of the mill property. Probably needing more capital for his milling venture, Daniel now sold his Chesterfield land to his younger brother Edward. It was in Powhatan County that Polly delivered her firstborn and named him Robert to honor her father.

As was true of many a man who had seen the productive soil of the Bluegrass country, Daniel yearned to return westward across the Appalachians. In the opening weeks of 1785 he concluded to move to Kentucky and plant his roots firmly in the new society rising in the West. The spring and early summer were taken up with a preparatory visit to Fayette County, where he intended to settle.

August found Daniel back home in the Piedmont enmeshed in the tedious details preliminary to transferring beyond the mountains his family, his household plunder, and a supply of mercantile goods. It was then that he experienced a profound religious conversion that would serve him as a lodestar through all the years to follow.

Early that autumn Trabue, his family, and other companions journeyed through northern Virginia over the well-used route to the Monongahela and down that stream and the Ohio to Limestone. On this trip, filled with drama and suspense, the travelers followed the only waterway into Kentucky—made popular and supposedly safe by the recent Treaties of Fort Stanwix and Fort McIntosh.

When Daniel transplanted his young wife and child from the Virginia Piedmont to the Kentucky wilderness, he subjected them to the delights and dangers of the frontier. Such an experience meant enjoying the beauty of the forest, dreading the presence of stealthy red men, living in a log cabin, and depending on wild meat to supplement the produce of field and garden. Here in Fayette County near the Kentucky River the Trabues struggled to make a home and to raise their offspring. It was perhaps in 1787 that Mary gave birth to her second child, named John to perpetuate the memory of Daniel's deceased father. By the death he would suffer, this son was destined to bring ineffable grief to his parents twelve years later.

In the summer of 1788 Daniel fixed his name to a petition circulated in the western portion of Fayette, requesting the Virginia legislature to divide that county and to establish a new jurisdiction. The petitioners argued that the long distances from their homes to Lexington, the county seat, increased the costs of litigation far beyond their resources. The large population of Fayette, alleged to be three times that of any other Kentucky county, not only gave rise to a crowded court docket and the consequent delay in the administration of justice but also weakened the principle of proportional legislative representation. Too, the expanse of the county prevented its militia officers from taking vigorous action against marauding Indians.[6] People in the backcountry had bombarded legislators on the Atlantic seaboard with this rationale for over a century to soften their opposition to the expansion of frontier government. These arguments had the desired effect that fall, because the General Assembly authorized the forming of Woodford County out of western Fayette the next May.[7] Now the conveniences of local government would be found closer home.

Roads, a bridge, and a mill were the first tangible benefits the new political unit brought to the community of Grier Creek, where Daniel lived. His plantation consisted of some two hundred acres on the north bank of that stream not far above its mouth. Determined to resume his trade as a grist miller and to build a new mill, Daniel sought title to an acre of land across the creek from his proposed site. This additional area was needed for the abutment of the dam. In September 1790 the Woodford County Court issued a writ of *ad quod damnum* by which a jury assessed the damages to be expected by the construction of the enterprise and evaluated the acre taken for this public purpose.

Joseph McClain, owner of the land opposite Trabue's, took exception to the decision of the panel to allow a dam fifteen feet high and to appraise the acre at 10s. In June the following year a second jury lowered the height of the dam one foot, raised the value of the acre to 14s. 5d., and set the flooding damage to McClain's adjacent land at 9s. 9d. The court now licensed Trabue to erect his mill and dam. This business establishment and Trabue's Bridge, some sixty feet below the dam, became prominent landmarks in the Grier Creek neighborhood, to which Daniel's mother, his brother Edward, and some of their Dupuy uncles had also moved. Prospering because of the allowable tolls of one-eighth of the corn ground into meal and one-sixteenth of that made into hominy, the proprietor kept this business while he remained in Woodford County.

During the Revolution when stationed at Logan's Fort, on the headwaters of Green River, Daniel Trabue had probably heard about and even hunted on Skinhouse Branch in Beech Woods Valley some forty-five miles to the southwest. In this idyllic region, the virgin forest was filled with beech, sugar maple, ash, buckeye, walnut, and hornbeam; the stream banks were overgrown by vigorous stands of cane. Thus there was mast for bear and turkey, cane for buffalo, deer, and elk. A picturesque three-mile stream fed by limestone springs of crystal water, Skinhouse is a shallow branch of Caney Fork, which flows into Russell Creek (a southern tributary of the Green). About midway along this branch on its right bank a party of Virginia backwoodsmen from the Holston and the New rivers had maintained a hunting camp during the fall and winter of 1770. Part of a group known later on the frontier as "Long Hunters," these men erected there a bark-covered hut as a storehouse for their supplies and for animal pelts gathered from the surrounding area.

Next spring when only three hunters were in camp, Indians assaulted the station, carried away the skins and furs they wanted, and, stripping the bark from the skin house, left the balance to be spoiled by the elements. One of the hunters escaped, the other two were captured. When the absent adventurers returned after some weeks, they found a desolate camp.[8] One of them carved on a large beech tree the following record: "2,300 Deer Skins lost; Ruination by God."[9]

At his mill seat on Grier Creek, Daniel Trabue perhaps often talked about these frontier events; at any rate, he and others of his family agreed to secure land on "Skinhouse Run" in the recently formed Green County and to make their homes there. It was probably in the spring of 1795 that Daniel and his brother Stephen, their father-in-law (Robert Haskins), and their brother William's widow (Elizabeth Haskins Trabue) contracted with Zachariah Johnston, a land speculator of Rockbridge County in the Great Valley and a fervent advocate of religious liberty who had formed a partnership with Adam Craig of Richmond, to purchase for £748 the tract of 666 2/3 acres which included the site of the Long Hunters' skin house.[10]

Back in Kentucky, Daniel paid the taxes on this acreage in August 1796 but was hindered by "a spell of the billious fever" from going down to the Frankfort land office to settle with the surveyor who had laid out the tract. He proposed that the sellers meet him on Skinhouse Branch the next spring and divide the tract among its new owners. Then, he reasoned, "Each of us Can pay our own Taxes, etc." By September 24 Trabue had sold his Woodford home and was intending "this fall to be a living on the Skinhouse Run and be Ready for you when you Come their," he wrote Johnston in Virginia.[11]

On August 9, 1792, a few weeks after Kentucky had achieved statehood, Daniel had been commissioned a captain in the Eleventh Militia Regiment of Woodford County and three years later had advanced to a majority. In preparation for his departure from the county, Major Trabue resigned his military post before October 26, 1796.[12]

During the first week of November, Daniel finished straightening out his tangled business affairs on Grier Creek. It may have been shortly thereafter that he and his family moved to Beech Woods Valley in Green County.[13] Within the next three years his brother Stephen, leaving behind his brother Edward and their mother in the Bluegrass, joined Daniel on Skinhouse Branch. By 1798 Daniel's aging father-in-law had made the arduous trip from the Virginia Piedmont to Green County, Kentucky. Robert Haskins, bearing the burden of over threescore years, brought with him his family, including his widowed daughter Elizabeth Trabue and her two teenaged girls—Nancy and Phoebe.[14]

The upper Green River country in 1796 was more primitive and less populous than the Kentucky River region the Trabues had left. Only six years had passed since Jesse Gray had established a defensive station about two miles north of Daniel's land. It stood near the ford on Caney Creek where crossed the Indian path running between Glover's Station on Green River and the future site of Columbia on Russell Creek.[15] Notwithstanding the initial usefulness of Gray's Station, two events in 1794 had greatly reduced its importance. William Whitley's successful expedition against the Cherokee Nickajack towns on the Tennessee had rendered Green County immune from southern Indian raids; Anthony Wayne's psychic victory at Fallen Timbers on the Maumee had put a quietus on northern Indian threats to the state as a whole. The happy conclusion of these incursions against the Indian released a flood of migration from central Kentucky into Green County.[16]

The Trabues and their kin, who were in the van of this popular movement, divided the skin-house survey into four tracts with two on each side of Skinhouse Branch. Daniel and his widowed sister-in-law's farms lay on the left bank, while the others were situated across the little stream. The land chosen by Daniel and his father-in-law made up the western and southern portions of the survey.

In this new backwoods community, honor and responsibility were quick in coming Daniel's way. Along with his father-in-law and ten other frontiersmen, Trabue became in 1798 a trustee of New Athens Academy, which was established at Greensburg, the county seat. In December, Governor James Garrard, a Baptist preacher turned politician, commissioned Daniel a justice of the peace in his newly adopted county. This post carried with it a seat on the county court, the vital agency of local government. From July 16, 1799, to February 16, 1802, he sat on the bench of this monthly tribunal with considerable irregularity.

In July 1799 when Major Nathan Montgomery resigned his command of the Second Battalion in the Sixteenth Militia Regiment, James Blane, the Green County representative in the legislature, was appointed in his place. The new major soon tired of the position and resigned. On December 21 Daniel Trabue was recommended to Governor Garrard by local leaders as a fit replacement on the basis of his military service in Woodford County, which he had discharged with "propriety." Appointed to the vacant majority, he approached his task with vigor, organizing the next spring two new companies in his battalion.[17]

Many of the Trabues and Haskinses had experienced religious conversions and joined Baptist churches in the Old Dominion when the postwar fires of the Great Awakening were sweeping across that state. Now in Kentucky on Skinhouse Branch, some of these pious folk, including Daniel, called together their relatives and neighbors and formed the Russell's Creek Baptist Church as early as June 1800.[18] Indeed this community had been stunned and sobered by the wanton cruelty of the Harpe brothers, who murdered and mutilated Daniel's twelve-year-old son in April the preceding year. Here was the catalyst to set men to pondering the ways of the devil as well as the mysteries of God.

A log meetinghouse was soon built for the new church at the farm of Stephen Trabue on a gently rising slope overlooking the location of the Long Hunters' skin house. In 1804, when the owner donated the church site of 1¼ acres, Daniel Trabue and his father-in-law became trustees of the property.

Elder John White, who had been licensed in 1798 by the Green County Court to celebrate the rites of marriage, was probably the first pastor of the Russell's Creek Church.[19] As a security, Daniel signed the bond that the minister posted on June 19.

The church on Skinhouse Branch and nine other congregations organized the Green River Association of Baptists in June 1800, following a preliminary conference twelve months earlier. Daniel's first recorded attendance as a "messenger" of the Russell's Creek Church to the association was in July 1801, when he traveled with Pastor White, his brother Stephen, and his brother-in-law Henry Hatcher to its three-day session at the Dripping Spring Church in Barren County. These annual meetings regularly began on a Saturday and ended with a business session on Monday. The Lord's Day was given over for the most part to public worship, including several sermons.

By July 1802 the Russell's Creek Church had acquired both a new preacher and a new name. Elijah Summers came from the pastorate at Trammel's Creek in Green County to serve the thriving congregation on Skinhouse Branch, which changed its name to Mount Gilead. The effects of the Great Revival, then moving mightily over the state, were seen in the growth of the membership of the Skinhouse church during the past twelve months from fifty-eight to eighty-six. Within that period thirty-seven people were baptized and fourteen joined the congregation by letters from similar societies. In the churches of the Green River Association 519 persons entered the waters of baptism during that time. On every hand there was a powerful stirring of the Spirit. The voice of the backwoods preacher was being heard, calling men to repent of their sins and to seek the eternal God.

Like the lush vegetation in the surrounding forests, the Green River Association grew apace. By 1804 the associated congregations totaled thirty-eight; the believers, 1,876. The time now seemed ripe for a division of the group. One offshoot, which included the churches of Cumberland County to the south, took the name of Stockton's Valley Association. Messengers from Mount Gilead and nine sister societies formed the Russell Creek Association. These churches, east of the Little Barren River, were in Green and Adair counties. At the organizing session in September, Daniel and his brother Stephen were among the messengers from Mount Gilead, the group's largest congregation—numbering eighty-nine souls. The remnant of the Green River Association retained its original name.

By 1800 the tide of migrants rolling into the upper valley of the Green River swelled the number of tithables in Green County to 1,545. The county had spun off in 1796 a new jurisdiction—Cumberland County—which lay along the Tennessee border. The area to the north of Cumberland was filling with people along the fertile bottomlands of Russell and Big creeks and of Glens and Pettits forks. The legislature cut off this region from Green in December 1801 and formed Adair County. The boundary between Green and Adair was fixed so that Daniel Trabue's house stood in the new county one-quarter of a mile below that line.[20] Thus Daniel's fortunes were to be tied to those of Adair County.

After Governor Garrard signed the bill establishing Adair, he laid off a militia regiment for the embryonic county, numbered it the fifty-second, and promoted Major Trabue to be its colonel. The governor was encouraged in this action by Colonel William Casey, leader of the first settlement made within the area which became Adair County. Colonel Trabue, the title by which he was popularly known in the Green River country thereafter, routinely performed his military duties as head of the Adair County regiment until his resignation in September 1805. Thus ended Daniel's long militia career, which had stretched back to his teenage years in the Old Dominion and had included devoted service in four Kentucky counties.

Anticipating the formation of southern Green County into a new political jurisdiction, Daniel Trabue and two kinsmen by marriage, Creed Haskins and William Caldwell, purchased in 1801 fifty acres of second-rate land lying about five hundred yards from Russell Creek with the apparent intention of mounting a campaign to locate there the seat for the new county. The site, a few miles from where the Greensburg-Burkesville Road crossed the creek, is a low tableland above a small branch, which is fed by a number of springs and which empties into the creek. Near the branch were already located the makings of a small community—a tavern and the shops of a blacksmith, a shoemaker, and a saddler.[21]

The proprietors named their budding town Columbia and proposed to give "to the Public" the land for the public square, a bountiful spring located one block below the square, and the sum of one hundred dollars, if their village were designated as the county seat. Nor were they alone in this effort. James Walker, Sr., who owned considerable land in the area, offered to donate twenty acres adjoining the town on the southeast.

Trabue was among the eight men commissioned in 1802 by Governor Garrard as justices of the peace for the new county.[22] Daniel's appointment probably resulted from his brief tenure as a magistrate in the parent county. Thus he achieved on the Kentucky frontier a sociopolitical status never accorded his father in the Virginia Piedmont.

The eight justices solemnly assembled on May 24, 1802, at the home of James Walker, Sr., situated several hundred yards to the east of Columbia on a high hill overlooking the village. There they took oaths to uphold the federal constitution, to support the state of Kentucky, and to discharge faithfully their obligations as members of the Adair County Court. When they met the next day to locate the "Seat of Justice," they divided equally on their choices of two sites and, accordingly, postponed the decision until the following month. During the intervening weeks Trabue, Haskins, and Caldwell must have promoted their cause vigorously, because the court agreed on June 28 to fix the county seat at "the place commonly called the Public Square in the Town of Columbia."[23] Now Daniel and his two partners were assured of success in developing this land. They had indeed become the founders of Columbia.

Four months later the county court, acting under the authority of a 1796 state law, established Columbia as a town and appointed five trustees to lay off the streets and alleys and to sell the village lots at public auction. In this manner a system was set up by which the land of the three proprietors could be sold and the proceeds turned over to them.[24]

During 1802 Daniel participated in the county court on each of the thirteen days it met. Never again would he set such an annual record during his lengthy tenure on that tribunal. He also filled a number of other public posts throughout that first year of the county's existence—commissioner to recommend the course for a road to Greensburg, surveyor to open this route, judge of the three-day election in November, and presiding justice at the last session of the county court in December.

The erection of the public buildings on the square was an important phase in the development of Daniel's town. These structures gave it an air of permanence and perhaps helped the proprietors to dispose of their lots with less difficulty. A two-story jail, twelve feet square, was begun first. Built probably on the public square, it was completed by June 1803. In the meantime a pillory and stocks and a stray pound had been finished. The contract for a courthouse was let in 1803, with specifications calling for a 2½-story building, 24 by 37 feet, with a shingled roof and one chimney. The first floor consisted of a courtroom with one fireplace; the second, two jury rooms, each with a fireplace. Accommodating only the law courts, it would be a true courthouse in the English tradition, with the office of the clerk under some other roof. Various problems delayed its completion, but on December 1, 1806, the county court, meeting at the home of John Beard, Sr., heard a report from the building commissioners that the new brick courthouse, now ready for occupancy, measured up to their expectations. Probably with a sense of the importance of the occasion the court adjourned, traipsed over to the public square, and reconvened in the new quarters. The honor of presiding as the senior judge that day fell to Daniel Trabue, who with his two partners had worked so diligently to establish the frontier village.

With the town of Columbia set on its way to a modest growth Daniel turned in 1803 to the business of grist milling for the third time. He had purchased from John Craig of Scott County for $210 three hundred acres of third-rate land on the north bank of Russell Creek not far from the

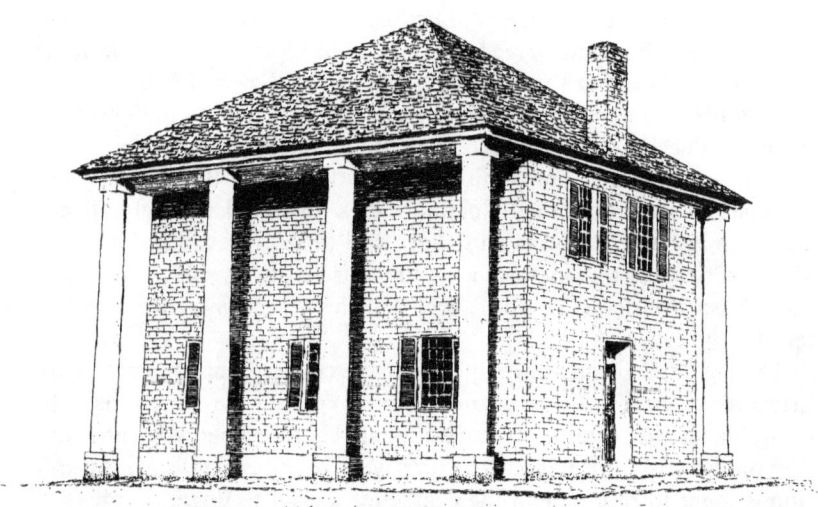

Adair County Courthouse, Columbia, Ky., 1806. Artist's conception of the structure based on an architectural description of it and a photograph made after its remodeling in 1847. Drawn by David Kent Humphreys.

county seat. Trabue planned to build a grist mill several score feet above where the Greensburg Road, which ran through his property, forded the stream. He was given leave by the county court on October 1, 1804, to erect the mill.

Probably soon thereafter Daniel began the construction of a stone millhouse on the north bank of the creek where a ledge of limestone projects into the water. On this rock base was set that portion of the house foundation which lay alongside the stream. This partial foundation is all that remains of Trabue's Mill except for loose stones scattered downstream in the creek bed.

Once the millhouse and dam were completed, Trabue's Mill became a profitable business as well as a landmark on the Greensburg Road. After Trabue had taken the federal population census in Adair County in 1810, he nailed a copy of the schedule to the door of his mill, which he designated "the most General public Place in the County . . . next to the Court House."[25] To an establishment with so large a clientele a well-kept road was essential. Trabue had been wise to locate his mill on the Columbia-Greensburg Road, traversing the community that had grown up around the Mount Gilead Baptist Church. He used his influence as a member of the county court to promote the maintenance of this route, as well as its relocation in some places between the mill and Columbia.

But Trabue was not all business. He developed quite a lively interest in the Russell Creek Baptist Association, to which he had been a founding messenger in 1804. A new, dynamic actor—a young Christian possessed of intense fervor—stood ready that year to stride upon the stage of Daniel's life. Sometime during 1804 Isaac Hodgen, a preacher licensed by the Nolynn Church near Hodgenville, wooed and won the heart of Daniel's niece Phoebe, who lived with her mother—the widow Elizabeth Haskins Trabue—high on a hill in the Mount Gilead community overlooking the meetinghouse on Skinhouse Branch. The churchman married this nineteen-year-old girl on December 27 and took up housekeeping in the home of his mother-in-law, where he continued to reside until his death. In 1805 Isaac was ordained to the Gospel ministry, and two years later he assumed the pastorate at Mount Gilead.

As Trabue's pastor and nephew-in-law, Elder Hodgen, it seems, exercised considerable religious and moral influence upon Daniel. During the first sixteen years of the Russell Creek Association, Trabue was a messenger of the Mount Gilead Church at half of the annual meetings.[26] When Andrew Broaddus, the well-known Baptist preacher of Salem, Virginia, passed through Columbia on his way to Hopkinsville in October 1817, he stopped briefly at the tavern of "old brother" Trabue and was "kindly and cordially" welcomed. Elder Hodgen, whom Broaddus characterized as a "zealous minister of Christ," had just concluded a preaching service in town, perhaps at the courthouse. He was at Daniel's public house when the traveler arrived.[27]

Hodgen was elected the moderator for thirteen of the nineteen annual sessions of the Russell Creek Association during his tenure at Mount Gilead.[28] With exceeding regularity the minutes of the associational meetings were published yearly. Each church usually sent a small sum of money for which it received a proportionate number of copies of the imprint for that session struck off in the shop of some county-seat printer. In 1821 there arose the practice to deposit these printed minutes in Greensburg with a faithful leader to whom the churches applied for their shares. In addition to the usual place of supply, Columbia was designated in 1825 and 1826. For the first of these years "Brother" Trabue's was specified as the location of the deposit.[29]

What manner of man was Daniel Trabue's pastor? Elder Hodgen was a handsome person, standing about five feet eight inches and weighing almost two hundred pounds. His square-shouldered physique and commanding appearance bespoke considerable strength. A man who knew him during nearly all his ministry compared his zeal for the Christian cause to "an overflowing fountain, issuing from such a depth that no change of seasons could affect its enlivening current."[30] As a pulpiteer Hodgen had few peers in early nineteenth-century Kentucky.

His sermons were plain; his delivery was vigorous and eloquent.

Although Isaac Hodgen usually had the simultaneous charge of four churches and preached in each on a given Sunday of the month, he considered his "great life work" to be that of a "traveling evangelist." In this capacity he traveled many thousands of miles.[31]

Hodgen's interest in foreign missions came to the fore in 1813, when the association appointed him to gather a fund for mission work in India.[32] Within a year he had accumulated twenty-four dollars. In 1815 Luther Rice, agent for the nationwide Baptist Triennial Convention, preached at the associational meeting and received for foreign missions an offering of $114.40, including what Hodgen had collected earlier.[33]

Not only did Elder Hodgen support overseas evangelism, but he also bridged the theological gap between the doctrines of predestination and the universality of the Gospel. He was helped along in such an adjustment by reading *The Gospel Worthy of All Acceptation* (1784), a work by Andrew Fuller of England, who posited a general atonement coupled with a special application of God's grace.[34] By this dogma Hodgen justified his inviting all men to heed the Gospel.

In the prime of life Elder Hodgen suddenly died on March 22, 1826, probably having been poisoned. He was buried in the family graveyard on the farm which his mother-in-law had settled. The admonition "Prepare to Meet Thy God" is carved on the limestone that marks his tomb. To Daniel Trabue, who had known this man of God for over two decades, the loss must have been keenly felt.

In addition to the grist mill on Russell Creek, during 1807-1810 Trabue operated a retail store, perhaps at his farm on Skinhouse Branch, where he had run such a business as early as 1799. He also managed his Skinhouse plantation until around 1811. During the preceding eleven years he kept an annual average of six Negro slaves, some of whom perhaps worked in his fields. By September 1802 he was marking his livestock with "a crop and slit in the right ear and a hole in the left."[35]

For capital to sustain his retailing venture Trabue may have relied heavily on the income he would receive as county sheriff during his two-year term beginning on April 1, 1808. The previous autumn the county court had recommended him for this post, "a Just Regard being had to Seniority in Office" as a justice of the peace.[36] Governor Christopher Greenup chose Daniel Trabue to be the sheriff, succeeding his eldest son, Robert. This appointment rotated Daniel off the county court, on which he had served for six years.

To restock his old retail store or to launch a new one elsewhere, Trabue sent his eldest son, then twenty-four years old, to the "Nothern [sic] Parts" to purchase goods on credit from wholesalers. It was the late fall of 1807 that Robert, armed with his father's power of attorney, journeyed into the Bluegrass.[37] It seems that the young man ordered large shipments of merchandise because three lawsuits involving debts contracted soon thereafter for over seventeen hundred dollars were filed against Daniel some years later.

The largest of these cases concerned a debt of $1,442.85, plus court costs and interest at 6 percent from October 1, 1808. An adverse judgment in this suit, handed down in March 1814, may have forced Daniel to sell his grist mill on Russell Creek, even though it was a valuable, income-producing enterprise. At any rate, he let it go for three thousand dollars to William S. Bailey of Rockbridge County, Virginia, perhaps in 1814. He had already gotten rid of his old plantation in Mount Gilead by January 1812; he moved into town "about the year 1814."[38] By January 1815 Trabue and his family were occupying a two-story log tavern in Columbia on Main (now Jamestown) Street at Pinckney Alley (now Reed Street) a short block off the public square. In April, William Worley, the first taverner in Columbia, sold this property to Trabue. The previous year Trabue had disposed of four of his nine Negro slaves. He probably paid for the tavern with money from these sales of realty and personalty.

When Daniel moved to the growing village, its population numbered around three hundred. He was no stranger to the townspeople. His public service as magistrate, as militia colonel, or as sheriff had brought him to Columbia many times each month during the first eight years of the town's existence. In fact, he had regained his seat on the Adair County Court in February 1814, having been reappointed as a justice of the peace by Governor Isaac Shelby. Even though recognized as a founder of the town, he now came as an innkeeper.

The county court granted Trabue a license to operate his tavern during 1815. That year whiskey was selling at 37½ cents per quart, French brandy and rum at $1.25. Wine brought $1.50 per quart. A night's lodging "in clean sheets" cost 12½ cents, a warm dinner of two or more courses 25 cents. Trabue renewed his license in 1816 and in 1818, and presumably in the intervening year. When he sold this tavern in 1819, he received only $920. The panic of that year struck with depreciating fury; he had paid $2,500 for the property four years earlier.

In December 1820 the Kentucky General Assembly subsidized Daniel Trabue and three partners—Charles Bennett, Adam Kearns, Jr., and Jacob Antle—in a business venture begun a number of years earlier. They were drilling for brine on the West Fork of Blackfish Creek, a tributary of the Cumberland River in Cumberland (now Russell) County. Their intention was to produce salt by evaporation. The aid from the state was the authority to patent a maximum of five thousand acres of "waste and unappropriated land" within five miles of their well as soon as they had produced five hundred bushels of salt. Trabue and his colleagues were to buy this land at the rate of ten dollars per hundred acres—half the regular cost.[39]

The one hundred-acre "Salt Well Tract," as the land on which they were drilling was called, had been surveyed in 1806 for William Stapp. On May 23, 1820, Trabue, Bennett, and Kearns acquired Stapp's interest in this acreage and formalized a partnership. Trabue owned one-half of this new enterprise and the other two entrepreneurs shared equally the remainder. The next month Antle was received as the fourth associate. Now each of them possessed even parts.

During the early 1820s Kentuckians were spending large sums of money for salt made in Virginia and Illinois. Given the economic depression and the consequent scarcity of coin, the legislature wanted to promote the production of salt at home. It thus justified the granting of special privileges to Trabue and his company. In fact, the General Assembly claimed that the unappropriated lands sought by the well drillers had "little or no value, only for timber—nor would that be of any value unless salt water is obtained."[40]

Other prospective saltmakers in the Cumberland Valley were also awarded benefits by the state. Martin Beatty, who struck brine in Pulaski County during the fall of 1822, was given two thousand acres without his paying the usual charges. A boundary of land was set aside for Marcus Huling, Andrew Erwin, and Peter Simmermon, who were likewise boring for salt water.

Still persisting with their drilling, Trabue and his partners had surveyed 1,816 acres within their reserved zone by November 22, 1822. As the end of 1823 neared, they had still not reached salt water, even though they had penetrated to a depth of almost 450 feet, reaching "a solid rock, the borings of which are somewhat salt—sufficiently so to encourage them to continue their pursuit for salt water."[41] As a further inducement the legislature reduced the price of the land to five dollars per hundred acres.

But Trabue and his associates were not to enjoy the rewards of their labor without controversy. William Patterson, Sr., William S. Patterson, and James G. Patterson surveyed 280 acres within the reserved area. Trabue's filing of caveats in 1823 halted the issuing of land patents to the trespassers. Three resulting lawsuits were continued in the Adair Circuit Court until March 1826; by then a new county had been formed which included the disputed lands. The court, accordingly, changed the venue of these cases to the Russell Circuit Court, where they were heard in July 1827. Sixteen months later the judge ruled in favor of Trabue, but the Pattersons contested this decision in the Court of Appeals. The rulings of the circuit court were finally upheld in April 1830 by the high court,

Trabue's residence, Columbia, Ky. This brick house was erected in 1821. Drawn by David Kent Humphreys.

which decreed four to one that the legislature was justified in encouraging Trabue "to persevere and expend his money in pursuit of salt-water, the finding of which is of public utility."[42]

Taking advantage of declining realty values caused by the Panic of 1819, Trabue bought that year a parcel of 3½ acres located a few hundred yards beyond the southeastern limits of Columbia. Lying on the south side of the Campbell's Ferry Road to the Cumberland River, the tract included the brow of a high hill overlooking the town. It was there that Daniel, who invested two hundred dollars in this acreage, planned to build a new home for his growing family. By December 1821 he had laid a stone foundation and completed a modest two-story brick residence with two rooms on each floor and with a chimney centered at each end of the house. Influenced by the early Georgian style found in the first brick houses of Kentucky, this extant structure measures 20 by 33 feet.

The new residence of Trabue was superior to the average home in the immediate neighborhood of Columbia. There were, however, at least ten brick dwellings in the area before he put up his, but by far most homes in the community were frame or log houses. A traveler who came into Columbia by the road from Stanford four years earlier had described some of the dwellings in the countryside as "built of flat logs and cramm'd with lime mortar," but most were "badly built and miserably finished (or rather unfinished) log cabins."[43]

Daniel and Mary Trabue may have been occupying their new house when on January 23, 1821, their son Robert, as an assistant to the federal marshal, tardily enumerated them in the 1820 census.[44] At any rate, the family crowded this little residence to overflowing. The three youngest in the household were boys: Presley O., age fourteen; James, age eighteen; and Daniel, Jr., in his early twenties. The youngest daughter, named Judith Dupuy, was twenty-three years old. There was also Sally, the oldest offspring at home, who was a spinster in her late twenties. Two of their children were married. Robert had taken Lucy Waggener as his bride in 1809. Mary had wedded Samuel Sublett four years later.

The cramped condition in the house was alleviated somewhat in June 1822, when Daniel, Jr., married Mary Jane Paxton, a granddaughter of Colonel William Casey, the pioneer settler in Adair County. The following year Sally became the third wife of the widower Garland Anderson, a farmer older than she by more than twenty years. She went to live on his estate in Mount Gilead. In 1826 Judith moved to Greensburg as the new wife of John Scott, sixteen years her senior.

Even though Daniel's new home had been constructed during a time of deflated prices, his possession of it aggravated rather than ameliorated his sagging financial status, which had steadily worsened since the selling of his grist mill on Russell Creek. While operating the tavern, Trabue had mortgaged in 1816 two of his four remaining slaves—Nathan and Matilda—to guarantee the repayment of a loan of $500 from a Danville bank. Three years later he had offered Matilda, then age twelve, and the three other slaves he owned—Aggy, age about thirty-six; Green, age about sixteen; and Shearwood, age one—as surety for debts totaling $750.

From the Bank of the Commonwealth of Kentucky, located at Frankfort, Trabue then borrowed a sum which had been reduced to $224 by October 1824. This money was perhaps swallowed up by erecting a new manufactory which he began that year—a bloomery and a grist mill. This debt had not been paid on the following March 9, when a suit to recover the loan was first heard in the Adair Circuit Court. The ninth was indeed a time of immense stress upon Daniel because he had to defend himself in eleven other cases before the court that day. The lawsuit by the bank was continued to June 7, by which time the debt had been brought down to $182.

The debt was still hanging over Trabue on June 7, 1826, when the court awarded the bank a judgment for the principal, the unpaid interest at 6 percent, and the costs of litigation. On the twenty-fourth the court issued an execution writ of *fieri facias*, commanding Sheriff Elijah Cravens to seize and to sell at auction enough of the debtor's property to satisfy the decree. Returnable to the court on August 12, the writ was endorsed by the plaintiff: "Notes on the Bank of Kentucky and its branches and notes on the Bank of the Commonwealth of Kentucky and its branches will be received in discharge of this execution."[45] Thus the bank's willingness to accept paper money negated a proviso in the Replevin Act of 1820 by which Trabue could have delayed payment of the debt for two years.[46]

Three days elapsed before this *fieri facias* was put into Cravens's hands. The writ came to the sheriff at three o'clock that afternoon, but he waited until the day he was obliged to return it to court before he levied on the acreage where stood the brick residence in which the Trabues had then been living for over five years. Still the officer neglected to auction the property that day. He claimed that he did not have "time to sell" it.[47]

In September the reluctant sheriff was prodded again to his duty by the clerk of the circuit court, who issued a writ of *venditioni exponas,* sternly charging Cravens to auction the unsold realty seized under the first writ. It was ironic that Clerk William Caldwell had to send out an order which so adversely affected his old partner in land development, who now stood to lose his home on the bluff, immediately beyond the fledgling village they had called into being. The steady, ample income of Caldwell, an officer of the two highest courts in Adair County, rendered him immune to such pecuniary devastation. In fact, the clerk was prospering while other men in the county were driven to the wall during the severe depression then in progress.

Storekeeper John Field, for instance, had mortgaged most of his property in town as surety for accounts owed a merchant in Georgetown, District of Columbia, amounting to $51,461.29 in September 1819. By a commissioner's auction Field had lost in 1823 nearly two acres of developed land in the heart of Columbia besides other valuable realty.

Benjamin Lampton (grandfather of Mark Twain) and John Montgomery, operating a store in Columbia under the name of Lampton and Montgomery, had owed over thirty-three hundred dollars for merchandise purchased in Pennsylvania during 1817. After the depression hit, this firm became insolvent; accordingly, it was dissolved and the assets were divided between the owners. It seems that Lampton assumed the obligation for the unpaid mercantile accounts. All his assets were sucked into the quagmire of debt in 1819-1821. Even though company did not compensate for his own financial misery, Daniel Trabue knew that he was not the only debtor in distress.

In due course as the law required, Sheriff Cravens advertised the sale of Trabue's house lot and on September 14, 1826, at the debtor's premises put it on the block. The highest bidder was Parker C. Hardin, attorney for the Bank of the Commonwealth of Kentucky; the amount was only

$210. By now the debt, the interest, and the costs of litigation came to exactly 12½ cents more than the bid. Daniel handed over this petty sum to the sheriff, and thus a sad chapter in the life of this struggling entrepreneur came to a disappointing end.

The Trabues continued to live in the house on the hill until September 1828. At what time they vacated it and moved into a dwelling within the town limits is not known, but they were residing in Columbia when the 1830 decennial census was taken. By now the household was reduced to only the parents, their youngest son, Presley O., and their sole surviving slave, a woman around thirty years old. Soon thereafter Mary, Daniel's wife of almost half a century, died in Columbia on September 25. She was buried at Mount Gilead in the graveyard on the farm of her daughter Sally Anderson, now a widow of thirteen months.

Mary's death had compounded the sorrow of a grieving father. In August of the previous year Daniel's youngest daughter, Judith Dupuy Trabue Scott, had died in Greensburg soon after delivering her only child. John Scott named his daughter Judith Dupuy Scott in memory of his wife.[48]

When Daniel Trabue lost his brick house in 1826, financial darkness had indeed gathered. Early in 1824 he had proposed to erect a bloomery to produce wrought iron and a mill to grind grain, both powered by water. This enterprise was located in Adair (later Russell) County on Greasy Creek, a tributary of Cumberland River, on land leased for ten years from Jessee Wooldridge. The would-be manufacturer of iron contracted with Jacob Antle, a mechanic associated with him in making salt, to construct the water wheel and the tilt hammer and anvil. The dam, the furnace, the grist machinery, and the necessary buildings were to be built by other workmen.

Antle fulfilled his contract before the end of May 1825, but his workmanship did not meet Daniel's approval. The water wheel, lacking a sufficient number of buckets on its rim, did not run fast enough to power the tilt hammer adequately. Thus the machinery operated at so slow a speed that water, coal, time, and labor were wasted. The legs that supported the tilt hammer were only about ten inches square. Lacking a proper base, the hammer trembled when it fell upon an iron bloom on the anvil; the resultant product was not wrought as smoothly as good craftsmanship required.

In spite of the inefficiency of this water-driven equipment, Trabue accepted it. Around July 4, Thomas True, a millwright who had never seen a bloomery before, was hired to evaluate the work of Antle and of the dam builder. This craftsman estimated the tilt hammer and the water wheel to be worth $167 paper; the dam, $120 paper. Jacob Antle, however, disputed True's calculation and in the Adair Circuit Court sued the proprietor for breach of contract. He was awarded damages of $187.50 plus the costs of litigation. The financial circumstances of Trabue were so grave at the time the enterprise on Greasy Creek was begun that within twenty-one months he had pledged its entire value as security for his indebtedness.

In spite of the pecuniary burdens that weighed so heavily upon his shoulders, Daniel Trabue mustered up the requisite spirit to enter a movement afoot in 1827 to organize a Baptist church in Columbia. The town was encircled by four Baptist congregations in the countryside, but there was none within the village itself.

Trabue, the most prominent Baptist in the village, may have supplied the impetus that brought together a band of immersionists in Columbia in the summer of 1827, as he and his kinsmen had done on Skinhouse Branch more than a quarter-century before. In any case, he and his wife, Mary Haskins, and seven other Baptists met at the courthouse on Friday, July 6, to establish the Columbia Baptist Church. Beside the Trabues the charter members were John White; Peter T. Conover and his wife, Jemima; John Holladay; Tabitha Minter Pittman, a niece of Trabue and the daughter of a minister; and Herbert Green Waggener, Jr., and his wife, Elizabeth Carlile.[49]

The town church was constituted by four visiting ordained ministers: Herbert Green Waggener, Sr., William Burbridge, and Larkin F. Craig,[50] from the Zion Church; and John D. Steele, from the Mount Pleasant Church. The latter was chosen moderator of the meeting; Daniel Trabue, clerk. Elder Steele was the first pastor of the Columbia Church and may have been called to the office at this initial meeting of the congregation.[51]

The church adopted as its statement of faith the doctrinal "Principles of Union" of the Russell Creek Association.[52] Two months later when the association convened at the Mount Pleasant Meetinghouse, the Columbia Church was received as an affiliate of this union.

Daniel Trabue probably continued to fill the position of church clerk until he moved to Green County in 1835. In any event, he occupied this post in 1834, the last full year of his residence in Columbia.

In 1830 a festering doctrinal sore that had been plaguing many Baptist churches in Kentucky for seven years came to a head. It was the reforming movement of Alexander Campbell, a former Presbyterian minister who had become an immersionist and who purposed to restore Christianity to its apostolic condition. His chief disciple in central Kentucky was a Baptist preacher named John "Raccoon" Smith. A son of the frontier, Smith had grown up in the region to the southeast of Adair County but now lived in the Bluegrass.[53]

Within the bounds of the Russell Creek Association, John D. Steele, the initial pastor at Columbia, had become the principal advocate of Campbell's views. Whether he still held the county-seat pastorate at the beginning of 1830 is not known, but he was then the minister of the Union (now Milltown) and the Mount Pleasant churches. Steele may have been also the pastor at the Mount Gilead Church for part of the time between Hodgen's death in 1826 and the associational confrontation with the reformer in 1830. At any rate, Steele simultaneously shepherded four churches within the Russell Creek Association during the latter year, he had been a member at the Skinhouse church in 1814-1815, and he still exercised considerable influence with individuals in that congregation in 1830.

The association had not been blind to the variance between its accepted doctrines and the reforming tenets preached by Elder Steele and his cohorts. The foremost innovation of the reformers appeared to be their aversion toward creeds—positional statements about dogma or, as the associational constitution called them, "principles of union." But the "no-creed" stance of Campbell's adherents was a subterfuge for their more significant doctrinal changes as well as a rejection of the Calvinistic contents of Baptist creeds. The "Circular Letter" adopted at the 1830 associational meeting asked and answered crucial questions concerning the reformers: "Have they no Creed? If not, why so severely, and uncharitably, censure others? If they have no Creed, or belief of their own, differing from that which they oppose, where the necessity, or expediency, of this great war of words? The truth is, *they have a Creed*, and wish all to submit to it. . . . Now this . . . *latent Creed*, of our *No-creed* friends . . . is not written, but purely, mental."[54]

To Russell Creek Baptists the most serious doctrinal alterations made by the followers of Campbell had to do with redemption. First, Baptists held that the moral law of the Old Testament served as a standard to make man aware of his transgression. The reformers taught, from the opposite point of view, that this law had been abrogated and that Christians lived under the New Testament only. Second, Baptists insisted that the Holy Spirit was the immediate agent who changed the heart of an unconverted man and turned him toward God. The innovators believed, on the other hand, that faith came through the preaching or reading of the Word of God. Third, Baptists maintained that immersion neither converted the heart of a sinner nor conferred the Spirit of the Lord upon him. The adherents of Campbellism contended, however, that baptism "holds an important place in conversion, that it is a prerequisite to the forgiveness of sins and the gift of the Holy Spirit."[55] Thus, a wide dogmatic breach existed between the groups.

The Columbia Church, among others, had been "afflicted with the leven of Reformation."[56] On the second Saturday each month and the Sunday following, Daniel Trabue and his fellow worshipers had often heard Elder Steele expound his reforming views when the church assembled in the courthouse. The duration of his pastorate is not known, but by September 1830 he no longer occupied this pulpit. The congregation queried the association that month about ministerial aid, because it was without a preacher. Trabue was not a messenger at that annual meeting, but he must have keenly felt the impact of the dramatic events of the immediately preceding months in which the Campbell movement reached a critical stage.

Elder Steele had been dismissed from the care of the Union Church by a small majority on a charge of having "changed his views respecting the Law, Original Sin, the Atonement and the Call to the Ministry." Shortly thereafter, Elder John Smith rode down to Columbia to rescue Steele. At the same time, the Columbia Church invited Elder John S. Wilson of Todd County to preach in the community in support of the Baptist position.[57] Growing up near Columbia, Wilson had been converted as a teenager and at Mount Gilead had been baptized by Elder Hodgen. Now at age thirty-five, he returned to his boyhood home to debate the defender of Campbellism. No building in the county seat could accommodate the crowd that excitedly gathered; therefore, a stand was constructed in the woods near town. There these worthies upheld their divergent doctrines with great fervor.

On leaving town, Smith, accompanied by Steele, began a dogmatizing circuit which first carried them to an appointment in the Mount Gilead community. Meeting in a private home, these schismatics formed the Mount Gilead Christian Church. Nine charter members "confessed the Christ, and were baptized for the remission of their sins."[58] Among this group were Elizabeth, a daughter of the deceased Elder Hodgen, and her husband, Robert H. Caldwell, who later became a minister in the evolving denomination. All nine of these recusants may have been members of the Baptist church in that neighborhood.[59]

The next stop on their tour was the Mount Pleasant Church, in which Steele yet held his membership. After preaching there and in Kentucky counties to the southwest and in the adjacent parts of Tennessee, Smith returned homeward. Steele was subsequently excommunicated from Mount Pleasant, charged with "rejecting the principles of the general Union." At the close of the business session at which he was excluded, he organized the Mount Pleasant Christian Church with ten dissenters who accepted his doctrinal position.[60]

This chain of events had probably unfolded in July, August, and early September, well before the 1830 session of the Russell Creek Association. It was an anxious body of messengers from twenty-two churches which gathered at the Pitman's Creek Meetinghouse in Green County on the eighteenth of the latter month. When Elder Steele, who had been selected the previous year to deliver the introductory sermon, arrived at the meeting place, many of the brethren were caucusing in small groups in the churchyard. In a short while one of them announced that it was time for the delegates to assemble in the house, but that the sermon would be canceled. When the association convened, it agreed not to hear "Mr." Steele, because he had embraced the heretical views of Alexander Campbell.[61] To that degree the Baptist union unfrocked the schismatic.

The two churches that Trabue had helped to organize—Mount Gilead and Columbia—sought the advice of the association "relative to Campbellism." It declared that if any member discarded its "principles of Union" and maintained "the propriety and expediency of uniting upon a bare profession of a belief of the Scriptures," he was at war "not only with the ass'n, but with the whole connexion." Churches were advised to exclude such a person from membership.[62]

The sundering of his beloved church on Skinhouse Branch and the general turmoil within the Russell Creek Association during 1830 may have caused Trabue to renew his devotion to the work of the union. He attended its next four annual meetings as a messenger from the Columbia Church. The 1831 session was conducted at Mount Gilead—a gesture probably designed to encourage the Baptists there who had remained faithful to the union and its doctrine. Trabue must have received a good deal of satisfaction by traveling into the countryside with his fellow Columbians for the last associational session he would attend at the Mount Gilead Church. For the remainder of his days Daniel Trabue continued within the Baptist fold, faithful to that light which had shone upon him in the Old Dominion while on his way homeward from Richmond.

If any man ever needed the solace which religion affords, that man was Daniel Trabue. Financial ruin like a wintry storm was now beating down upon him. He had compromised his title to the iron bloomery and grist mill on Greasy Creek by giving three mortgages to his creditors. By March 1828 there were in sight no means by which he could pay his debts except by the sale of this property. Within twelve months his sons Daniel, Jr., and James, holders of mortgages that covered the major part of this property, had secured their foreclosure by friendly suits in the Adair Circuit Court.

Even though Kentucky law provided no other remedy for the settling of a mortgage, there was a more compelling reason for using this judicial procedure. To safeguard Daniel Trabue's reputation and to verify these creditor-sons' claims, it was important that the circuit court sanction the transference of these assets to Daniel, Jr., and James. Otherwise, it might have seemed that the debtor was passing this realty into the hands of his children in order to escape the demand of some actual creditor.

Shortly a deed of trust held by three Columbia merchants for the remaining fourth of the ironworks was doubtless foreclosed, and all Daniel's developed realty had then been sacrificed to the wolves of debt.

By this fashion Daniel Trabue's checkered career as an optimistic entrepreneur came to an end. Having attained his seventieth birthday, he now faced the years of decline. He has prospered in his early days as a sutler during the Revolution and later as a grist miller in Powhatan County, Virginia, and in Woodford and Adair counties, Kentucky. As a land developer, he and his two colleagues had founded the town of Columbia. His efforts as a merchant and a taverner in Columbia had been marked only by slight success. The boldest ventures he had embarked upon—saltmaking and iron founding in Russell County— were begun in the decade after the Peace of Ghent, when the supply of currency greatly diminished, the value of real estate sharply declined, and a depression fell over manufacturing in Kentucky.

In his quest for profit Trabue had assumed great risk. Circumstances, however, had gone against him; his investments had thus been swallowed up in the abyss of deflation.

His optimism had gotten the best of him. Had he been more cautious in making investments, had he concentrated on one enterprise, he might have succeeded in business. The career of William Hurt (1757-1842), the first man to settle south of Russell Creek beyond the protection of a fort, contrasts decidedly with that of Daniel Trabue. In addition to farming, Hurt engaged successfully in distilling, grist milling, blacksmithing, tanning, and shoemaking—all of which were carried out as activities of a self-sustaining plantation. Whereas Trabue accumulated excessive debts to his undoing, Hurt made it a rule never to borrow money. In fact, he spent no money except to purchase land or slaves. All other types of property he acquired through barter. And he prospered by reason of his financial policy.[63] Hurt was cast in the mold of the agrarian who valued the land and who lived on it in a state of self-sufficiency. He was at one with Jefferson's party of Republicans (later called Democrats). On the other hand, Trabue was more at home with the economic ideology of the Federalists and their political descendants, the Whigs.[64]

In spite of the fact that Trabue was generally an unsuccessful entrepreneur, his method of operation was more the wave of the future than was that of Hurt. The nation, bent upon an industrial destiny, was hurrying along the road that Trabue had traveled, even though his section of Kentucky would retain its primary allegiance to agriculture.

In a Kentucky county during the first half of the nineteenth century, the two justices of the peace whose commissions bore the earliest dates were customarily recommended to the governor as candidates for a two-year term as county sheriff. In this fashion the members of the county court, who served without salary, could look forward to appointment to this very lucrative position.

When Daniel Trabue began his second term as a magistrate in 1814, his name was placed at the bottom of the list of members of the Adair County Court. Seven years later he had advanced to the fourth place on a roll of twenty justices. In 1828 he was third among nineteen, in 1829 second among eighteen.[65]

On October 4, 1830, Andrew Ewing, the presiding judge, and Trabue were suggested for the sheriff's post. Ewing received the gubernatorial appointment and in January 1831 assumed the position. Now Squire Trabue became the presiding justice. Two years later he was the first of the two nominees for the sheriff's office. Governor John Breathitt named Daniel as the new sheriff for a term of two years. He was sworn into this office on January 7, 1833; thus, his nineteen-year stint of faithful service to the public as a justice of the peace came to an end.[66] This period together with the six years of his first term on the bench (1802-1808) amounted to an even quarter-century given to the administrative and judicial functions of this post. Each term as a justice of the peace ended with his appointment as sheriff. In this way the county government fittingly rewarded the magistrate for his service to the people. And Trabue's selection as the enforcer of law and order and the collector of county revenue in 1833 came at an opportune time for the aging public servant.

When the Congress belatedly provided in June 1832 a pension for Revolutionary militia officers and enlisted men who had served for at least six months,[67] Daniel Trabue was already beset by poverty, infirmity, and old age.[68] This pension, however, would fit his need well, because it could not be attached by any legal process but was intended solely for the personal benefit of a former soldier. With keen expectation of this federal assistance, the venerable old man set to work to prepare his application with as much verve as if he were putting up a grist mill.

The Pension Office of the War Department required an applicant to go before a court of record, there to declare under oath his military participation in the American Revolution and to present other evidence. Trabue, accordingly, appeared before the Adair County Court on August 6 to make his formal statement. Even though he was the presiding justice, he observed the rules of propriety and did not sit on the bench that day. The septuagenarian recounted, probably with must gusto, his tours of duty with the Chesterfield militia in Virginia and his three-year sojourn in the Kentucky wilderness.

Four days later Trabue again stood before this tribunal to testify concerning such minor but necessary details as his discharges from duty and his places of postwar residence. More important were the affidavits he presented which had been secured from four fellow veterans who substantiated his service. At the same time five prominent citizens of the county appeared on his behalf.[69]

On August 18 Trabue's application cleared the Adair County Court and soon was on its way to the War Department in the Federal City—as the nation's capital was oftentimes termed in those days. But by early November action on his claim was temporarily delayed by reason of certain flaws in the attestation of the affiants' reliability. These errors were remedied only by great effort, because Daniel could not "Ride about much in winter time." To secure a statement from a magistrate concerning one of the deponents, he sent a young man fifty miles to Lincoln County. The attempt was to no avail, for the official "was Gone from home a long Jurney."[70] Even so, an amended declaration passed the seal of the county court on December 5. Trabue wrote a covering letter the next day and mailed the application to Washington a second time.

The wheels of the Pension Office turned slowly. A pension for Trabue was approved late in December at $260 per year, but it was June 26, 1833, before the first payment was made. The amount was $520—the sum for two years, beginning at the retroactive date of March 4, 1831, as the act of Congress provided. His pension was the largest annual grant ever made to a Revolutionary veteran in Adair County.

Well before the federal bureaucracy granted his pension, Trabue had set his mind, with equal vigor and optimism, on an even larger perquisite from Uncle Sam. The month following the passage of the benefit to Revolutionary militiamen, the Congress financed a program by which Virginia could keep a promise, made in 1779, to give "half-pay for life" to the military officers of her state line.[71] Daniel reasoned that his eighteen-month stint as a deputy commissary in Kentucky qualified him for this bonanza.

Trabue turned to a kinsman for help. Unable to secure through friends the information he needed from the public archives in Richmond, Virginia, he toyed with the idea of going there to do his own research. Elder Chastain Haskins Trabue, a Baptist preacher and a son of Daniel's brother Stephen who then lived in Adair County, thought about accompanying Uncle Daniel to the Old Dominion. The nephew promised to assist him in gathering affidavits in Kentucky, and they planned such a trip for early April 1833.[72]

In great earnest Daniel undertook the task of presenting to the Treasury Department, to which responsibility for pensions had been shifted from the War Department, the best possible case in support of his claim as a commissary officer under George Rogers Clark. Probably attended by Elder Trabue, the aging veteran began in April a long swing through the Bluegrass country, perhaps on horseback, to take depositions from his ancient colleagues. By May 17 he had been provided with affidavits by acquaintances who lived in Bath, Franklin, and Mercer counties.

After Daniel Trabue returned to Columbia from his arduous trek, several months slipped by before the proper attestation of the affidavits was completed in the various county courts. By then he had decided to employ Christopher Tompkins of Glasgow to lay his claim before the government. Tompkins, now a Kentucky congressman, had been the judge of the Adair Circuit Court from 1809 until 1824.

In Barren County on November 8, Trabue appointed the legislator his agent to demand and receive the compensation due him for his services as a deputy commissary in Clark's Regiment. Despite this prolonged effort, Trabue's claim for "half-pay" was summarily rejected by the bureaucracy. The secretary of the treasury ruled that his case was "not embraced by any act of Congress."[73] The government had thus decided that when Daniel performed his Kentucky duty during the Revolution he had not been an officer under Clark.

This turn of events was followed by a brief lull in his attempt to increase the financial assistance being received from the federal government. After having resided in Columbia and its vicinage for over two decades, Trabue moved to the countryside in 1835 to live in the home of his daughter Sally Anderson, a widow of over five years. Presiding over a 480-acre plantation in the Mount Gilead neighborhood of Green County, she had inherited considerable wealth upon the death of Garland Anderson.

Maybe Trabue moved to Green County within a short while after his second term as sheriff expired early in January. Also his change of residence suggests a continuing physical disability. The governmental pension notwithstanding, Trabue's estate had dwindled by then to a record low. All that remained were a horse and one thousand acres of third-class land in Clay County on the Middle Fork of the Kentucky River which he had entered as early as 1794.

On the other hand, Daniel may have feared another outbreak of Asiatic cholera, such as had hit Columbia with exceeding fury in 1833. That devastation had been the first epidemic the village ever experienced.[74] The ex-sheriff's removal in 1835 was perhaps flight from this disease.

Originating in India, cholera had first appeared in the United States and in Kentucky during 1832. This dread, enteric disease causes dehydration, cramping, and profuse diarrhea. Its attack produces paleness and a pinched expression in the face. Usually during this epidemic a collapse occurred, often followed by death within three days.

The 1833 epidemic in Columbia had probably ended with the onset of cool weather. Cholera did not visit the town the next year, but it reappeared in the summer of 1835. By then Daniel was safely ensconced in the countryside, but his youngest son, Presley O., who had been practicing law for over eight years, was brought low by this malady. He had filled the office of attorney for the commonwealth in Adair County for more than three years.

This promising young lawyer probably represented clients at the June 1835 session of the Adair Circuit Court, which sat from the first through the twelfth. The June session was one of three annual convenings of this tribunal in Columbia. At such times, attorneys and other visitors from nearby counties as well as people from Adair usually taxed the public facilities of the town.

When Presley came down with cholera, he rode from Columbia to his sister's countryseat in Mount Gilead. So near collapse was he that he had to be helped from his horse upon arriving. Judith Dupuy Scott of Greensburg, the only child—then almost six years old—of Presley's deceased sister Judith Dupuy Trabue Scott, was at the Anderson home visiting Grandfather Trabue. As soon as the sick man reached the house, the family began to pack the girl's belongings in order to send her home. Before leaving, Judith, whose mother had died twenty-three days after giving birth to her, was taken to her uncle's room to say goodbye. The dying man remarked, "Judith, I will soon be seeing your mother. Is there anything you want me to tell her?" So terrified was the child that she ran out of the bedroom screaming.[75]

Aware that the disease was usually fatal, the family put slaves to work digging a grave for Presley even before he died. The end came on the twenty-fourth, and his dehydrated body was laid to rest in the Anderson Cemetery to the left of the grave of his mother, who had been dead almost five years.

But for his daughter Sally Anderson, the sorrowing Daniel—who had suffered the loss of his youngest daughter, his wife, and his youngest son within six years—would have felt very much alone. The scourge that had swept Presley away must have instilled as much dread in the father's heart as had the vicious action of the depraved Harpe brothers, who had slain little John Trabue thirty-six years earlier in that selfsame community.

Failing to secure "half-pay" as an officer under Clark, Daniel Trabue petitioned the Congress "in his old age and poverty" for "some reasonable compensation"—probably implying, in lieu of what had been denied. He did not mention that he was already drawing a yearly pension of $260 under the act of June 1832.[76]

On February 1, 1836, the House of Representatives referred his appeal to its Committee on Revolutionary Pensions. Reporting unfavorably on March 26, the panel concluded erroneously: "His services at Fort Logan were of a private character, and not in any respect connected with the State or continental service."[77] Even so, it reported out a private bill to allow Trabue an annual sum of twenty dollars.[78] Either the committee was unaware that he was receiving a generous federal pension, or it conceived of the new amount as an addition to the old.

The bill cleared the House on June 13, the Senate twelve days later. On the day it passed the second reading in the House, 105 other such bills were considered.[79] President Andrew Jackson signed this "Act for the relief of Daniel Trabue" on June 28.[80] The next month the Pension Office instructed the Northern Bank of Kentucky, in Lexington, to put Trabue's name on the pension roll at the rate of twenty dollars per year.

In the course of time, Congressman John Calhoon of Kentucky dutifully sent Daniel a certificate for the new pension, informing him that it supplemented his earlier and larger annuity. Now the old man's mind was vexed with the thought that it might be unfitting to receive this additional sum. Even so, the legislator later urged him to "draw it and not hesitate." Sherrod Williams, another Kentucky congressman, gave the same advice. Former Congressman Richard A. Buckner asserted that "there was no impropriety" in accepting the second pension.[81]

Under the terms of the special act of Congress, the pensioner eventually received a lump sum of $110, covering the $5\frac{1}{2}$ years ending September 4, 1836, and later one semiannual payment. But in the summer of 1837, both the old and the new pensions were abruptly suspended by the Pension Office in Washington. Writing in November from Burkesville, the seat of Cumberland County, Daniel, Jr., surmised on behalf of his elderly father that the annuities had been stopped because of "his drawing on 2 pension certificates."[82] But another fly had gotten into the ointment. The commissioner of pensions had ruled, in error, "that there was no record evidence of his Service, and that there were no Stationed troops at Logan's Station in Kentucky during the war." Thus, the pensions of all privates who alleged service at Logan's Fort were discontinued.[83]

After Trabue refunded on January 1, 1838, the $120 he had drawn under the private act, the commissioner of pensions restored the smaller annuity. Still unaware of the real cause of the revocation of the pensions, Daniel, Jr., wrote the official in his father's stead that the annual pension of $260 was the one the veteran wanted and not the $20 one "unless they will pay both."[84] The son's plea notwithstanding, the commissioner did not reinstate the earlier annuity, now considered illegal by the government. Believing that some benefit was better than none, the father petitioned the official the next year to resume payment of the smaller pension, because the Lexington agency had not received the commissioner's order to do so.

Other letters passed between Lexington and Washington concerning this peculiar case, which was further complicated by an act of April 1838 requiring pensions unclaimed for eight months to be paid at the Treasury Department in Washington and not at the regional agencies. The old veteran never received any further payments. The larger annuity of $260 had been paid him for six years—a total of $1,560. This sum seems paltry when laid alongside the labor Trabue had expended from the fall of 1831 to the summer of 1837 in trying to establish his claims. On the other hand, the money came to him at a time when he was plagued with poverty and ill health.[85]

Daniel Trabue was fortunate to have a daughter like Sally with whom to spend his declining years. She owned ample wealth and labor with which to provide for her ailing father.

The last three years of Daniel's life are relatively a closed book. The fact that he was a messenger at none of the annual meetings of the Russell Creek Association after 1834, not even the one the next year at Mount Gilead, may indicate his continuing debility.

When the census taker came calling at the Anderson farm in 1840, he listed Daniel as a member of his daughter's family and as a putative pensioner of the Revolution, noting his age of eighty years.[86] As many as fifty-five pensioners of that war had once lived in Green County, but the number had now dwindled to twenty.

On the tenth of September that year the tired warrior, hoary with age, was gathered to his fathers. Trabue was buried to the right of his beloved Polly in the graveyard on his daughter's farm.

A brief obituary appeared two months later in the principal Baptist paper in Kentucky. He was characterized as a descendant of Huguenots, a veteran of the Revolution, a "Pioneer of the West," and "a member of the Baptist church for the last fifty years."[87]

When Daniel Trabue died, only four of his eight children survived. Mary Sublett had been dead for over three years. Sally Anderson was the only daughter who remained. The three sons were widely scattered. After having lived at the seat of Cumberland County for a while, Daniel, Jr., had returned to Adair and was now situated three miles from Columbia on the Burkesville Road, where he operated a store and tavern. James had been a prosperous wholesale merchant in Louisville since 1834. Robert, who had served as a justice of the peace in Russell County until early in 1828, lived later at Mount Sterling, Illinois.

In time, Daniel, Jr., was designated by the Adair County Court as the administrator of his father's estate. It was a meager, material patrimony the children received—the boundary of virgin timber in Clay County and the faint prospect of additional gratuities from the federal government.

The legacy Daniel Trabue transmitted to his heirs and to posterity, however, was far greater than these tangible benefits. Man's allotted threescore and ten years had been lengthened for him to fourscore, and he had lived a full and rewarding life. Beyond his economic contributions as an optimistic entrepreneur, he had rendered remarkable service as a public servant, a Baptist churchman, and a militia officer. As a county official he had been known as Squire Trabue for a quarter-century and as Sheriff Trabue for four years. As a deacon, a church clerk, and an associational messenger he had been called Brother Trabue. But it was by the title of his highest militia rank that he had been the most widely known—Colonel Trabue, a title inscribed on his gravestone.

Daniel Trabue had indeed been a pioneer in the land beyond the mountains. As a settler there, he had helped to wrest Kentucky from nature and from the Indian's tenuous hold and to plant the white man's culture in Trans-Appalachia. He had done all this, and of equal importance he had left a rich and meaningful narrative about much of what he observed and did.

The Narrative of
DANIEL TRABUE

Memorandom made by me D[aniel] Trabue
in the year of 1827 of a Jurnal of events
from memory and Tradition

1
The Huguenot Heritage

The Biography of Daniel Trabue.¹ I was born March 31, 1760,² as per Register, in chesterfield county, Virginia, 15 Miles from the city of Richmond. My Progenitors was from France. My Grandfather Anthony Trabue Fled from France in the year of our lord 1687³ at a time of a bloody persicution against the Desenters by the Roman Catholicks.⁴

The law against the Desenters was very Rigid at that time. Who Ever was known to be one or Evin suspected—if they would not swear to suite the priest—their lives and estates was forfited and they put to the most shamefull and cruel Tortue and Death, and worse than all they would not let any One move from their kingdom. They say it was the Dreadfullest time that could poseblely be conceived of. Gurds and troops was stationed all over the kingdom to stop and ketch any that might run away. At Every place where they would expect those persons might pass, their was Guards fixed and companys of Inquisetors and patrolers going on every road and every other place Hunting for these Hereticks, as they called them.

And where their was one that made their escape perhaps their was hundreds put to the most shamefull Tortue and Death and their estates confiscated.⁵ When the Decree was first passed a number of the people thougt it would not be put in execution so very hastely, but the priests, Friers, and Inqusiters was very intent for their estates and they rushed quick.⁶

I understood that my Grandfather Anthony Trabue had an estate but concluded he would leave it if he posibly could make his escape. He was a young man and he and a nother young man took a cart and loaded it with wine and went on to sell it to the furthemost Guard. And when night came they left their horses and Cart and made their escape to an Inglish ship who took them in. And they went over to ingland, leaving their estates and native country, their relations and every other thing for the sake of Jesus who Died for them.

My Mother was a Daughter of John Jams Dupuy. His father [left France about the same time.⁷ The circumstance was he was an officer in the army and he went home. And before he got home he had heard that his wife⁸ was turned Herriteck and when he got home she]⁹ told him all a bout the matter. She said she believed that [th]e catholicks was rong and that she had experienced the true [re]ligion of Jesus christ and she could not renunce it. She said the priest had been to see her and threattened her very sverly and told her he would be their again the next Day and if she Did not renounce her sentement and swear thus and so they would put her to the cruelest Death that they could think off.

That night she thought she was in a Dreadfull condition. She was looking for her husband at home but was not certain he would come and if he Did come she Did not know how he would act with her as he was a Catholick himself. She fasted that day and prayed to god almighty to Direct her what to Do. She did not ceace to pray all night.

The next day she saw the priest and the inquisitors coming. She had time to fall on her knees a minute or two before they entered her house. She prayed to Jesus christ the mighty God to be with her in this time of great need and strengthen her and Direct her what to Do. She said it came to her not to Deny her saviour.

She Jumpt up and meet them at the Door and told them to come in. They asked her if she would now Do what they wanted her to Do yesterday. She said she had not altered her oppinion. They told her she was a fool, she was Deluded by the Devil, and they would kill her as she was not fit to live any longer, and she would go to the Devil instantly. She said if they despised her and Cast her off and put her to Death her Dependence was in Jesus her saviour, who would receive her soul in heavin. They told her again she was a fool and a herytick (and many other names they called her), and that the way they was a going to serve her was to pull off all her finger nails with pinchers. And they said, "Look out at the door," that their was a big fat wild horse. "We will tye your hair of your head to that horse's tail and let him go. And then what will be come of you?"

She said, "I am a lone woman. You can Do so if you plese. I cannot help myself."

One of them said, "Let her alone to Day. It is thought her husband will come home to Day and he will tell her better." So they went away and left her.

The same Day her Husband came home. She told him all that had passed. He loved her much. She was a hansom young woman—newly married and no child. My Great Grandfather Dupuy was a strict Catholick[10] but thought this persecution was rong, and that he would take her over to ingland and leave her their untill times would alter, and he himself would come back and enjoy his estate as he was rich. It was said their was petitions going Every Day to the king to alter the Decree. My Great Grandfather thought the Decree would be altered. He imediately got a suit [of] men's cloaths that would fit his wife, give her a sword; and she passed as his servant in a man's regimental cloathing and a sword by her side. And they went to ingland.

As he was an officer, had on his Regimentals and sword, he could pass any where and shwing his commission if nessisary. He had no time to Dispose of his estate. He had once been offered, as I understood, as many Dollars as would go round his farm or lot by laying them Down flat and the edge to tuch. They said he had a valuable Vinyard. He and his wife got safe over to Ingland.

He soon understood that the priests and Inquisitors was Displeased with him as they suspected he had taken her away. He wrote back several times and got many letters from France but nothing to his benefit. His land and other propety was confiscated and went to the benefit of the Diabolical craft.[11] My G[reat] Grandfather Dupuy was much freted and perplexed about his estate, but concluded that it was certain that the king would alter the Decree some Day and restore his estate to him.

And in ingland they came across a number of Refugees who had made their escaps, although it was only hear and their one who made their escap. Yet when they got to gether it was a goodly company. They could tell one another of their trials and Dificulties.

The king of Ingland offered to these poore Refugees (if they would go to America) he would Do something for them, as he wanted to populate this new country.[12] And in the year 1700 my Grandfather Anthony Trabue and my Great Grand Father Dupuy and many others agreed to embark in the cause of going to the new world, as they then called it. Their was one of their Ministers also went with them. This Anthony Trabue was married this year to a French Girl in holand that was also a refugee and of his sect.[13] Many of these French people went to holland but Returned. My G[reat] G[rand]father Dupuy thought he would go to America and would return himself to France some Day if times was altered.

They all sat sail and landed and settled in America on James River about 15 Miles above the falls of James River.[14] This falls is where the city of Richmond now is. The king gave every one of them land[15] and corn for the first year. They laid off a town on said river and called it the manican Town after an Old Indian town which was at this place. This town was laid off on the south side of the river which was 15 Miles above said falls. It was a Desireable tract of Rich and furtail land. They went Emediately to hard work, building houses and clereing and tilling the earth.

They soon built them a church. They had a minister of their own.[16] These French people was the scect of Disenters that is called Congregationlists.[17] The king of Ingland alloued these people free liberty of Conscience as to their Religious worship and it was never took away from them. And they was never compelled to pay any thing to the established church[18] and pay their own Just what they was pleased to pay.[19]

Some of these people fetchd some little mony with them but the most of them was poor people.[20] Their industery and hard work soon got them to live very well. The nearest mill they had was at Col. Bird's, who lived at the falls of James River which was 15 Miles.[21] So some of them made use of hand mills. I think they brought some hand mills with them from Ingland. Their was a great many wild Deer in the woods but as these French men was not accumtomed to hunting they did not attempt it or but very little but soon Raised cattle and hogs a plenty.

Their was a number of wild horses in the woods in those Days and was claimed by Col. Bird and he incourged these French Men to ketch them and break them for working and Rideing for which they was to Give Col. Bird some small Trifle for Every one they caught. And they made Pens or pounds (at noteble places where their was what is called Deer licks) with gates that would fall too and shutt when the horses Got in. They would then halter them and break them for working and rideing. I have seen of this breed of hoses that the French folks had which they said was of the wild breed. I have seen the Remains of some of these pens. They was little horses and mostly natural pacers but indurable good horses.

The houses they built was posts in the Ground made of post oake which lasted a long time and sills framed to these posts and studs in the sill to the upper beam or plate and weather borded with clap bords. I have seen some of the houses they built, almost the first that was built. They had framed woodin chimneys and the inside Daubed with morter so they Done very well. The body of their houses was clap boards nailed on the out side, the inside lathed and filled with morter so that they were quite comfortable.

These French men worked their fields mostly with hows as they did not at first understand much about ploughing. They made Tobaco for Markit after a very little while.

It was said when these French men first settled their they did not know that green brush would burn. So they would hall or drag it out of their little field and make great high piles and after it got Dry then burn it. The trees and logs they served the same way. They rolled them entirely out of the field and left them in piles and when Dry they would burn easey. They cut Down every tree. They was so industrus that they would work late at night, and the men would Frequently get up before Day and make firs by a tree and cut it Down.

I was told these Frenchman—a number of them—went to Col. Bird's mill 15 Miles Distant, and they would had to encamp on the way as it was not a settled country. They made them up a fire and put their Sacks all in one pile. And That night their came rain and a sleet, and the bags was froozd all to gether; and when morning came it took them a long

THE HUGUENOT HERITAGE

time to get them a part. I have many a time heard them laugh and tell how aukeard they weare when they first came to James River.

They all lived near the bank of the River and on a certain day they Discoverned a man Ride Down to the operset shore and roade in the water. These French people was much alarmed, Thinking the man was Destracted and would soon be Drowned. All the town folks run out to see him, but to their great supprise the man Forded the river very well. This man was an old hunter and knew of this ford. After this these French people could ford the River likewise at a low time. They had lived their a considerable time before they knew the river could be forded.

As these French men was mostly very industrys they soon got to live well.[22] This Col. Bird was a great man in those Days and laid off these Frenchman's land and furnished Corn, etc., and Regesterd all their names.[23] And some of the French names appear so strange to Col. Bird he altered some of them, and their land titles or grants was according to the way that Col. Bird spelt them.[24] My Grand Father's name was Anthony Straboo but Col. Bird set in [it] Down Anthony Trabue and so we write our names to this Day. My Grandfather brought a certificate with him wrote on parchment from France that was spelt Straboo as well as I can recolect.[25]

Anthony Trabue had 3 sons—Anthony, Jacob, and John James.[26] John James was the youngest son (who was my father). First Anthony Trabue also had two Daughters. Jacob had many children and so had the two sisters. My father John James Trabue was marryed to Olymhy Dupuy. They had 7 sons and 8 Daugters—To wit, James, John, William, Daniel, Edward, Stephen, and Sammuel; Magdelum, Pheby, Jane, Mary, Martha, Elizebeth, Judith, and Susanna.[27]

I was sent to school in 1767.

In the year 1769 or about that time their was a great Fresh in James River, Much the largest that had ever been heard off. It carryed off the most of the houses that was on what they called the lowe grounds. It swept off the most of the Tobaco ware houses with the Tobaco in them; and as these Tobaco Ware houses all belongd to the publick, the publick had the Tobaco to pay for. Mony was very scirce at this time. The assembly of Virginia struck a paper curency to pay for the Tobaco which made mony plenty.[28]

And in the year of 1771[29] the baptist came in our county and they was much opposed by the church of Ingland and our rulers.[30] Their was 7 baptist preacher in chesterfield prison at one time for preaching,[31] but the more they was persicuted the faster they Gained prosalites.[32] At last they let them alone but not until the british war Commensed.[33]

In the year of 1774 on the 4 day of May their was a Great Frost that killed all the fruite, all the wheat, Rye, Barley, Oats, etc., and the corn also. But the most of the Grain put up again from the Ground. It was really a solemnly looking scean to see the orcheads, the fields, the woods that was so all forward and Green one Day and the next day to see it all black. Anumber of the trees was entirely killed.[34]

In the Same year 1774 their was an Indian war against the shawnees[35] and Govenor Dunmore went out him self.[36] My Brother Jams went with Dunmore as a Lieuftenant.[37] He raised some of his men in our county. They had Cockades of red ribond. I admired the looks of these soldiers so much I would have been glad to have went with them if I had been old enough. When brother James and the solders came home they told us about the battle at the mouth of the Kenoway [Kanawha] on the 10 of October, etc.[38] They also told us about Kentucky, a new Decovered wonderfull country. Brother James said the govenor said we was certain of a war with Britan, and their was[39] nothing elce talked about scircely but the war.[40]

Our church parsons and Merchants was mostly schoch men and Inglish.[41] I recolect I heard our parson[42] tell my father that the people was Deluded by some of their leaders. They was not only rong but fools. The people wuld Die like rotten sheep for the lack of salt. And what would they Do for Iron etc., powder etc.? He further stated their was as many men in the City of london as we had in north America.[43] He further stated that the Indians was all alreadey ingaged on the King's side by Dunmore and other of the king's officers and that the negros would also rise in Rebelion,[44] and if the people Did Rebel they would all be subdued and Defeated and all the leaders would be hung and every one that had any hand in it would suffer much by high fines and Taxes, etc.[45]

Their was meetings Called to consult about the war.[46] Their was Fast Days appointed.[47] The baptist and Prespeteruns was ancious for the war. Then it was that most of the men had hunting shirts and had "Lirbety" marked on their hunting shirts and bucks' tails in their hats. And the Mejority of the people said, "We will fight for our lirbety."

Their was a law passed that every one shoud take an Oath to our cause which was called the test Oath or leave the country by some given Day.[48] Some left the country. Others that would not leave the country and would talk in favour of the king was handled very roughly.[49] Some was
tard and featherd.[50]

These scoch Merchants hid their salt so that no salt could be got. People gethered in companys and went and hunted up the salt where it was hid and Divided it in many instances by paying them a reasonble prise. All law was stoped except breaches of the peace, etc.[51] Numbers went to the bays and boiled salt. Some saved their meet chiefly with hickery Ashes. Some people Dug up their smoke houses' floores and put the Dirt in hoppers and Dript the Dirt and boiled the water and made salt. One man my neighbour Gave 1,000 pounds of Tobaco for one bushul of salt.[52]

This year 1775 my father and grandfather Dupuy boath Died.[53]

And in 1776 the law was the young men at 16 y[ears] Old was to be put on the muster rool and put in Divisions for Duty when called for.[54] I was enroold and Drawed Number 1 and went one tourer Down the River against Dunmore.[55] And in 1777 was called on to gurd powder and move the Magezeen, etc.; and their appeared not much to be Done or wanted Doing in virginia.[56] At this time no sail for produce.

Brother William and myself concluded we would Join a company that was a going to the North under General Washington.[57] I was taken with a long fever and Declined to go to the northern army. Brother William went with a number of others.[58]

2
A Martial Introduction to the Kentucky Wilderness

The same Fall or begining of Winter Col. G. Rogers Clark from Hanover[1] was Fixing for a Campaighn to go Down the Ohia to the Falls.[2] The Virginia Legislator had authorised him to raise an army and go westward,[3] and my Oldest brother—to wit, James Trabue—agreed with him to inlist some men and go with him as Lieut.[4] I agreed to go with him. I got well and hearty and in the last of January or February 1778 we set out for our Jurney.[5] The most of the men that had enlisted with my brother had gone on to kentucky before christmas.

Their was only 7 of us and a negro boy went throug the wilderness together in March 1778. We all had good rifles and good Ammonition.[6] On Holston we took provision for our Jurney.[7] We understood a little provision would Do as we could kill a plenty on the way. We entered the wilderness in high spirits. I was truly Delighted in seeing the mountains, Rivers, hills, etc.,[8] spruce, pine, Laurril,[9] etc. Every thing looked new to me. Traveling along in Powls Valley where the Indians had broak up some people, seeing wast Desolate Cabbins I began to feel strange.[10]

We went on our Jurney and came in sight of the noted place called Cumberland Gap. We encamped all night (yet we was 3 or 4 Mile off) in a wast Cabin, and it was a Rainey blustry night. When Morning came the weather was clear, and after we ate our breackfast a little after sunrise we persued on our Jurney. When we got near to the Gap at a lorril branch[11] where the indean war road[12] comes in the Kentucky road[13] (this indian Road Crosses the Gap at this place from the Cherekeys[14] to the shoney town). And at this branch where the indian road comes in we saw fresh Indian tracks.

James Trabue ordered us every one to alight, prime our Guns afresh, and pick our flints[15] if they needed it, and put 2 bullits in each man's mouth. And if we could come up with the indians we must fight our best. The Indians' track was fresh and was Just gone the way we was going.[16]

James Trabue and one other man went on foot about 100 yards ahead. And our orders was if they Discoved the Indians they would Jump one side behind trees. And when we saw that we must all Dismount and run up to fight, and the negro boy must stay and mind the horses.

45 A MARTIAL INTRODUCTION

We had one man with us that was named Lucust. He said he wishd he could come up with the indians. He wanted so bad to have the chance of killing them. He said he knew he could kill 5 him self. He Could shoot. He could Tomerhack and make use of his bucher knife and slay them.

We still persued the indians. Their track was plain in places and after we got through the gap going Down the mountain the Indian tracks was still their. It looked like I was going out of the world.

When we got Down the mountain my brother called on me and a nother man to go before and told us to go fast. We walked very fast and some times run. When I was on before I could have a plain view of their Tracks, and in one place where the indians crossed a mirery branch I saw 3 Trails.[17] I then supposed that their was many Indians as they was apt to step in one another's tracks.

When I was returnd from going before and others in our places, I told my brother about the 3 Trails and told him my fear about the quanity of Indians. He said he had paid perticular attention to the sighn and he Did not think their was more Indians than white men. He said we all had good guns and good powder and we could beat them if we could git the first fire, unless they was Greatly over our number and he Did not think they was. And he said the main thing was to have a good resolution.

I was Giting very fraid we would be Defeeted, and as we went on I talked some with Lucust again. He still talked the same way of killing several of them. I for my part began to feel chikinhearted. I was afraid I should be killed in this Drary howling Wilderness but I never mentioned it to any one. I thought if we come in contact with the indians I would keep behind or in the reare, but I thought that would not Do as I might be called a coward. I thought, "I wish I could have courrage like Lucust. I would be glad." Mr. Lucaust was my main Dependence and a poor Dependence he was. I then wished I was back in Old Virginia.

We came by this time neare the indians, and the water was mud where they woud cross the branches. I knew although I was only a boy I was as active as any we had in loading and Shooting or runing, and I would try and have resolution but my heart would go piti pat.

All at once I saw the 2 men that was before Jump out of the road and was behind Trees. I Jumped of[f] my horse as quick as a cat and run with all my might to the exprorers that was before looking ahead. And Just before I got up to the 2 Men I saw the Indians before runing and Juming and Dogeing away. I run with all my might and tryed to git a shoot at them. I had liked to have got a shoot once or twise. I observed these 2 men as I passed by them was also trying to run a head and shoot.

It appeared the indians was seting Down in the road Ateing and they never saw the 2 men until they saw us, and as we was runing up we appeared many. We supprised them and so they Dashed off. I passed where they had been seting Down. I Descovered plunder lying their but persued after them. My brother Spoke to me and said, "Daniel, Take a tree!" I then Jumed behind a tree until the men got evin with me. I had never looked behind until this time to see where the rest was.

My brother said, "Boys, scatter to the Right and left. Let us persue after thim a little further but look sharp." Their was fully as many Indians as their was of us. We went on a bout 200 yards and called a halt.

And when we got back to the Indian plunder we found 7 packits, 5 boughs and arrows, 3 shot bags and powdir horns, several blankets, several new shirts, new fine leggans full of silver Broaches, brich cloaths full of silver broaches, one brass kittle, and many other things.[18] And when we was picking up this plunder and laughfing out a loud, this negro boy picked up a something a little on one side made with Feathers like a ravin. The negro boy said, "Lord! Lord!" with a loud laugh. "What is this?"

James Trabue said, "This is their thing they pow wouw with or cunger with, but," says James, "I thought I told you to mind the horses."

The negro said, "Lucust is their and I thought as he stayed their with the horses I would come and see what you was Doing."

James T[rabue] then hollowed and sayed, "Lucaust, look sharp on the other side and Don't let the indians git the horses." We could see him behind a tree near the horses but he came runing Down to us half bent. James T. said, "Why Did you not stay to mind the horses?"

He answered, "I was afraid to stay by my silf."

"And why Did you not come agreeable to my order?" said James.

"I was afraid," said he, "they would Git my horse," said Lucust.

James would swear when he was angrey. He cursed him for a D[amned] Coward.

We picked up all the plunder and ate their Meat that they was eating. We Deprived them of Finishing their Dinner.

The men praised me very much for being a brave soldier as I was the foremost man until stopt. I then thought that all Dangers wa'n't Death. I Did not tell them for some time after we come to talk about it of my fears. They was more of them that was very much afraid that their was too many Indians for us. We kept 2 Men a head as before until we had got past their war road.[19]

We went on much Gratyfyed and carryed all this plunder with us to Boonsburrough.[20] Our provision Give out. We could not kill any thing to eat.[21] Thursday morning [April 16, 1778] about Day light we ate the last of our provision, which was one Rasher of hog bacon to each man. And not a nother mouthfull Did we git until sunday (which was easter sunday)

47 A MARTIAL INTRODUCTION

about 2 o'clock when we got to Boonsbourrah on the Kentucky River.[22] The people[23] all ran out over Joyed to see strangers come to their town or Fort.[24] They Give us something to eat. They quickly asked us when we first spoke to them if we had seen any Indeans on the road. We told them all about it.

We sold the Indean plunder in the Fort on Munday at vandue and it Fetched Fifty shillings for each man.[25] Lucust got no part of the plunder. The negro boy got his shear. I bought some of this plunder, some nise wamp um and a shot bag and powder horn, etc.

I was much pleased to be on the banks of Kentucky River—the River that had been so much Talked about. We got bear meat and buffilow[26] and venson aplenty in this fort to eat, but not any bread to be had and not any salt.

My Brother James expected to have found some of his men hear but it was not so. 2 of his men Did go their—to wit, Thomas Brooks and William Brooks.[27] And they went with Col. Boon[28] to the Blue Licks[29] to make Salt and the Indeans took them all Prisoners—to wit, 27 men including Col. Boon.[30] Some of Brother James' Men was Gone to Logan's Fort.[31] We concluded to go to Logan's fort in a few Days but we would stay hear and rest a while.

We had to turn our horses in the woods. And the very next Day when James and my self was hunting our horses not fair from the fort, wee killed a very fine Deer and some of our company killed Deer, Turkeys, etc.

The people in the fort was remarkable kind and hospetable to us with what they had. But I thought it was hard times—no bred, no salt, no vegetables, no fruit of any kind, no Ardent sperrets, indeed nothing but meet.[32] Yet we was well off to what we was in the wilderness before we got hear. The sunday before I got hear[33] I was so hungry that if mony could have got it I think I would have gave $10 or 20 for one Diet. It was easter sunday and that was a noted Day in Old Virginia, and I thought, "If I was only their how I could eat. But I Don't Doubt but it was an advantage to us to suffer for food on the Road as the fair we now have will Do, as hunger is the best of sause."[34]

In about one week we went on to Logan's fort about Forty miles through the woods without any road. We found the way very well. When we Got their we found some more of our company and their was Great Joy. The people in this fort lived much better than at Boonsborough fort. They had plenty of Milk and Butter and some Bread. I was very much pleased and Delighted with the people and our fair too.

In a very few Days I went to the woods with some hunters to hunt. I was much plesed with the land and we killed some Bears. I had brought with me from Old Virginia a first-rate bull Dog that would seize any Ox or bull or horse. And the first bear he come up with was near where we could see him and he was a very large Old he bear, and my Dog run up when the other Dogs was abaying him. My Dog sezed him, and the bear Raised up his paw and knocked the Dog Down a hill many yards. It Disabled him so we was obligded to leave him in the woods. We got the bear and he was a fine one. We made out our loads and went to the fort and in about 2 Days the Dog came home.

And after that he become to be one of the best hunting Dogs at the fort. He would never after that seize a bear by the head but would seize by the hinder part and when the bear would turn to him he would Jump back. Every one in the fort would get my Dog when they was a going out. They Generally took several Dogs to the woods. They was very beneficial in killing bears and Buffaloos. I thought the beautyfulest sight I ever Did see was to see a parsil of Dogs in full chase after a bair and they a yelping every Jump. They would soon stop him and then the hunters would shoot him. I soon got so that I could eat meat without salt very well.

In a few weeks a number of men came from Virginia for to go with Col. Clark. They was stationed at Logan's and Hirodsburgh,[35] redy when they might be wanted.

Ben logan was then a Capt.[36] The fort was on his land, and inside of the fence thir was land not cleared and he was willing for us to raise Corn. My brother James and myself cleared up about one acre of land and planted it in corn to see how it would grow and it made a fine crop.

We went several times in the woods exploreing the country and hunting, but as the indeans was in the habit of waching the roads they had to be very caucious and not to go any road in Day light.

I soon lost my horse and several others. It was supposed the indeans got them. Their was an Old Duchman[37] lost his horses and he and myself concluded, although we could not hear off or find our horses near about the fort, we would go some Distance in serch of our horses. So we set out on foot, took some provision with us.

We hunted all Day but could not find them. I suppose we went 15 or 20 Miles eastard, thinking they might have gone to wards the Old Settlement. We took up camp in the woods, was afraid to make fire, wropt our blankets around us, and went to sleep and slept very well.

When Morning came this Duchman said to me, "Do you stay hear while I go one side." He took his gun in his hand and went out of my sight. He stayed some time. I would have been uneasy if he had not left his blankit where he had lay. After a while he came back and with a smile said, "I have made all things fast so that no indean can hurt us this day."

I said, "Mr. Lail,"[38] as that was his name, "how can you Do this thing?"

He said he was endowed with such power, he could spell their guns and Do many things.

I then told him I was faithless about these things.

He said as I was young I knew no better but he knew better.

"Well," said I, "will We find our horses to Day?"

He said he had been trying for that but something was rong. In that matter he could not tell, but one thing was certain. The horses was not on that rout. We would go back to the fort by takeing a rounderbut rout.

So we set of[f]. We was on foot. We walked very pert, stoped to eat when we was a hungry, and when we came in about 2 or 3 Miles of the fort we came to the road. Mr. Lail was before and he took the road. I said, "Mr. Lail, let us not keep the road. It is too Dangerous."

Mr. Lai[l] said,[39] "Te cane preak[40] is so pad to co through, and ted I not tel you tat no Indin in De nation coud hurt us dis day?"

I said, "Mr. Lai[l], I am afraid to go along the road. Let us take thrugh the cain."

Mr. Lai[l] said, "You are unpeleafer. I tel you Dere is no tanger. So com long."

So off we started and when we got about 100 yards from that place Mr. Lail's gun wint off accidently and he was so bad Frighted that he Jumped out of the road, leaving his Gun and big brim hat almost equal to an umberel lying in the road. I hollowed to him to stop.

He said, "Was tat you who shoots?"

I said, "No."

"Who was it ten?"

I said, "I Don't thing any body shot."

He said, "Wat was tat ten like a cun close by mine head?"

I said, "Mr. Lail, what do you leave your gun in the road for? Come and pick up your Gun and hat."

He came part of the [way] and would turn back, wanting me to explain to him the matter.

At last I picked up his gun and said, "Your own gun went off." He then came all in a trimble and took his gun and started in the cain. I said, "Load her," to which he Did.

He then said, "Some ting is gone rong. We must not keep De road."

So we kept through the cain to the fort and we never found our horses. No Doubt but the Indeans Got them. Capt. Logan said he saw a trail of horses where the indeans took them off. Capt. Ben Logan would frequently take men out of the fort before Day and go to notable places and wach for Indians. I went with him many times.

Mr. Lindsay[41] was commissary for the garrisons we had, and when Col. Clark landed at the falls of Oheia in June he began to erect a garrison at that place and sent to us to come on.[42] We hastend to him and Joined him. And this Mr. Linsay was now employed by congress to go to

New Orleans with a bill of Credit to git Goods for the soldiars' Cloathing for the united states army from the spanish Government. He went and got the goods the same year and fetched them up in a large ceal boat or boats.[43]

My Brother James[44] now was put in as Commessary for the 4 Garrisons—to wit, Boonsbourough, Logan's fort, Herodsbugh, and Lewisvile or falls of Ohia.[45] I imediately under took to be Debety Commessary at Logan's fort.[46] I took possesson of the publick stoore and publick horses, etc. at Logan's fort. My brother James had Deputies at every Garrison and he would go from one place to the other.

Col. Clark went on with his campaighn.[47] He took the Govener Roseblock at the Elinoise at Caskaskey.[48] This Gov. Roseblock was a French man but could speak Inglish that you could undestand him. This govenor was a French man. He was fetched through Ky. and sent on to Virginia.[49] Col. Clark also took the O[hio] post now Called Vinsains.[50]

James Trabue was very active in his Duty at the Defferent Garrisons and soon had them well supplyed with provisions by haveing hunters out, etc. And when he Received the publick stoors their was a quanity of powder at each of these Garrisons that had Got spoilt so that it would not Do for Rifles to kill indeans or to hunt with. James Trabue emedeately employed men to Work this powder over.[51] He understood it him self and shewed them how to work it. So we soon had a plenty of good powder, and when Clark's men came back Returning home we could suply them with provisions.

The Commanding offecers was much plesed with James Trabue. He was almost constant agoing from Fort to Fort, and some times he would send me and then he would attend our Magazene or publick stoore. James Trabue was very perticular with his Deputies. Very often he examind their books of the provisions and ammuntion and their Vouchers of Delivery and urge them to accurecy, etc.

This business kept me very busy and I was willing to be kept busy. My wages was prety good. I got the same pay as a Captain got or More.[52] Some times when I could spear the time I would go out my self with a hunter or two and fetch loads of Meet in to our stoore.

3
Disruptive Indian Incursions

The indians was very troublesome this summer. They was almost or very often waching the roads, killing Men, or steeling our horses, or killing our cattle.

Col. Harrod lived at Hirrodsburgh. His wif's father and mother lived at our Fort—to wit, Loga's Fort. Thir name was Cobern.[1] They moved to Herodsburgh and anumber of men conducted them when they moved but they Did not Remove all their Goods, etc., and old Mr. Cobern came up for the ballance of goods and had only 2 Men with him—To wit, Mr. Walker and Mr. McCoy. And in the morning when he was packing up to Depart Capt. Logan told him it was not prudent for him to go with so few men, if he would stay to the next day he would make some arangement for him to have a guard.

He said he wanted no guard, their was no Danger, the Indians was not always a waching the road, that it was not long since the Indeans left this place. He said, "Some time hence their may be Danger but their is none now. I will go and you need not give yourself any uneasyness about us."

So they bid us adieu and left our Fort, and in about 2 hours Mr. McCoy came back with the Dreadfull Mellencholy knews that Mr. Cobern and Mr. Walker was killed and he Narrowly made his escape. This happened about 2 Mile from Logan's Fort.[2]

Capt. Ben Logan emedeately went to the place with about 13 Men. When he Got their he found Mr. Cobern and Walker killed and skulped. They found that the indeans had persued McCoy some Distance to wards Herodsburgh and they (the endians) thought he was gone on that way. So they concluded the people at logan's Fort woud not know it, so they put the plunder in a cain break and hoppled the horses and then was gone to wards the fort. The conjecter was from the sighn their was 9 or 10 Indeans.

Logan sent back Alexander Montomery[3] to tell Capt. May[4] to take some men and go to the big lick[5] and wach their, while he would stay with the plunder and horses. James Trabue and Capt. May and about 8 other Men went emedeately. I got my gun to go but soon found their was none but Mr. McCoy to be left in the fort and none wanted to stay.[6]

Brother James[7] said, "O Dan, Stay! We must not all leave the fort." So I stayed with only one man—to Wit, Mr. McCoy. We quickly bared up the fort gates.

Capt. R. May and the men went to the lick and went on the back side in a Gut and lay concealed, and after a while they saw the indeans coming. Their was 9 indeans. Capt. May said, "Boys, now Don't shoot until I give you some Itam.[8] I will give the word. I want the endeans to come near to us."

James Trabue says, "Boys, look! Don't you see that Indean their with a Naked belley? Don't none of you shoot at him. I want to kill him my self."

While the men was a waiting for the indeans to get nearer and for Capt. May to give them the word they heard May's gun snap, and they looked at Capt. May and his gun was snaped. They all emedeately thought that Capt. May wanted to cheet and have the first fire to kill one Inden and they emedeately all fired. Brother James Trabue's white belly Indian fell and 2 or thre more fell and was badly wounded.[9]

The indeans Jumpt to trees and cursed our men and said, "Dam son a bich, come hear." These wounded Indians appeared to crawl off or was helped off. They was at the edge of a cain break.

They [the whites] got no indian. They come to the Fort and so Did Capt. Logan and his men as it was night.

The next morning by times Capt. Logan, Mr. Whitley (who was after this the Noted Col. Whitley),[10] and about 18 Men in number (I made one of this number) went to the place and had anumber of Dogs. They thought they could track them with Dogs through the cain. We saw plain where 4 or 5 bled Freely and as the cain was so thick we could not Discover them. We was a hunting them the hole of one long summer's Day. In the cource of the day we passed by wheare Mr. Cobern and Walker was killed. We stoped a few Minuts only and put logs over them to keep the wolves from geting them. We made no Descovery of Indians this day.

Mr. McCoy stayed several Days with us until he got a good chance to go home to Herodsburgh.[11]

I think it was some time in July we was to have the first court that was to be in Kentucky County.[12] The Court was held at Logan's Fort.[13]

Several men came from Herrodsbourgh to court. And when they arived they Give intelegence that the Indeans had fired on them about half way to Harrodsburgh which was Ten Mile from logan fort[14] and one of thir men was a missing—to wit, Mr. Poge.[15] It is yet a mistery how these men come to ride away from Poge and leave him for their was 18 or 20 Men and only about 5 indeans; but the fact was the indeans was in a cain break and our men Did not know how many their was.

Capt. Ben Logan called out, "Boys, Git ready! We must go their and see what is Done." He and his men started in a few Minuts on foot. They went brisk a bout 13 Men. The fact was at that time their was but few men belonging to the fort as some were gone with Col. G.R. Clark.[16]

The court meet and Done some little businss and adjurned to the next court in cource. As well as I can recolect Col. Bowman, Capt. Reddle, Col. Richard Calleway, and Capt. Ben Logan weare the Majezstrats of the Court of Ky. They chose Levy Todd for their Clerk. Col. John Todd was their Lawyer.[17]

Capt. Ben Logan was gone and went to where Mr. Poge was. They found him in the woods badly wounded. They made a litter and carryed him home to Harrodsburgh and got their the same night. Mr. Poge lived a few Days and Died.

The next Day when this Valueable Capt. Logan and his Valuable Men was comeing home near the same place where they [the Indians] shot Poge they fired on Logan and his men and wounded Hugh Leeper.[18] These men Returned the fire. The Indians were in a very thick cain break; but Logan and his men rushed in the cain after them and they fled. They got Pog's gun their with these endeans. The endeans bled much and from accounts by Prisoners their was but one Indean that got home. The rest killed but got none of them.

Logan and his men made a litter and started home with H. Leeper. They was afraid to come along the road with this wounded man so they took the woods and Dark caught them when they was 5 Miles off in the night.

Capt. Logan waked me out of my bed and told me he could not git no body to go to the assistence of these poore fellows. The fact was we had no more men.

I told him I would go.

He said I must go by the little flat lick which was about 3 Miles, then through the woods North course about 2 Mile.

I had 2 publick horses in a horse pen. I took them. A negro man and a Duch boy with horses accompanyed me. We took some provision for the men, as they had nothing to eat since Morning when they left Herrodsburgh.

Capt. Logan sayed he was very Doubtfull[19] I would not find them but he said he could not help it, he himself was tired Down and so was the men. But he said to me, "If you Don't find them in the night when Day comes you can by sirching about their." But he said, "Try to bring the wounded man in to night if posible but I am Doubtfull that he is mortally wounded."

So I went on with my Rifle. The Negro and Duch boy also took guns. We went on brisk. We had a path to the little flat lick. I then steered my cource as well as I could. I thought it would be a mere Marricle[20] if we found them in the night but we found them.

We saw their fire and went to them and talked as we apprached on them. Archer McKinney[21] was seting up with Leeper to give him water, etc. And when they heared us a comeing, Mr. McKinney said, "They are a coming."

One of their men was a yankey by the name of Phillips, understood as he was a sleep that the Indeans was a coming. He Jumed up and cryed out, "O lord! O lord!" and frighted the other men. They Jumed up, run to trees, and cocked their Guns.

I hollowed to them and said, "Don't shoot! We are friends." I looked at my Brother soldier Leeper and saw how he was wounded. I was very sorry indeed.

The men eat of the provision we gave them. They concluded they would not go until Morning. It was not long to Day and Morning Came we set out for the fort. Hugh Leeper was put on a horse and Archer McKinney road behind him and held him on the horse and we got in safe early in the morning.

Mr. Leeper was shot through the body near the left brest with 2 bullets—one about one Inch above the other.[22] The bullits went clere through his body. It was thought he would Die but he survived and got soon well again.

Our Court Jentry went home on this day.

The endians stole almost all the horses we had belonging to Logan's Fort.[23] Some men had been to the indean towns and stole horses and had good suckcess in the adventer.[24]

Alxander Montgomery and Simon Kenton[25] asked me if I would go with them to the Indian town to steal horses,[26] and I and G. Clark[27] agreed to go. We 4 agreed to go to Scioto wher Chillicothey now is.[28] We made preparration to go, got some nise halters made with grained raw Buffelow hides. We procured Deer lether lagons, parched corn Meal, and some Jirk. With 2 pair Mockinsons to each man, etc., our Guns and ammonition in the best Order, the next morning we was to start.

My Brother James was gone to Boonsbourough about his Comnessary business. Capt. Logan was to keep the publick stoore for me until James Trabue got back. We did not look for him under 2 or 3 Days but he came that night. He was quickly informed of this Matter. He came to me and talked to me about this Matter.

I told him that he knew the indeans had got my horse and we could go and steel horses from them. It was much better to Do that than to give my Mony for a horse. And he could keep the Magezeen until I Returnd and if he had not time to Do it Capt. Ben. Logan would Do it.

James Replyed, "It is a Dangerous attempt. I am not willing for you

55 DISRUPTIVE INDIAN INCURSIONS

to hazard your life in that way. One man's life is worth 100 horses and you have got mony a plenty that you brought from home with you." And said he, "I have als got mony. A horse can be got when you want one to go home on." And he further said, "I have got a good horse. I will give you him, for," said he, "if any thing would happin to you how could I Ever see our Mother? She would say, 'James, how come you to lit Daniel go on such an errand?'" I concluded I would not go.

The next morning [Monday, September 7] A. Montgomery, S. Kenton, and G. Clark started. They went to the Chillicothey town [September 9] and got 4 or 5 very likely horses,[29] and when they got to the Ohio the wend blowd and the waves was so high they could not Get thur horses to Cross [September 12]. It was about the middle of the Day when they got their. They made many attempts that Day but none prevailed.

Whin morning [September 13] came the waves was as rough as ever. They attempted to cross again but to no effect. They then left the horses in the bottom to feed and they went on their back track to see and wach. And they got such a nice place to wach if the Indeans had Come they could have Defeeted a smart[30] number. They stayed and wached until nearly the middle of this day.

They then concluded they would go and git the horses and go Down the Ohia perhaps to Luisvile. They went to gether up their horses. A. Montgomery had got on One of the horses. The Indeans came on them and fired on them and badly wound Kenton and took him a prisoner, shot Montgomery at a Distance of 100 yards through the head as he was riding from them in a Gallop and killed him. Mr. Clark run under some Drift wood and conceald himself till night; after night he tyed some logs to gether, laid his gun and things on this raft and shoved it before him and swum over and made his escape. And he came home with this Melincholy knews.

Mr. Kenton Tarryed some time with the indeans. He got well of his wound and they sold him to the british officers at Detroyt and he run away from them and Came home.

Col. Clark got back to the falls of Ohio and sent letters up to our Forts for some of the Jentlemen and ladys to come to see him.[31] He would make a Feast.

My Brother James Requested I should go and Do his buseness at that place. Some of us went from Logan's Fort. We went by Harodsburgh, stayd all night.

In the morning Col. Harrod and his Lady, Colonel McGarry,[32] and several other Jentlemen and ladys started—about 20 Men and about 6 Ladys. When we had Got a bout one Mile from the Fort I Descovered Indeans in the woods and runing to Get before us. I told McGarry of it.

He halted the compay and he went to examine the sighn. He came back, said he saw the indeans, and said we was not able to fight them while we had these woman.

And we retreated to the Fort. A party of men went from the fort and found the indeans had gone away.

The next morning we set out again. We had about 15 Men and 3 ladies on our next rout. Mistress Harrod Killed a Buffeloe as an exploit on the rout.[33] We got safe to the falls of Ohio.

Col. Clark had got back and fetched up with him a Keel boot with some Rum and sugar which he got from Caskaskey. He had a large new room Just built, hewed logs in the inside, a good plank or punchem Floore.[34] That same evining he made a ball.[35] A number of Jentleman and Ladies attended to it, and when these Fort Ladys come to be Dressed up they did not look like the same. Every thing looked anew. We enjoyed our selves very much. Col. Harrod and his lady opened the ball by Dancing the first Gig. We had a plenty of rum Toddy to Drink.

We stayed their some few Days. I made some agreement with Clark for some little salt for our Forts and took it up with us at that time. This salt Clark had fetched from Caskaskey but informed me he would try and have some made at bullits lick[36] for the publick's use. And after a while Col. Clark Did have some Salt made. I fineshed the buseness I was sent to Do and got a man to go with us and pack up the little might [mite] of salt we got. It was a bout 2 bushels to each Fort which was a great thing to us. With that salt we saved a vast quanetety of Beare Meat. We Returned home again.

4
The "Big Siege" of Boonesborough

James Trabue started to Virginia[1] to go home and also to go to Williamsburgh at the seat of government to get Mony for to pay for the provesions we had bought.[2]

About this time Mr. Hincock,[3] who had lived at Boonsbourrough [and] who had been a presoner with the shoney Indians and at Detroyt, made his escape and Came to boonsbourough and informed them that the Indeans in a great army[4] was a coming to take boonsbourough; that Col. Daniel Boon was at Detroyt[5] and had agreed with the british officers[6] that he would come with the Indians, and that the fort should be give up, and that the people should be taken to Detroyt and live under the Juresdection of his graceous Majesty king Gorge III. Mr. Hencock stated that it was with Great Difficulty and hazard that he made his escape and he would not have risked his life if it had not been to give them this Notice.

The people at Boonsbourough imediately sent to our fort and Herrodsbourgh for some of our men. We had about 40 Min. We sent about 15 and some went from Herodsburgh.

Col. Daniel Boon Came to Boonsbourough and told the same tale that Mr. Hencock had stated. Only sayed he was a Deceiving the Britesh officers and Indians, he was now come home to help his own people fight and they must make what preperration they could[7] but the indeans would certainly be their in a few Days. But they would have time to go against Jest some indians that lived not far over the Ohio, and if a few men would go with him he would conduct them to this little Camp,[8] and as these indians was rich in good horses and beaver fur they could go and make a great speck [amount] and Git back in good time to oppose the big army of Indians. Several men agreed emediately to go with Boon. Col. Richard Calliway[9] apposed the plan with all his might but they went.

If I remember about 20 Men went, and before they got half way to the place that they started to go to they meet with a company of Indians a coming towards boonsbourough. They had a smart engagement with them and Returned to boonsbourough with all thur Might,[10] and they got their only a few hours before this great army of Indeans got their.[11]

When the Indians Got their, a white man or half Breed[12] came up to the fort with a white flag and called for Capt. Boon. Boon went out to the Indians and Returned to the fort, stateing that they could make peace with the Indeans, that the officers must all go to the indeans' camp and make a good peace, to which he (boone) said he was willing and thought they could make a good peace. But the good Old Col. R. Calliway apposed it and wanted the endeans to come up to them.[13]

At length the indeans agreed that their Chiefs would come up near the fort gate, and our officers would go out their and meet them. And accordingly this was agreed to and they meet accordingly.

Preveously to their going out Col. Calloway told the people in the fort they must be Redy with their guns, if the indians useed any Violence to fire on them, etc.[14] He also told them for the Woman to put on hats and hunting shirts and to appear as men and git up on the top of the walls and as they might appear as a great many men. And the woman did so and the men in the fort did also git on the walls and Cabins and showd to a good advantage. Their was about 75 white men in this fort and about 1,000 Indians around the fort.[15]

About 30 of the indian chiefs[16] came up in about 50 yards of the Fort, Col. Boon with them, and our Officers—about 15—went to them and they had a long talk. And the Indians made or pretend to make a firm peace with the white people and said we must shake hands for frindship, to which the white people agreed to Do.[17] So they shook hands. The Indians then said, "Shake hands again," and so they Did. Now the Indians sayed, "Two indians must shake hands with one white man to make a Double or sure peace."[18] At this time the Indians had hold of the white men's hands and held them.

Col. Caleway objectd to this, but the other Indeans laid hold or tryed to lay hold of the other hand, but Col. Calleway was the first that Jirked away from them. But the indeans seized the men—two indeans holt of one man or it was mostly the case—and Did their best to hold them, but while the men and Indeans was a scuffling the men from the fort agreable to Col. Calliway's Orders fired on them. They had a dredfull skuffil but our men all got in the fort safe. And the fire continud on boath sides after that.[19]

Col. Calleway[20] had made a wooden Cannon and took wagon tyre and wropt it, and the indeans had agreeable assembld several to gether at a Distance. Calleway loaded his Cannon and put in 20- or 30-ounce balls and fired at the Indeans. It made a large Report equal to a Cannon. The Indins squndered [scattered] from that place much frighttd and it was thought several killed or wounded. This Cannon was fired the second time and burstd. The last time it was fired was at a grope of Indeans at a Distance and it made them skamper perdidiously. Whether they was hit

59 THE "BIG SIEGE"

with the bullits or whether it was the big loud Report it was uncertain, but one thing is a fact they never was seen in gropes right after that time.

The indians some times would hollow aloud to our men and curse them and said, "Why Don't you shoot your big gun again?"

Our men Did answer them, "Go many of you together and we will shoot it, but it is not worth while to shoot at one Indean when he is runing or Doging" [dodging].

This fort was close on the bank of the Kentucky River, and it was Descovered from the fort that their was an old cedar stick or pole that come up out of the bank perpendecular and it was observed to shake: our men knew then the endeans was Digging a passway (this was a project of a Canadian french man,[21] as was thought) under the fort from the River under the bank but they could not be seen from the fort.[22] Col. Calleway imediately had our men at Diging a ditch oppersite the Indians' Ditch.[23]

Capt. Holder, a large strong man, took big stones and cast them from the fort over the bank, expecting they might fall on some of the Indians.[24] One of the woman of the fort said, "Don't Do so, Capt. It might hurt some of the Indians and they will be mad and have revenge for the same."[25]

And the Indeans and our men did almost meet under the fort a Digging. They could hear one another a Diging[26] and when the indeans heard that, they thus quit, supposeing our people might or would put their big gun their.[27]

The siege continued for 10 Days and nights.[28] Our men received but little Damage from the Indians' fire but it was thought their was several Indians killed.[29]

William Pattin, who lived at Boonsbourough, was in the woods at the time the Indians came to this Fort; and when he came home the Indians was all round the fort, and he lay in ambush until the siege was almost over.[30] He would go at a Distince on some high hill and view the Indians, and some times in the night he would approach tolerably near; and on the last night he stayed, the Indians made in the night a Dreadfull attack on the fort. They run up to the fort—a large number of them—with large fire brands or torches and made the Dreadfullest screams and hollowing that could be imagind.

Mr. Pattin thought the Fort was taken. He came to our Fort—to wit, logan's Fort—and informed us Boonsbourough was taken and he actuly Did hear the Indians killing the people in the fort. "They took it by storm," he said, etc. He heard the woman and Children and men also screaming when the indeans was killing them. We beleaved every word he told us as he was known to the people to be a man of truth.

Now Capt. Ben Logan had made great preparations against the Indians. He had Dug a Deep Dech from the fort to the spring and covered it all over so that water could be got in a pinch.³¹ He told the men, woman, and childrun imedeately to bestir themselves and bring in the fort rosten years,³² punkins, fill their vessils all full of water. He said their was but little Doubt but the indeans would come to our Fort.

He called on me about the qunety of provision I had on hands. I informed him I thought we had a plenty as I had lay in meet on the purpose in case of a siege. He said, "Let me see." The stoore was oppined and he viewed it. He Replyed, "You have got a good qunety but it is uncertain how long we might be beseeged, and I think you had best go out to the big lick and Drive some cattle up and we will stop them up in the fort as we may need them. If you will go I will send men with you."

I said, "I certainly will go and I have 2 horses hear ready. I will go this menuet. Whear is your men?" The men was ready emediately—about 6 or 8. And we had got but a few steps before Capt. logan said, "Stop! I am afraid for you to go. I will go by my self.³³ Go back in the fort. I will hunt the cattle and Indians alone. I will keep in the cane the whole way. And," says he, "have as much new corn as posible brought in the fort and look sharp."

The men, woman, and children was as industrus as I Ever saw people in my life. They had abundance of corn in every house and punkins and Every pail, tub, Churn, kittle, and pot filled with water.

And in about one hour Capt. Logan came back badly wounded. He was rideing a white horse. The horse was very bloody and his wounds was in 2 or three places very Dangerous, one of his arms brok. It was a bad affair. He said about 9 or 10 Indians all fired on him with in a few steps of him when he was in the cain on a small path.³⁴

We had no surgen but Ben Pettit and he knew nothing about it, only from nessessity.³⁵ Mr. Pettit applyd Sleppery Elm bark.³⁶

We had a brave man in the fort whose name was John Martain.³⁷ Capt. Logan got him to go with all speed to holston after men to come to our assistence. I wrote the letter for Capt. Logan to a friend of his to come and help us in this our need, also refurd them to M[r]. Martain.

We had Only about 24 Men in the fort besides Capt. Logan. We expected the indians would besiege us but Did not think their Main body would come under a day or two. Their was great Distress in our fort not only for our selvs but for the people of Boonsbourough and in perticular for the 15 Men that belonged to our fort that went their to help them. We thought we was in a Great Perdickament. If the Indeans took Boonsbourough with 75 Men what will become of us with only 24?

A little after Dark Capt. Logan sent for me to come to him. He said that we appeard to be in Great Danger but it was best to Do our best and when the Indeans Did come, for he said he Did not Doubt but they would come and try to take the fort, he thought we ought to fight until the last man was killed and try to kill as many of them as posible. And says he, "I am certan if we can keep the fort 15 or 20 Days Men will come from Holston and help us." And says he, "It is certain if the indeans takes the fort they will kill me and all the sick and wounded and perhaps won't speare any. Try to encourage the man and boy in your house." I lived in Mr. Smith's house and he had a son about 12 or 13 years old, and Capt. Logan said, "Tel Mr. Smith to come hear." I Did and he went. He told Mr. smith the same tail and so sent for Every one of the men one by one and told them all about the same tail.

Some time in the night the indians came up near the fort and did steal one horse that was tied near the fort. Our senteries fired on them. When morning came the cattle come runing up and we could see them at a Distance and they would Dash off and run around about, so we could see and know that their was Indians around us. We expected every minut to be attaced. It was a Meloncholy Morning. When the cattle would come up to the fort some of them Had arrows in them and they would keep looking back. We was afraid to open the fort gate to let in any cattle for fear the indeans might rush in. The cattle that had bells on them, as an Indian said about a big fat hog, come up a missing as the Indeans had killed them for their bells. So they never come up any more.

We had port holes in our houses. They weare block houses.[38] What is ment by a block house? The uper story to be much biger than the lower story and to Jut over so that you may be up on the uper floor and shoot Down if the indeans was to come up to the walls, and they cannot climb up the walls of these houses. All the houses at this fort was built this fashion that was on the out side, and wher their was not block houses it was stockaded very well. We had an excelent Fort. They had no chance to cros our walls except they had ladders.

As Mr. Smith and his son was in their house I very frequntly would go over the fort and look at the rest of the people. They was a couragus people but yet I will say they all looked very wild. You might frequntly see the woman a walking around the fort looking and peeping about, seeming that they did not know what they was about, but would try to incourage one another and hope for the best. Capt. Logan boar his wounds with a great Deal of patience and fortytude and the men would often go in to see him. He would still encourage them.

The Indians did not attack us on this day and we thought the reason was their had not been time for their main army to get hear from boonbourough but yet they would come. About half the men stood all night at their posts and so would relieve on[e] another.

The next day I heard a great cry out on the side of the fort next to wards boonsbourough. I said, "Mr. Smith, stay hear. Look sharp! I will go and see what is the matter."

He said, "Yes, go."

I heard them say, "Yes, yes, the indins is a coming."

The woman, all runing to see, they weare a peeping through small holes, some of them saying, "Lord, have mercy on us. Yonder they come."

I had my gun in my hand. I run up in one of the bast ends wher their was men ready for fireing. I looked towards boonsbourough. At the Distance of perhaps 300 yards I saw them a coming. We could not see how many as we Could not [sic] see only the front of them and they weare only in one file, what is called Indian file, one Deep.

The men—some of them—said, "Dam you! Come on!" I heard the same thing repeated along the side of the fort next to wards boonsbureough wher they could see them. I actully felt better at this time than I had felt for these two Days. I told these men I thought I could soon make a good shoot and they all said they would try to make shore shoots.

When they advanced nigh the fort some of the woman was the first that spoke out and said, "It is our boys." And as they come nigher we found out it was our boys shore enough. The fort gate was flung open. "Come in! Howdey, John, Dick, Sam, harry, Tom, Jarret, Manifee," etc. Some a crying for Joy, some a laughing for Joy as they had [been] thinking their brother, husband, or relation was killed or prisoners with the Indeans was come now home alive. "Are you all alive? Are you all hear?"

"Yes! Yes! Yes!"

"We heard you was killd. Mr. Patton said the fort was taken."

"No, it was not," they said.

They was told Capt. logan was badly wounded. "Run in to see him and tell him the knews." Some of them went emedeately to Logan and told him the knews. Capt. Logan smiled for the first time sence he was wounded. If ever I had seen people glad, it was at that time.

These men told us all about it and said they was not supprised at Mr. Patton for thinking the fort was took, for the Indians at that time did rush up to the fort and did make the Dreadfullest ados that was ever heard off, and as it was in the night he could not tell from the Distance he was. These men informed us the Indians was Gone from Boonsbourough. Some gone to wards the Cherrykees, some towards the shoneas' town. Some had gone toward Harrodsburgh and about fifty or sixty had come to this fort.[39]

This same Day some of our men went of[f] from the fort and found the trail of Indians was gone from our fort. They had Done much Damage in killing Cattle, hogs, etc., and stole some few horses but their was not many to steel as they had got them nearly all before. I then thought all Dangers want Death.

63 THE "BIG SIEGE"

I think it was about three weeks the men from Holston Came—I think about 100.[40] We had a plenty of provision provided for these Holston men such as fat buffelow and bear meat and new corn. These Holston men was very Desirous to Join and go a campaighn against some one of the Indeans' town. The officers was sent to from Boonsbourough and Herrodsburgh to council about this Matter. It was finally concluded it was not practible at this late season of the year. So after a week or two these men went home again.

Colonel Richard Calleway brought up a Complaint against Capt. Daniel Boon, who is now Called Col. D. Boon. Their was a court Marshal[41] called to try him. He was tryed at this time at Logan's fort. I was present at his Tryal.[42]

Col. Richard Calleway's Charge first was that he (D. Boon) took out 27 Men to the blue licks to make salt, and that the Indians caught said Boon 10 Mile below these men on Licking,[43] where he was a ketching Beaver, and they was not going to wards these men. And Boon told them of these men and took the Indians to the men and told our men, "You are surrounded with indians and I have agreed with these Indians that you are to be used well; and you are to be prisoners of war and will be give up to the British officers at Detroyt, where you will be treated well." And these men against their consent had to go with the Indians to Detroyt.

And at Detroyt he (Boon) Did Bargan with the British Commander that he would give up all the people at Boonsbourough, and that they should be protected at Detroyt and live under British Jurisdiction.

And that when Boon came home he incouraged some Men to leave the fort to go away over the Ohio River. Boon went with them to an Indian town and that before they had got near the town they meet with some Indians and had a small fight with these indians was a comeing to boonsbourough. When the men saw them our men hurryed back with all their might and they only got to the fort a few hours before the Indean army got their.

And he (Boon) was willing to take all our officers to the Indean camp to make peace out of sight of the fort. Col. Calloway says Boon was in favour of the britesh goverment, that all his conduct proved it.

Capt. Daniel Boon sayed the reason he give up these men at the blue licks was that the Indeans told him they was going to Boonsbourough to take the fort. Boon said he thought he would use some stratigem. He thought the fort was in bad order and the Indeans would take it easy. He (Boon) said he told the Indians the fort was very strong and too many men for them, that he was friendly to them (and the officers at Detroyt) and he would go and shew them some men—to wit, 26—and he would go with them to Detroyt and these men also, and when they come to take Boonsbourough they must have more warriers than they now had. Boon said he told them all these tails to fool them. He also said he Did tell the Britesh officers he would be friendly to them and try to give up Boonsbourough[44] but that he was a trying to fool them. Col. Calleway insisted he was in favour of the britesh[45] and he ought to be broak of his commission. Boon insested other wise. The court Marshal Deseded in Boon's favour and they at that time advanced Boon to a Major.[46] Boon after that time appeared alwaise to be on the side of this government. How ever, Col. Calleway and Capt. Ben Logan was not pleased about it.[47]

This same Fall[48] Capt. Rogers[49] was going up the Ohia from Leusivil to fort Pit[50] with a keal boat with many men in it, and when they got to the mouth of Licking they Decovered some Indians on this side of the River. They run their boat ashore and landed their men and fired on the Indians, but their was more Indians than they expected and they got completely Defeeted. Some few of the men run back to the boat and shoved it off and made their escape.[51] Their was many killed on the ground.

One man[52] had boath of his arms broak and run of[f] in the woods and he come across a man by the name of Dulain. This wounded man followed Dulain and Dulain run and he kept up with him. At last Dulain told him he must not follow him, as he was a bleeding the indians would follow him by the blood, and another thing he said he could not travel as far in a Day as he could. The wounded man insested to go with him, and if he Did not keep up or could not travel as far in a Day as he could he might then leave him: he insested to go with him, that if he was left by himself he must perrish; but Dulain told this man not to follow him any further, and run off and left him.

This poor creature did not know what course to take. At length he concluded to go back to the battle ground, and when he got their he found a man in the bushes with boath of his thighs broak.[53] They condoled their casses with one another. They tied up their wounds as well as they could. This man with the Broken thighs had a good rifle gun and plenty of powder and bullits. He ketched fire and the man with the Broken Arms would kick up the wood, and they made fire as it was in October or November and the weather was cold. A number of Turkeys pirched on the trees where they weare. This man with the gun would shoot the turkeys and the man with his arms broak would kick them up and they ate them and made use of the flesh also to apply to the wounds.

The Turkeys came their almost every night and they lived this way about 9 Days when a boat came Down the River agoing to Leuisvile.[54] And "broken Arms" saw it and went on the bank of the Ohio and told them of their cituation and beged them to come and take them in. The people in the boat was afraid it was to Decoy them and would not stop.

THE "BIG SIEGE"

"Broken Arms" run Down on the beach and Down the river, beging and beseeching them to have pity on them, Declaring their was no Deception with him. At last one man in the boat said he woud run the risk. He took a canoe and went to them and fetched them to the boat and took them Down to the falls of Ohia. These men was nursed and Doctered and boath got well.

As to Dulain that left the wounded man in the woods and refused to let him go with him, [he] was at the Fort at the Falls of Ohio, and when he first got their he told them about "broken Arms" and said he had nursed and waited on him untill he Died. He then covered him with logs, etc. The people in the fort and command was so Displesed with Dulain that they made him ride a rail throgh the fort and the boys flinging at him and then Drumed him out of Camp. This affair about the broken Arms and Broken thighs, etc., was told to me by an acquaintence of mine who was then liveing at Leuisvile by the nam of T. Phelps.[55]

Our hunters brought in a great many fat Bears. Many of them weighed 400 neet. We had got a litle more salt that was made at Bullits lick, and very little salt would save fat Bear meet. Sometimes I could spear the time and Did go out with the hunters to kill bears, which amusement I took great Delight in. As the weather was cold we made large fires and our Dogs was all the sentry we had. If they would bark one man go around and see what it was. We was often in the night Disturbed in this way by the wolves.

Some time in December [1778] Brother James got back to our Fort with mony to pay the people for their provisions and the hunters for Meat Furnished. It was now agreed that I should go home and Return again Shortly but I could not git company and it was too Dangerous to go alone. Their was 2 other men in our fort wanted to go also, and we concluded as it was now winter their was not so much Danger of Indians and we would make the venture.

And the Day before christmas we set off when their was a smart snow on the ground. We had each a good horse, Rifle, and Tomerhock, etc. Some of the people in the fort said we would perish with the cold as we had no big axx to cut fire wood at night. Some thought we might come across Indians and it was Dangerous for us three to go by our selves; but, however, we started and took provision for our selves and some little corn for our horses.

Christmas Day in the evining one of our men—to wit, Daniel Mungrel—killed a cub Bear. We took it along to our camp. We stopt about sun set at a very Good place for wood and water and cain for the horses. We getherd a plenty of good wood before Dark to keep a big fire all night. We skined our bear and it was a very good one. We roasted a part of it for our christmas Diner and we feasted on it most bountyfully. I thought it was as good a christmas Diner as I had ever eaton. We was some little afraid of Indians, and as their was snow and a crust on it no one could aproch without being heard. So we concluded that night one to keep awake at a time to listen and we Done so every night.

When we got to Powels Valley I meet with John Clarry[56] and one of his brothers that had lived in Logan's fort with me, and they overpersueded me to go by their father's up clinch River about 75 Miles.[57] They said it was none out of my way, and I went with them and stayed and rested 3 or 4 Days. They had aplenty of corn and fodder for my horse and aplenty to eate and whiskey to Drink. The Indians had not pestered that neighbourhood that year so they made good crops.

Old Mr. Verdemon[58] was a near neighbour, who was father to Jerymiah Vardemon.[59] Old Mr. Vardemon had a Daughter liveing in Logan's Fort—to wit, William Manefield's wife. They (the family) was very glad to hear that their Doughter and family was well as they had heard about the Indians being very Troublesome in Kentucky.

I started on my Jurney along a small path that had not been much Trod. And one night I came to a poor man's house, and their was no other house for many Miles so I petitiond for qurters. I was told I was wellcome to such as they had. I stayed all night. My horse had aplenty of corn and foder. They had nothing to eat but homminy. This man had a wife and 7 or 8 children and all his Deppendence for Meat was hunting and he had no powder. So the family had to go without meet until he could get powder. I had a little meet with me. That night the family and I finished it. That night their came a bundence of Rain and raised a creek that I had to cross, so that I was water bound.

This man and I went to hunting but could not kill any thing. Every meal we had hominy. I had to stay their 2 Days. I would have went round the creek but it was so mountainous a cuntry it was not practiable. I was now very sorry I had left the main road to go with Mr. Clary. The whole of this road from Mr. Clarry's was nothing but hills, Dales, and Mountains all the way to new river. The water fell and I left this poor man's hominy house. I made some presents to the children as they weare kind to me with what they had.

I Did expect to git to new river at Inglishe's fery[60] this night, but the road was rough and bad and the Day short. I got to a house about Dusk and it was a snowing very fast. A old man and his wife lived their by them selves. They told me about 2 mile from their was a tavern[61] where I would strike the big road[62] and I could easyly find the way. The path only forked once and then I must take the right-hand path.

As these people was very poore and not willing for me to stay and I wanted to git to some good publick house, I made the venter and started on my way but I saw no right-hand path. I went about 5 Miles and came

67 THE "BIG SIEGE"

to new river. I hollowed several times but could hear nothing but the roaring of the water. It had been snowing all this time very fast and the snow was very Deep and it very Cold. I could see no house, hear no Dogs bark, and I Did not know what to Do. If I was oblidged to sleep in the woods, I thought it wuld be a bad chance for me to make fire in such a Deep snow.

It had snowed so fast I expected my back track was covered with snow but I turned back to find the way to the last hous I left. I at last found the house, tyed up my horse until morning, slept by the old man's fire after eating some mush and the sowerest milk I have Ever tasted, payed the Old man in the morning and went on my Jurney, found the way to the tavern, got a Dram.

I told the lady I was almost perished with cold and hunger and to give me a worm breackfast like coffey, Eggs, saussages, etc. And all these I got and my horse well feed and I was now on the big road. I now felt well satisfyed and got much Recruited.

In about two hours I went on my Jurney again. I now had a main big road to travel. The weather remained very cold but I could git a good house at night, so I thought I would Do well. I went on and arived in chesterfield at my Mother's, found her well and the family. And they were much Delighted to see me well and in good health, and so was I much plesed to see them all onece more.

They asked me a bundence of qustions about kentucky and the Indians, etc. I told them all about it. My Relations and the neighbours all would come to see me and I must go to see them in return. When they come to see some plunder I had, which we had got from the Indians when we Defeeted them, they was astonished and much gratifyed. I had a cousin by the name of Daniel Trabue and after this they would call me "Kentucky Daniel" and the other one they called "River Daniel," as he lived on James River.[63]

After a while I Received a letter from my Brother James from Kentucky. He informed me Col. Richard Calleway would be at my Mother's in the spring of the year [1779], and he wished me not to come back to Ky. until Caleway would come and help him to pack out powder and lead. Col. Calleway come to my Mother's, went to the Legislater at Williamsburgh.[64] He was a member from Kentucky.[65] He promised to come to my Mother's when the assembly adjurned[66] and I promised to go with him to Ky.

Several of the neighbours insested on us that when Col. Calleway should Return from the assembly to let them know it as they wanted to see him, and several Did come and see Col. Calleway. They thought it was a great affair. Calleway Did tell them about their fort being besieged and his and boon's girles being taken by the Indians and how he persued the Indians and retook them. He also did tell them many things about the Indians and about Ky. Several of these neighbours Did buoy land warrents and got land in Ky.

I took a negro boy with me and went with Col. Calleway. We gethered 40 pack horses, got some powder in the Magezene near where I lived, got the lead at the lead Mines on new River.[67]

This very session the legislater passed a law for takeing up the land in Ky.[68] Men was very easy to get to go with the powder and Lead, as they wanted to see the country and get land when the office was to be opened the next spring. Upwards of 40 Men volenteered them selves to go.[69]

Col. Caleway was very caucious in the wilderness, kept up sentrys every night, and marched in great order. We got to Boo[n]sbourough safe with the powder and lead. Col. Calliway lived at this place.

An express was sent to Logan's Fort imediately, and Brother James and Capt. John Logan[70] with 30 men came for the propotion of powder and lead that was for Logan's Fort. We took it safe to our Fort.

I was truly glad to be at Logan's Fort again. Their was many more people at this fort this year than the year before.

Col. Bowman Had Just Returned from a campaighn he had against one of the Indians' town. He made a broken trip of it, got some of our best men killed, and killed very few Indians, and returned home again.[71]

5
The "Hard Winter" of 1779-1780

Two of the men that came out with the powder and lead which lived near Col. Calleway when he lived in Bedford county by the name of Moses Mcilwain[1] and Ambres White.[2] They stopt at Boonsbourough and in a few Days Mr. Muckilwain and Mr. White went to the woods with some other men to explore and see the rich land on the other side of the Ky. River. A party of Indians found them out and way laid them. Mr. Muckilwain was took prisoner, also Mr. White was taken prisoner and badly wounded. The Indians took them to their towns and in about one year Mr. Muckilwain got away from them and got home to his family in Bedford County, Virginia.

Mr. Muckilwain had a large Family—to wit, a wife and a number of children and servants. He was a very respectable Jentleman and well of[f]. Mr. Muckilwain informed me the plan he took to effect his escape. He was a big fat man and could not undergo fertiague [fatigue] of so long a Jurney on foot.

He stated their was an Indian man in the Town that had but few frinds if any, as he was a bad man and rouge withall and a great lier. The rest of the Indians Despised this one. Mr. Muckilwain was Determined to befriend this Indian. He would give him some of his victuals. Some times he would steel Bred and Meat and slip it to him secretly, etc. At length this Indian Asked Muckilwain if he wanted to go home. Mucki[lwain] told him he Did and if he would take him to Fort pit he would give him $300. They had long talks about this Matter and made a solmen bargain. This Indian was to let M[cIlwain] know when he was ready. He was to furnish him with a horse also.

So one night he tells M. to go with him. And he took him a little Distance and hid him in a thicket and told him to stay their until he Returned. In a Day or two this Indin would Return and tell him to keep conceald and have patience, he would git things fixed to suite their progick [project] after a while. So one Day he came to him and had 2 horses, one for M. and one for the Indian. They also had provision. The Indian had a gun, and they set out and arived at Fort pit.

Mr. M. Told the commander at the Fort Pit all about this Matter.[3]

They wanted to kill this Indian but Mr. M. insisted other waise. Now this Mr. Muckilwain was a very sensible smart man and a slick toung [tongue], so the people agreed to what he said. A Mr. Broadhead, a Merchant, paid the Indian in Merchandise—to wit, Blankits, etc. When the Indin got Ready Mr. M. escorted him some little Distance and bid him fare well and boath cryed. The Indian let Mr. M. keep the horse he road. Mr. Broadhead made the Indian pay three prices for the goods he let him have and told Mr. M. he would only charge one-third. So Mr. M. got on his Indian horse and soon got home to his family, to which their was great Joy in the Meeting. When Mr. M. Told me of the Narretive he laugfed and cryed Too. Mr. M. sent the mony to Mr. Broadhead and paid him. Mr. M. after that moved his family to Ky. and enjoyed the Rich land in Fayatte county.

Mr. Ambros White lived with the Indians some years before he could effect his escape.[4] He lernt their habits and customs and got to be much of a hunter and woodsman. And at one of the Indians' Great Feast Days when they weare all Drunk Mr. White and   others all got each of them a good horse, bridle and saddle, good guns, and Amonician, etc., and made their escape, came home by the way of Fort pit and then home. Mr. White's wife and parrents still lived in Bedford County, Virginia. His wife lived with old Mr. White. The family had heard from him and believed he would come home some Day. When he (Mr. A. White) went to his father's he saw his father, Mother, and wife, and he knew them but they Did not know him.[5] After a while he told them all about it and their was great Joy. Mr. White has told me a great Deal of his Dificulties with the Indians. He now lives near Frankfort and is well of[f], has a plenty of propety, etc.[6]

I will Return to Logan's Fort. My Brother James informed me we had very much writing to Do and I went to it. My Brother had to go to the other Garrisons to make settlements with his Deputys. We soon got our books and accounts all in good order. People had moved to this country this fall more than ever. The commissinors that was appointed by the Virginia Legislator to grant preemtions also had come out.[7] Their was so many people had come and was a coming,[8] the conclusion was to Discontinue keeping up the soldiery at the Forts. So they weare all Discharged about the last of this year 1779; the publick stoors and the Magezeans locked up for the present in January 1780.[9]

James Trabue went to Virginia again to Draw mony to pay for the provisions which we had purchased.[10] Previous to his Departure he said if I could their ought to be meet procured this winter for next spring.[11]

The conclusion was that we must try to git some salt and kill wild meet. We understood that a company of men was to start on a certain day from Herrodsburgh to go to Bullits lick to boyle and make salt. The conclusion was that I would go, Foster would send A negro man with me, and we would take pots and kittles with us. And Mr. Smith also sent a young man and we made up a little company—to wit, Jeffery Davis, William Maxey,[12] the negro Man, and 2 or 3 others which I have forgot their names.

All set out. We had good guns and ammonition. When we got to herodsburgh their was nobody a going from their. I told these men with me that we would go on, so we set out. We went on some Distance and stoped to eat and let the horses Eat some Grass. We ate all the provision we had.

These young men said they was afraid to go on with me. They was afraid of Indians, was also afraid as their was no road or path that I would not find the way, and another thing was we had nothing to eat we might starve to Death.

I told them they ought to have brought provision with them and as to the Indians we had to run that risk. As to finding the way I was not uneasy about that as I knew about steering in the woods. I could find the way as I had been their. At any rates, whther they went or not I would go on with negro Jo. We went on our Jurney and at a little before sun set we stopt and took up camp. Told the negro boy to hopple out the horses and all the men as quick as they could to go out a hunting and try their best to kill something. We was encamped on Chaplens fork[13] on no path.

When I Returned, I had killed a large fat Rackoon. The men had killed nothing. The negro had a large good fire. The koon was soon prepaired for cooking. The men began again with their woefull tail. Said they, "We are in a wilderness without any path, nothing to eat but a koon for 6 or 7 Men without Bread or Salt, liable every moment to be Masscreed by the Indians. If we can only be spared until morning we will return to Logan's Fort." One of them said he would return to Old Virginia as quick as he could and them that liked Kentucky might enjoy it but he would not stay in such a country.

This was a very prety moon light night. After we got things prity well settled I said, "We have 2 good Dogs. I know mine is an exception for game. Let us go out a hunting." All of the men refused. I told negro Jo to take his axx. I took my gun and off we went, and in going only about 200 yards wheare some of these men had been out a hunting I saw 5 turkeys on one sycomere tree over the creek. I mooved to a place where I got the turkey between me and the moon, Drawed my sight and killed one, and loaded and fired until I killed all 5 of the largest fatest Turkeys that I had ever seen.[14] When I got to shooting I made shore the men would come to us, but they stayd where they was at the camp looking at their koon a rosting.

We took our turkeys to the camp and I said, "Now pick and

clene them and eate some of the best eating in the government." I soon had one a rosting. The koon was ready for eating.

They asked me to come up and eat some of it.

I Refused saying I would choose Turkey. The turkeys was all cleaned and some of them cooked for the night and the next morning. We all ate heartyly.

The neaxt Day we went on our Jurney and no one turned back. I went on before. I killed that Day a fine Deer and one or two turkeys. We put the meet on the pack horses.

One of the men we had with us was a young Irishman who was constant contending and Disputeing with the other young men that was from old Virginia about words and customs, etc. So some time that morning I shot a Buffelo bull and he fell down. We all went up to him. Some of the men had never seen one before this one. I soon Discovered I had shot this buffelo too high and I told some of the boys to shoot him again.

This young Irishman said, "No"; he would kill him and Jumed at him with his tomerhock and strikeing him in the forehead.

I told him it would not Do, he could not hurt him, the wool and mud and skin and skull was all so thick it would not Do. But he kept up his licks, a nocking a way.

The buffelo Jumped up. The man run, the buffelo after him. It was opin woods, no bushes, and the way this young Irishman run was rather Desending ground and every Jump he cryed out, "O lard! O lard! O lard! O lard!"

The buffelo was close to his heels. The man Jumed behind a beech tree. The bufflo fell Down, his head againt the tree, the tuckeyho[15] boys laughing, "Ha! Ha! Ha!"

One of them went up and shot the buffelo again and killed him. The Irishmain exclaimed againt them, saying this was no laughing Matter but that these boys or young [men] (he said) was such fools they would laugh at it if the buffelo had killed him.

These young men would Mimmick him, "O lard! O l[ard]!" etc. and breack out in big laughter.

This Irishman said he would go no further with such fools. He said he had nothing against me but he would not go with such fools as these boys weare.

When I saw he would go back, that I could not persuid [persuade] him to go further, I advised him to take a load of this buffelo meet as it was very fat and he was welcome to it, to which he agreed to it as we Did not need it. We look a little of it and bid him a Due [adieu], leaveing him a buchering his buffelo.

We went on our Jurney and before we got to Bullits lick I killed a

73 THE "HARD WINTER"

buffelo Cow—as fat a cow as I ever saw, I think, in my life wild or tame. We took a goodly part of it with us. We arived to the lick, found some people their making salt from the falls of Ohio.

A Mr. T. Phelps—an acquaintence of Mine—was their, had a furnace of small pots and kittles. He wanted to go home and hired his small establishment to us for 2 weeks for which we was to pay him in salt. We fixed up our pots and kettles in addition to Mr. Phelpes' and we went on very well, imediately making salt. The water we had was standing in the lick. Their was a hole or well only about two feet Deep that had been Dug out.[16] I was their previous to any Diging and the water stood their in a puddle so that the buffeloes would go their and Drink it. We Did see buffeloes every Day in sight of our works. We killd them when we needed them.

We had been their 3 Days when some men came their from herodsburgh that had started 3 Days before us. They had been lost. We had cold weather. These men also turned in to making salt. We was very glad of more company. The fact was I was very Dubious of Indians.

In about 2 weeks or little more we had got to each hand about 2 bushels of salt and I bought a little more from Mr. Phelps and so we made ready for our return.[17] And their was 3 or 4 Men from the falls of Ohia came to us and was agoing to the upper Forts, and wishing to go with us as company was good in these times they waited until we was ready. We went on and that night Just before we camped one of these strangers (his name was Saullivon) who killed a cappital Buffelo, and as we had a plenty of salt we lived well that night for meet. It had clouded up and that night had feel [fell] a Deep Snow.[18] The next morning was very cold and we had a good fire. Did not start early.

One of these Jentlemen, a stranger, observed, "This morning is very sutiable to set in a good tavern and have to drink good rum and hot Tea or Coffey for breckfast."

Mr. Swollivin observed that he thought a pan of fryed hommany would suite him best. It was taken as an insult. Blows insued. They had a very smart scuffle in the snow. We parted them and our Tuckeyho boys laughed heatyly [heartily] at it. We got home safe with our salt.

It was suppriseing to see the quanity of people that had recenty moved out to Kentucky and they weare more yet a coming. Mr. Smith, Mr. Foster, and these same young men, and several others, and myself started for the woods. Took some of our salt and 2 negro Men with axxes to cut wood, for the hard winter had began. The snow was Deep and the weather cold.[19] We went to Green river and soon killed some Good fat Buffeloos. Mr. Foster and some others took their loads and went to the fort. We continued hunting and killing and sending them home.

The weather at last got so intencly cold that we had to lye by for several Days. The snow was fully knee Deep. Our meet that we had kept for our own eating faild. The Turkeys had got poore. They would set on the treers all Day and not fly Down.[20] Many of them fell of[f] from their roosts and never more recovered. We could kill as many of them as we wanted but they weare too poore to eat. We made socks to go over our shews with Buffelo skins puting the wool inside and we had woollen gloves. But yet we could not stay away from our big fires, for if we Did shoot it was Imposible to load our Guns again.

The weather had altered a little for the better. Mr. Smith and I concluded we would go out and try our luck once more as we had nothing to eat. We put on 2 pair of gloves and buffeloe socks on over our shews. We had not got fair before we found 11 buffeloes in one Gang. Shot Down one. Set on the dogs after the others and going about one Mile they stopt them. We boath shot at once and killed 2 More. They broak and run off. The Dogs run off after them, stopt them again. We concluded to shoot the leaders—to wit, the Old cows—and then the younger ones would not leave them.

The next time we done so by giveing the other notice when he was ready for fireing. We killed 2 More and the rest stayed their fighting the dogs. And we kept shooting them down as fast as we could until we got them all killed but one and that was a calf. He run away.

We went to the camp, took the men and horses. And as we went on to the main body of buffeloes we went by the first ones killed. We guted them first ones that was killed and went to where the main body was a lying. When we got their, their was the buffeloe calf. The dogs took after him. The snow was Deep. He ran off round about and returned. And as he run over the dead buffeloes he fell Down and the dogs ketched him and we tyed him. Made up a good worm fire and guted all our buffeloes before we went to sleep.

We had fine fun with that buffeloe Calf the next Day. Their was a long rope cut of buffeloe hide and put around the horns and one of the boys would git on his back. The buffeloe was let Go. He would run the length of his rope which was held by 2 of the other boys. He would kick up and Jump until the man would fall off but as their was snow their was no Damage Done. We at first thought we would tame him but after several such frolicks, thinking he would be too troublesome we killed him and Slaughtered him. So we killed the whole Gang which was 11.

We thought by this time we had meet enough. Mr. Smith and my self and some others went home with all the horses packed with meet while the other men was to stay their and save the ballence by salting and Drying some of it. They had a camp covered with buffeloe hids. We took our meet to a cabin of Mr. Smith's 2 Miles from Logan's Fort on Gilberts creek.[21]

75 THE "HARD WINTER"

I left my negro boy with my meet and I Returned to Green River with the horses. Some Men that was not hunters went with me to green river and helped me with the horses. I killed several buffeloes on the rout and loaded all their horses. They offered to pay me but I Did not charge them any thing.

One Day as I was before and the dogs before me runing in the path near the river, the snow Deep, a swon was in the path. And as he was large and had to flop his wings several times before he could rise, the dogs ketched him. I took him to our camp. He would not eat any thing we had. He was as high as a common woman with a black bill and black feet. I killed him and skined him and gave it to a lady in the fort. She made a good pillow of the feathers.

This hard winter began about the first of November 1779 and broak up the last of Feberary 1780. The turkeys was almost all dead. The buffeloes had got poore. People's cattle mostly Dead. No corn or but very little in the cuntry.[22] The people was in great Distress. Many in the wilderness frostbit. Some Dead. Some eat of the dead cattle and horses. When the winter broak the men would go and kill the buffeloes and bring them home to eat but they was so poore. A number of people would be Taken sick and did actuly Die for the want of solid food.[23] The most of the people had to go to the falls of Ohio for corn to plant which was brought Down the Ohia.[24]

Brother James Trabue with a number of our relations and acquaintence came out in the spring [1780]. I had, I thought, a plenty of good fat salted buffeloe meet for them but had no bread. But a good many hands makes light work. Our meet soon failed. These Old Virginians—several of them (uncle Bartholomew Dupuy[25] was one)—went with us to the woods to see the land and hunt. We killed some very good Bears but they was soon eat up.

Gorge Milpon Smith,[26] half-brother to G[eorge] S[tokes] Smith, came out also. He was an active man with a gun. These 2 Smiths and I was often out together hunting, while the others was preparing the ground for planting corn. We killed several Bears and Deer but they weare soon eat up. We was much engaged in prepairing ground for planting corn.

I was one saturday very busy. The 2 Smiths, out a hunting, came home without suckcess. We had nothing to eat. In the night we went afishing in Dicks river[27] with a light and giggs. Caught some and frid them and eat them but not a sufficuncecy. The 2 Mr. Smiths was a going the next day to preach at some place on Munday. They said they would go a hunting.

Sunday morning Jeffery Davis and myself got our horses and guns and thought we would go to some Deer licks about 6 or 7 Miles Distant and see if we could not git something to eat. We sat out and looked sharp for game from the start and went to the licks, wached all Day and Did not see any thing to kill. When we was lying and waching the lick Mr. Davis said, "If we was only now in Old Virginia. At this very time their is preaching at Dupuy's Meeting house.[28] So many prerty Girles their. If I was their I could go with some of them and eat a good Dinur, have something good to Drink. But hear we are. Nothing to eat in this Dreary Wilderness, and we Don't know when we shall if ever get anything to eat."

We moved to Different Deer licks and hunted Dilingently all that Day without suckcess until after sun set. We had got nearly insight of our fence. I saw a bear. I Jumpt of[f] to shoot him. Mr. Davis said, "Don't shoot! It is Jones'es little black horse." He spoke lowe so that the bear did not hear him as he was nearly 100 yards Distant. I could not see very well as their was bushes in the way but thought it was a beair and thought if I was not quick I might loose him. And at that time I would rather have a good beare than 2 little horses as that of Jones'es was. I fired and killed him. Mr. Davis road up to him and shot him a second time in his head. He road to our cabin and about a Dozen of our men came runing, and glad they weare as they had been keeping a fast Day for the want of something to eat. It was taken home and some was soon prepared for eating and we made up for some of our back rations. This bear I suppose would weigh 200 neat, but as we had no bread it would not last more than 2 days.[29]

[The two] Mr. Smiths and I went off a hunting, was 3 Days out, killed a little Deer which Just served us and the dogs. We started home wards and hunting as we went. We got in about 6 or 7 Mile of home and stoped to eat and then concluded to start home but every man to take a Different cource, that 3 courses was better than one. So we Divided and started.

It soon began to Rain. I saw a large bear before me. He was a runing so that I could not git a shoot. I was on a very good brisk horse. I lit out after the bear and could keep up with him. He went a good cource for home. After a while the Dogs that was with Mr. Smith got on our trail and came to me. They soon stoped the bear. It was raining. I was afraid to git my gun wet. So I road close to him and stooped over the gun and fired at him not taking sight. Away went the bear. The dogs soon stoped him. I went off to a large tree and loaded, and the next time I thought I would go very close, and road up close and my gun flashed. The bear Jumped at me, sccared the horse so he Jumed side way against a Dog wood. I took up the Dog wood, Dropt my gun. Away went the horse and bear. I picked up my gun, ketched my horse, and went to the bear. My gun was wet. I could not git it off. I made Many trials but all in vain.

THE "HARD WINTER"

The sun shined out. I Did not wont to loose my bear as we veryly needed it. I then thought off Driveing him home. I called off the dogs. He run right from us. We kept close behind him and when he woud go rong I would set the Dogs on him and he would stop. I would ride round and call of[f] the dogs. He would run straight from us. We Drove him nearly home when he run up a tree. Mr. G.S. Smith heard us and came to us and shot him. We took him home and Glad our people was as they was entirely out of food. He was a large fat bear.

We had many hunts and killed a great quanity of meat. Some times we sufferd very much for food. When we had what is called bad luck we made our business for to hunt for the rest, while they was prepairing for planting Corn.

I will mention one more of our hunts. We went on paint lick creek[30] and on a Ridge we killed a buffeloe and hung it up and went on to hunt more, and went round about and came on the same ridge again and got on our trail that went to where the buffeloe was a hanging up their. We saw Indian tracks gone on to where the buffeloe was hanging, knowing the Indians was in the habit of waching hunters' Meet. While we was consulting about this matter two buffeloes came runing from that way, and stopt and looked back to the way where our meet and the Indians weare.

G[eorge] S[tokes] S[mith] said, "Let us kill them," but [George] M[ilpon] S[mith] opposed it; however, S. S[mith] and myself shot boath of them Down.

M. S[mith] said it was presumtion but S. S[mith] said, "We might as well die by the sword as famin," and he knew the Indians would be waching the meet that was hanging up and we would take this. M. S[mith] and the dogs was to wach and S. S[mith] and my self was to bucher. It was about sun set when these buffeloes was killed.

It was after Dark before we got the meet ready for starting and it was very Dark. The buffelo that was a hanging up was less than a half mile off. It was so Dark we could not see to travel. The moon did rise a little after midnight. So the conclusion was to hopple our horses and opin our bells, and when the moon would Rise we would start. When the moon Did rise the horses broak and run, skeard very much. We knew the indians was after them. We kept close to gether and tryed to get around them. We heard and saw the Indians. When our horses run up to us they stood still. We stoped our bells and stood still. We heard the Indians again. We took our horses to the camp. The Dogs barked very much. We put on our saddles. The dogs quit barking. The conclusion was that the Indians was Gone to where the meet was a hanging and would wait for us their. We loaded our horses and started when day came. We kept in the cain the most of the way home.

M. S[mith] said he would not run the same risk again for a hansom sum. I have ever thought we was rong, as the Indeans when they go to war has several in company. But we Did escape and got our meet home safe and it was realy needed. The next Day the Indians Defeeted some hunters not fair from that place, it was supposed the same Indians.

6
The Captivity and Escape of Two Trabue Brothers

It was concluded upon, that I should conduct uncl [Bartholomew] Dupuy, Col. Sherwin,[1] Docter scott, all from Amelia county, Virginia, to Leuisvile to see the country and git provisions to go to virginia. Mr. S. Smith also sent a young man with us. We took 2 or 3 pack horses.

We called on Col. Floyd on bear Grass.[2] Floyd informed us the Indians was very Troublesome in small companies, Done much Mischief in steeling their horses and killing people. Floyd said he was Determined upon waching on perticular places on the Ohia for them and kill one or more. I understood after that Floyd Did wach for them and Did kill some.

Col. Floyd had a black walnut Tree that these Virginians Did much admire. It was 33 feet in circumpherence and the trunk was about 60 feet to the limbs. Col. Shirwin said, "If that tree was in Old Ingland they would make saws on purpose for that tree to work it up." They (these Old Virginians) was so well plesed with this land on bar grass they said they could hardley believe their own eys.

We went to the falls, stayed their a day or two. We got our loads of flour, corn, and bacon, and started home. In going along the path in about one mile of Linn's Station[3] I was in front. I saw an Indian before us behind a log. He sqated down. The Indian was about 100 yards Distant. I Dashed off in the woods and hollowed, "Indians." The company followed my example and Dashed after me. The pack horses kept up with us. When we got in sight of the station I stoped to tell them what I had seen. I told them their was a large log near the road before us and I saw an Indian's head Dodge Down. We went to the station.

We heard guns fireing where we had been alarmed. In a little time 3 Men come riding up. 2 of them was wounded, had lost some of their hats. It was sun set and too late for any body to go after the Indians. The men gave accout that their was 9 or 10 Indians.

The next Day after Breackfast we set out for home. Was afraid to keep the path. I went before and pilated the company. We was 6 in number. On the rout Col. Sherwin and Docter Scott lost their horses. We lost one Day hunting them. Did not find them. We put their things on our horses and started. Col. Shirwin said he put a bottle of Old brandy in his saddle bags in Virginia and thought he would not tuch it or let any one know he had it unless he got in a strait and now was the time. So he pulled it out and it was Really good.

I was sorry for Col. Sherwin. He was a fat man and walking did almost kill him. Just about sun set we found their horses and they was Glad enough of it. Shirwin's horse was one of the Valuableest harses in those Days. We got home safe and these Old Virginians all started home.

My Brother John Trabue came out this spring [1780]. He was a Deputy survayer under John May.[4] Made several survays for the people near Logan's fort.

The land office was opened this spring at Wilson's Station[5] for entering land warrents.[6] James Trabue and I went their to make some entries, but their was so many people their we had to cast lots.[7] And according to lot he (James Trabue) made some few entres, and it would be several Days before he could make any more.[8] And it would be several Days before I could make my entres as my warrents was not on the first day.

So we went home[9] and James Trabue told me he would make my entreys for me when he made his, if I would stay at home and attend to howing our Corn planted. I agreed to it and gave him my warrents and a memorandom where my land was to be laid. It was 2,000 acres and choice land.[10] James Trabue said he would go to licking on his Commessary business.[11] He was very much [needed] their and could be back to Wilson's Station in time to lay our warrents.

So he went to licking and got to Ruddle's Station[12] at night. And when Morning [June 24, 1780] came their fort was sourounded by Indians;[13] and Col. Byrd, a british officer from Detroyt, soon arived with a cannon.[14] He (Byrd) sent in a flag to the fort, Demanding them to surrender to him as prisoners of war, etc., to which they Refused. The cannon was fired twise.[15] Done no Damage except knocked one cabin log so it was moved in about 6 Inches.

Capt. Ruddle insisted it would be best to Cappitulate. Capt. Hinkston[16] and James Trabue insisted to Defend the fort. At length Capt. Ruddle got a Majority on his side and petitiond Col. Byrd to caputula[te].[17] The flag was sent Back and forward several times before they agreed and the articles was sighned and agreed to. James Trabue was the man that Did wright in behalf of Ruddle and the people in the fort. The terms of Cappitulation was that Col. Byrd and his white soldiers should protect the people that was in the fort and march thim to Detroyt as prisoners, and that the indians should have nothing to Do with them, that the people's Cloathing and papers should be kept sicure to themselves with some little exceptions.

81 CAPTIVITY AND ESCAPE

The Fort Gate was opined. The Indeans came rushing in and plundered the people, and they evin striped their cloaths of[f] them and Dividing the prisoners among the indians. In a few minuts the man Did not know where his wife or child was, nor the wife know where her husband or either of her children was, nor the children where ther parrents or brothers and sisters weare, all contrary to the cappatulation. Nor they had no chance of seeing Col. Byrd, as the Indians kept them to themselves. They went and took Martain's station also.[18]

Capt. Hinkston made his escape from them and came home and told the knews. The Indians was troublesome in many places. This was Melencholy knews to me, my land Warrents gone that had cost me a great Deal, but that Did not Distress me like the loss of my Brother.

Col. [George] R. Clark proposed to go a campaighin against the Indians. It was agreed upon. Preparation was made. The day set for our march. I was to go as Commissary for Col. Ben Logan's Redgment.[19]

My pack horses and bullocks ready, when brother John Trabue Told me he wanted me to go to Virginia on some perticular business as he or James Trabue had to go; and as James was with the Indians, some one— him or me—would have to go. And he said he had been talking to the Logans, and they was entirely willing for me to go to Virginia and John to go on the campaighn as their Commessary. John said his main reason was as he had been an Indian trader he was some acquainted with their language and customs, and if they could take any prisoners he thought he could by some means git Brother James Ransomed or exchanged. I wanted him and me boath to go but he said it would not Do. He said our brother William[20] was now a prisoner with General Scott at Charlestown[21] by the   british, Brother James with the Indians, Brother Edward in the suthern Army. He thought it was my Duty to go to Virginia and Do his business and see to our Mother that had no son of any size, only a parsil of children and many Nigros that was not easy to manage.[22] So I agreed to go to virginia and John Trabue went the campaighn as Commessary.

Col. Knox,[23] Col. Tom Marshal,[24] G.S. Smith, and myself started to Virginia, and before we left the crab Orchid[25] we had a smart[26] Company. After we Crossed Cumeberland River my horse was taken with a Collick, it almost night. Mr. Smith Took my saddlebags and big coat, etc., and went on a head to stop the company. I was left behind with my sick horse. He got no better. I tryed to git him a long but in vain. I pulled of[f] the bridle and saddle and left him lying Down a rooling. I was very fraid of the Indians. I went on about 3 mile before I came up with the company. Colonel Knox and the Company told me they would wait on me a little while in the Morning for me to get my horse.

I went back before Day and could not find him. I Don't think I ever had such feelings. I was by myself, looking Every minut for the Indians and no horse, only the one I had borrowed to take my saddle in case my horse could not. As it was in the summer time, the grass high, I could easyly see the horse was not about their, that he must have followed the company. And I took my saddle and bridle and started. And as I went on it was hard for me to see where he could have left the road, as some of the men the over night had road out of the road on boath sides. I insisted on the company to waite a while longer on me as the horse was well, he could not be far from the road, and he could be found. Mr. G.S. Smith also insisted but to no avail. They would not wait.

There was a man that had a led [lead] horse that let me ride him and take my saddle, etc. He charged me a Dreadfull extortinate price, yet I was glad of that chance. I Road him to Holston. I meet a company. I told them about my horse. They found him and took him along. The Indians Defeated the company and got my horse.

When I got to Holston I stoped to buoy me a horse. The company all went on and left me. I bought a capital horse the next Day and went on my Jurney by myself.

As I went on a long Holston and knew [New] River the men was fixing to go against the torrys and British. They was very ancious. I Did almost conclude to go with them. These were the very men that killed and Defeated Forgisson on kings Mountain.[27]

When I went through Bedford at new London they had about 150 men[28] in custedy, Trying them for Toryism.[29] The fact was the british had taken Charles town and our army that was their[30] and sent some secret agents to Virginia with Lord Corn Wallice'[31] proclameton, proclaiming in the name of Gorge the 3rd that whoever would now throw Down their arms of Rebellion and Join his Gracious Majisty king Gorge's army he should have free pardon and his great crimes of Rebellion blotted out, and also that when the Rebels shall be subdued shall have a good proportion of these Rebils' estates.[32] These 150 Men had Joined in With this proclamiton and they ware arested and in order to get clear the most of them enlisted in the american army for two years.[33] So the biter Got bit. I know some of these men to this day.

When I went but a little further all along the Road the men had but Just started to go with General Gates[34] to take Corn Wallace.[35] General Gates seemed to be sure of Victory. When I Got to Chesterfield near Richmon they—the men—was gone from their also with G[eneral] Gates.[36]

When I got to my Mother's in chesterfield I had to tell them the bad knews as to Bro. James, but it was a great Consolation and gratification that Brother William was at my Mother's. He had Just got home. He made his escape in the following manner.

He was Orderly sargant to a company in the Virginia line and had marched from the North from Wasington's army to CharlesTown,[37] and

83 CAPTIVITY AND ESCAPE

when they was besieged 10 Days[38] they surrendered as prisenors of war. William Trabue said he expected at first they would soon be exchanged but no such news. The sickly season was a coming on, the men giting the fever. He was Determined to try to make his escape. He tryed to plese the british officers as a sergant of the Company.

So one Day he asked a british officer for a permit for himself and men to go Out of the fort to the town to buoy some nick nacks and get cloaths washed. He said he would. My brother said it was late in the Day, they would go to morrow, to which he agreed. So William told 6 of the men that wanted to make the venter with him that each of them to git cloathing that was not Ridgementals, settle up their little accounts with their brother soldirs, etc., "for to morrow we will try the skeam."

The next morning he got his permit for himself and six more. They took their napsacks and went to town. They went in a old wear house, pulled of[f] their Ridgemental Cloaths, and Tyed them and their napsacks Each in a large handkerchief. Then they did not look like the same men. They looked like cuntry men.

They went down to the River, bought some fishing hocks with poles, and went to fishing. Then they Got in a boat and rowed out of sight and landed and hid themselves until night and then took the Road and made brisk Tracks. Traveld all night and looked sharp and when Day come hid them selves in the woods and went to sleep and restd them selvs for the next night and then started. When they would hear any one a riding they would git out of the road and let them pass. The British had offered Rewards for all that could be caught and men was very often caught.

After a few Days they kept the road and traveld in the Day and their provision failed. They stoped at a house and got their breackfast. The innkeeper Asked them where they come from and where they was agoing.

They answerd, "We are from charles Town, was taken by the british as Militia men, and took protection."

He said, "Let me see one of your protection."

The answer was, "Before we go we will. We are hingry and want to eat and Drink a little rum." They got what they wanted and paid for it.

When they was about to Depart they was called on for to see one of their protections. The answer was, "Myne is not handy. I can tell you how they read," and told him. This did not satisfy him but they bid him farewell.

They went on viry fast for a while and stopt in the woods, lay down in the grass near the Road. And one did wach and the others slept. They had not been their long before they saw the same man and with many others with guns rushing along the road. They lay still until they saw the same men come back. They then kept the woods until almost night, went to a house, got something to eat, took the road, and traveled the most of the night. They had come to a Determind resolution. They would not be taken. If they was oblidged to Defend themselves they would fight to Desperation. Some times they would buoy bred and meet and take it with them. So it was they all got home safe and well.

General Scott has since told me[39] that after that time when these men left them the men got very sickly and many a Diing, that the sentrys was ordered to let our men pass any time in the night to bury their Dead. So our men would tye up a live man in a blanket, run in a stake or pole through the blanket, and two men cary him and some more with spads and then go on to the centry. He (the centenal) would cry out, "Who comes their?"

The answer was, "Corps."[40]

"Go by, corps," said the centenal.

And when they weare passed they would untye their man and all make their escape together. A great many got away on that plan in one night, but they altered the plan and made other arangements.

I went to Richmond and Done my business. Stayed a few Days at my mother's.

General Gates Got Defeeted[41] and several of these neighbours never stoped until they got home.

I started back to Kentucky and on my way heard the good knews about Forguson being Defeeted on kings Mountain. I called on Mr. Samuel Ewings[42] on new River. He told me I had better take something to feed my horse in the middle of the day and take something for my self to eat, that along on towards the head of cripple creek[43] they weare all Torrys for several miles. They weare Duch people.

I refused his offer, thinking I could make some shift, but when I came to inquire for something for myself and horse the answer was by a woman, "My husband is Gone to Philidelphia to get his mony he sold his land for, and I have nothing hardly for my poore children." I called on several. It was at every house the very same tail. I was now Determined to try a plan.

The next house I came to was a good looking house, Good barn, and Farm. So I road up and alighted from my horse and went in and said, "Maddam, can I get my horse Fed and something for myself to eat?"

She answered, "No, sir."

Question, "What is the reason?"

Answer, "My husband is gone to Philidephia, where we came from, to git his Mony that we sold our land for. He has been gone some time and he has not returned. I Don't know what we will Do."

Question, "You seem to have a plenty in your barn and a good crop a growing. Why not let me have what I now request?"

Answer, "This crop that you see I and my children make it and I cannot let any thing go."

"O, maddam," said I, "did you hear the knews?"

85 CAPTIVITY AND ESCAPE

"What is that?"

"It is General Washington and his Army is all taken by the king's men."

"You Don't say so! Is it a fact?"

"It is a fact and General Clinton[44] and General Scott at Charles town is all taken. General Gates is defeeted. The king has Done conqured the Rebels and we will have better times."

She said, "I am afraid you are a tory."

I said, "I Don't like to be called a torry, but I am on the side of king Gorge. He is a good king, etc. Fare well, Maddam."

"Stop," she said, "I will have your horse fed. John, feed this Gentleman's horse. Give him aplenty. Cattey, set the table and go Down to the spring house. Bring some good cool milk and butter and put it on the table and put on the chees meet and the Pys, etc."

I had a fine Diner and all the time I was eating she was talking about the times. She asked me many questians. I told her many fine tailes. She then told me her husband was then in the woods hid out; so was most of the Duch in that section and if I would only wait 2 hours she would send for her husband and let him hear some of this good knews, etc.

I told her I could not wait.

"Bring out my horse. What have I to pay?"

She answered, "Nothing, nothing! You have told such good news. You are more than welcome." I then told her the most I had told her was incorect and my reason for saying as I Did. She burst out in a cry and said, "You will now go and tell General Campbil."[45] I told her I would not, neither I Did.

When I got near the block house[46] on holston I met with Mr. G.S. Smith agreable to appointment to go through the wilderness to gether. We meet with more company, 10 or 12 of us on single horses, all well armed; and when we got some Distance in the wilderness we overtook a number of families a moving to Kentucky. They petitioned us to go with them, urging on us the Danger their woman and children were in as the indians was almost constent on the road. We consented and we was now 40 armd men and a number of women and children and Negros. When we got to cumberland River we stayed their one night and when morning came it was raining and continued to rain almost all Day so that we did not travel in the afternoon.

Major John Downey proposed that we—some of us—should go on the mountain and kill a bear for Meet for these people. Their was a mountain Just where we was on the North side of the River. Major John Downey, Mr. Ward, and myself agreed to go.

We went up to the top of the mountain. It was about two Miles to the top and when we got on the ridge we Discovered a vast qunity of chesnuts on the ground and a bundence of bear sighn. Their tracks was plenty, so we kept a long on the ridge still further from our camp, expecting Every minuet to see bears or Indians. It rained by this time hard. We was about 4 Mile from our camp. The ridge we was on was narrow.

We turned of[f] the ridge to our right to hunt some shelving Rock to keep the rain from us.[47] We turned to the Right to go Down the Ridge. Their was a Gap between two lofty Rocks. We went through the Gap and Down a few steps and we was on a bench 10 or 12 feet wide, and their was a shelving rock from the ridge which mostly covered this bench. This shelving rock which covered our bench was like a half-face camp and in the front about 8 feet high and on the back side about 2 feet high. In the front of this bench as we would look Down, this mountain from where we stood appeared to be Impassiable to go Down as it was about 25 feet Down to the next bench perpendicular.

We said, "Hear is a Jumping off place. This is a good dry place where we stand, but what will we Do if the indians comes on us hear?" We all concluded that it would kill any man that would Jump Down but that if the Indians did come we could keep of[f] 20 by shooting them as they would approach to us. This bench that we was on was about 20 yards long. We did not go to the other end to see it. We had no Idea that their was a gap at the other end of our bench. As it turned out their was.

Their was Dry leaves and sticks under our shelter. I stoped the tuch hole[48] of my gun with tallow and then did ketch fire and we made up a fire and Dryed our selves. I laid my gun Down on the back side of the fire to dry. We concluded that when it would slack raining we would go back the same way as we came and we would yet kill a bear as the sighn seemed to be plenty.

As we stood up before our fire we would look Down at this mountain. We all concluded it was the roughfest looking place that we had ever seen—big lofty looking Rocks, big guts, Dismal precipasses, etc. We was chitchattng, telling some mrry tails, Major Downey singing at times all though with a loe voice.

We had been their about 20 or 30 Minuts when we heard a stick crack at our gap. The word was, "What is that?"

One of us answered, "Chesnuts a falling."

Another answered, "I Don't like it."

I stooped Down to pick up my gun. I cast my eye that way towards the gap. I could see the Indians coming round. I said, "Indeans!" I Jumed up and went by Major Downey. He had his gun to his face presented to wards the gap. I was a going to pick the tuch hole of my gun and prime, which I could Do quick. We all had our faces to wards our gap, thinking to shoot them and Defend our selves.

At that time Indians Scremed Out on the other end of the bench and came rushing up. These indians to wards our gap answerd them with the dreadfullest yelling I had ever heard. All come rushing up on us together with their Tomerhocks in their hands.

I spoake and said, "Let's Jump Down!" We all Jumped Down. The Indians had got almost got nigh inough to strike when we made the leap. Mr. Ward Did Jump first. When Major Downey and I piched [pitched] off, ward was about half way Down. The bench we alighted on was rich soft earth and slanting and about two steps wide. So when we alighted we slipt so we went Down to the next bench which was not so fair. This was Done almost as quick as thoughts. So we was out of their sight. We went Down. I can't say we run Down but Jumped and sliped. So Down the mountain we went.

The Indians persued us. We suppose they started after us some other way than the way we went Down. We could hear the rocks tumbling behind us as we went Down. We also would Did [sic] start rocks as we went over them so they would rool down. We three men kept together for some time.

My shews was wet and too big for me. I kicked them off and went pass them. I thought off the silver buckels that was in them which was worth $6. I turned around and reached them. I then looked back. I Saw the Indians a coming. I saw one presenting his gun at me perhaps 100 yards off, others of them coming on. I felt bad. I turned to go again. I thought that the 2 men before me was as far before me as the Indians was behind me.

I soon ketched up with the 2 Men, and as I passed them Major Downey said, "Let's stick together."

I thought, "He did not think of that when I was behind." I said nothing as their was no time for chatting. I went on a head, only a few steps before them.

When we got Down the Mountain I stoped under a large Tree and primed my gun. Major Downey said, "Let us shoot them!" We could hear and see them a coming.

I said, "Come on." I led the way. We went on with all our mights. I believe I could have went a little faster but Did not like to leave them fair behind.

When we got Down the mountain we was on a creek.[49] We had to keep Down this creek as our camp was at the mouth of this creek on the same side. As we went Down the creek we was very often in a cain break. I thought it was best to cross the creek. I went over it. My companions followed me. We went Down on the other side. The Indians kept on this side. We saw them when we got almost to our Camp.

We croossed the creek oppesit our camp on a log. When we first waided it, it was to our mid sides. I then Drank water out of one of my shews. This was the first of my Ricolection that I had picked them up.

We was so much out Done we could hardly speak but told our min, "Indians," and they had followed us near the camp and that their was about 12 or 15 Indians. Our men (about 15 or 20) run with their guns but could not see them. It was almost night. We tyed up the most of the horses and give them cain to eat.

Major Downey never spoke but twise from the begining to the end of this affair. The first was, "Let's all stick together." The other was whin I was priming my gun. He said, "Let us shoot them." Mr. Ward never spoak one word all the time.

I spoak twise, first, "Let's Jump Down." The next was when I got my gun primed. I said, "Come on."

Major Downey said I saved his life by saying, "Jump Down," as he would not thought of it as we had concluded otherwaise.

Mr. Ward said he Did not Remember that I spoak at all at that time. He says the Indians made such a dredfull noise and come runing up on boath sides, he was so alarmed he Jumed Down, hardly knew what he was a Doing.

Major Downey left his hat, Mr. Ward his Tomerhock, and I my bucher knife and a handkerchief at our Shelter. We (each of us) Did conclude that if people could only see the way we went they would say it was a Marricle that we was not killed in going Down where we went. We think the Indians had no notion that we would Jump Down. We think the Indians' guns were wet. We think they followed us from our camp or they might have seen our smoak.

The next Day neither of us could scircly walk. Our friends had to bring our horses up to us to git on them. Major Downey was a very large boney man. No Dougbt if he had not Jumed Down but he would have killed some of them before they killed him. At any rates he would have tryed. Mr. Ward and myself was a bout common size.

We all got to Kentucky safe. I went to Logan's Fort. My broher John was Dead and buryed. I had heard of it before I got to kentucky. Col. Ben Logan and Wife and the other people of the Fort paid great Respect to him in the time of sickness. He was taken sick on his return from the campaighn. He was buryed very Deasontly. I paid off the funeral Expences.

Mr. G.S. Smith and my self had our corn Geathered. We sold some and cribed some and fed our horses plentyfully. Their was a wonderfull change of times between the time of planting this corn and the gathering of it, in Respect of provision. When planted partly starved, when gethered a bountyfull crop of corn, punkins, and potatoes, a plenty of Milk and butter, and the meet in the woods quite fat. The people quite cheery, getting quite sausey.

But I was very much Dejected. Brother John Dead, whom I loved and made great calcalations in him. He explored kentuck, Green River, and Cumberland in the year of 1775. Brother James now with the Indians or british and uncertain whether we ever would see one another again. My land warrents gone and the land located by others. My great calculation in Kentucky seemed to be blasted.

I hired out my negro boy. Mr. G.S. smith and myself started home to Virginia. Two of our young min—to wit, Samuel Hacher, a cousin of mine, and Jeffery Davis, who we had left in Ky. all summer and who had been out with Logan on the campaighn—went to Virginia with us.

When I got home to Virginia, in a few Days my brother James got home and their was Great Joy for him but lementation for Bro. John. The account that James gave of the surrender of Riddle's fort was that the british had agreed to pertect the whites from the Indians, as he wrote the capitulation himself. But as soon as the Fort gates was opened, they was all Divided and subdivided like a Drove of sheep or hogs amongst the Different tribes of Indians. Familys was Divided, the husband from his wife and children, etc.

One Indian sized James Trabue and claimed him as his prisoner. Their was Dreadfull puling and halling. And although one Indian claimed him and had him by the hand, a nother Indian run up to him and snatched the hat from off his head, which was a valuable beaver hat. My brother said when he lost his hat he was alarmed. He imediately puled out his wach and gave it to the indian that claimed him. As he could speak a little broken Inglish he told the Indian he might have it, and handed him his pockit book and told him he must return that again. The Indian said he would. He also gave the Indian silver buckils and some other Valuable things and told the Indian to keep them also. He was in hops as he was Generous to the Indian he would be to him and let him keep his cloaths and Return him his pockit book. But the other Indian that had no prisoner pulled of[f] all his cloaths and gave him one of their Raggad lousey shirts to put on that Did not keep the sun from burning his skin.

He told how they killed old Mistress Barger, an old Duch woman who we was acquainted with. As one company of Indi[ans] marched along, this old woman behind: one Indian behind her he would Jump up and wave his Tomerhock and cut a number of capers and then killed her. The blow came when this Old lady was not Expecting it. They finished her and skelped her and then Raised a Dreadfull yell. My brother said he often looked behind to see if they was cuting capers behind him.

They took him to Detroyt and sold him to the british. The men was mostly took to Detroyt and some of the woman, but the children was mostly kept with the Indians. My brother with many others was taken to Montreal.

When at Detroit he called on his Indian for his pockit book, promissing him something elce, and he did give some other little present perhap a loaf of bread, and got his pockit book again with the most of his papers.[50] He had paper continantal Mony in his pockit book. It was all gone but his land warrents was all safe. He fetched them home with him.

When he first got to Montreal he was informed by the people that he could git cloathing for labour in making fortyfications. He refused to work for 2 or 3 Days as he understood that some kind of work was much better price than others. After he had viewed the Different kind of work he informed the comander he wuld work with the stone masons. They askid him if he was a Mason. He answered he was a bricklayer but he thought he could work Stone.

He went to work with the Masons and got his Dollar per Day when common work was only 2/6. He soon got cloathing a plenty but pretended he was very fraid to be any indebt. These officers wood insest on these labourers to take up goods for their wages and was very willing for them to go alittle in Debt. He passed as a stone Mason and after a while they put him to brick laying and he satisfyed them at that also. He says he never worked at either before, but so it was he got his $1 per Day.

He made himself very fermilier with the people their and got hold of their Maps and examined into the Geographia of the country. He got to beleave he could make his escape. He communicated this to some of the prisoners and 7 of them agreed to embark in the Venture. He told these 7 Men to make ready, that the first Dark rainey night they would start, and try if posible to procure a Guns and ammunition, etc. They generally Drawed several Days' provision at a time and they saved and laid by such as they thought would Do for their Jurney.

A few Days previous to their Departure James Trabue went to their stoore to git some articles. He looked at some of their very best superfine broad Cloath. He told them when he got them enough in his Debt he must have a coate of that piece. They told him to take it now. It was cut off. He also took up 2 fine lineng shirts, breeches, and stockins, and Cravets, also trimmings. Had them all tyed up in a large handkerchief and took them to his logging, Determined to cheat them if he Could as they and thir Alleys—the Indians—had cheated him so much. He was in their Debt now about 75 Dollars.

Alexander Noel[51] was their a prisoner, told James Trabue he could not venter the risk of an escape, but if he (J. Trabue) could git home safe to write to his father and Mother in Essix county in Virginia about him. A number of the prisoners said the same, for him to write.

The first Dark rainey night they got all together. They had got no gun. They had flints and spunk. They concluded to go to the river to the centenal that was at the boats, and they would take the centenal with his

91 CAPTIVITY AND ESCAPE

gun and catridge box.[52] This Montreal was in an Island. When they all got near the river it was agreed that a duchman—one of their company—should go to the centry and be a talking with him. This centry man was a Hession,[53] and this Duchman could talk with him. And while the Duch man was to be a talking to him he was to take hold of him and the rest of the men was to lay hold and carry him with them. So this Duchman went and viewed the centry man and came back to the men and told them that this centryman was some little Distance from the boats, that he was puting some planks over an old frame to keep the rain off him.

They went to the boats, took one boat, got in her and roed her over. When they got nearly over the river they run aground and could not git her off. They thought They was Discovered as they saw a number of candles a passing about the landing and garrison. They waded to shore. The water before they Got out was up to their brests; however, they all got over safe and they bid a Due to Montreal.

They went on some Distance that Dark night and slept some little. When Morning came they then started, one man to steer the way and where ever he put his foot they all was to go in the same track. The man that was behind had a turkey's foot and a Deer's foot. If the least sighn was made this hindmost man was to either to make a Deer's track or turkey's track. They knew they would be followed and they must be very carefull so that they could not be tracked. They kept along on poor rocky ridges and puting their feet on rocks and stones and the rest to put their feet on the same tracks.

James Trabue went a head. He had a pockit compas. He would use it at times. He went along the poor ridges, and when he would git to water courses they would keep in the water for miles at a time. He was on a poor clift and a ceder tree that reached from a brook below to this clift. He went Down the ceder tree and down to the brook and then in the water for some Distance and then keep up some poore pint [point] and all the men following him correctly, so it was Imposible for the Indians to trail them.

One evining after sun set they came near to an Indian camp where their was a large army of Indians encamped. The Tomerhocks a cuting wood and their horse bells made a great Noise. They crept off to a hideing place to consult what to Do.

James Trabue told them these horses they had was horses they had taken from the white people from the settlement before them, and it was the best way for them for every man to take a good horse and take the Indians' back track. These horses would incline to go to their home. They could go a great Distance before Day. The men opposed this plan.

They then lay in ambush until the Indians was gone. The next morning they was afraid to keep the indians' trial for fear of meeting indians behind the main army. They, however, kept the course of the trail and when they would strike it would leave it again. They was very careful of makeing any sighn so that they could not be followed.

When they left Montreal the understanding was each man was to have 10 days' provision, and if they had have eaten as much as they could they might have eat it in 5 Days. However, on the 7 Day they had not one mouthfull to eat and no gun to kill any thing.

They could strike fire and would go in some hollow and make up a fire some times as the weather was cold. It was in october or november. They all had good blankits. When they thought their was Danger they made no fire.

As they had to take so much pains in not makeing sighn it took them longer than they expected to reach the settlement. The settlement they first struck was tyconderouge, which settlement had been broak up by these indians they meet.[54] They had been 5 Days now without eating any thing. They made Deligent serch for something to eat but the Indeans had Destroyed every thing. At one place they did find a few potatoes but not as many as one man could eat.

And in going about 40 Miles further they came to where white people lived which took them about one and a half Days where they got a plenty to eat. So they ware 13 1/2 Days from Montreal to the settlement where they Got something to eat. They suffered much for provision. If they could have found in this broken up settlement horse, cow, hog, Dog, or cat they would have eat it but found none. Every particle of corn, etc., was swept clean by these saveges, their horses taken away and cattle and hogs Destroyed and some of the people killed but the most of them fled.

These 8 prisoners all got safly landed in a christian country again which fully compenseated them for all their Dificulties they had underwent. These 8 Men went to the Govenor of New York or some General offcer in that country and [he] gave them orders to Draw provision at the Different publick stores as they went home.[55]

James Trabue could have got a good horse and saddle for his fine suite of Cloath and he could have road home, but he concluded he wood walk home and weare his fine cloaths. He got them made up and he was the finest Dressed Man in the country as their had been no Importation[56] for some time.

James Trabue gave account of several prisoners who we thought was killed. He wrote letters to their people. He wrote a letter to Old Mr. Noel in Essix County, Virginia, which was the first information of Alexander Noel being alive.

This Alexander Noel was liveing[57]   He with several others was a going to[58]   1780 and crossing Kentucky River Just belowe Frankfort at

Lee's town[59] the Indians fired on them[60] and took Alexander Noel Prisoner and took him to their towns.

This same Mr. Noel says that after James Trabue and these other men run away the british Officers Got 20 Indians to persue them and promised them $60 for each prisoner they would ketch. Mr. Noel said his heart aked for these men. These Indians and the officers too seemed to make sure of suckcess, but after 12 or 15 Days they Returned and said they could not trail them. They could not see which way they went after a few miles.

Mr. Noel is now a neighbour of mine and has often told me about it.[61] He states[62] his horse was shot from under him. They compelled him to walk when he was not able. He was starved for something to eat and when they passed through one of the Indians' towns the warriers of that town was all gone to war against the white people and they could get nothing to eat their. They went on a hungrey and after they got out of sight of the town they halted and some one of them Got a Mare that had a young colt. Ther was   Indians. They took the colt, killd it, and Divided it evin. The guts and liver was Divided. Part of the liver and some other part fell to Mr. Noel sheare. He said he thought when the liver was scorched on the fire—not half Done, the blood yet in it—it was the swetest eating he had ever eat in his life. And in a few Minuts every particle of the colt was eaten, hide not Excepted.

The indians took Mr. Noel to their towns and took him to Detroyt and sold him to the british. A british officer gave him an Old coat to put on as the Indeans had nearly stript him. They also gave him a loaf of white bread to eat. And as he was seting on the steps of the Doore eating his bread and very glad of it, an Indian snached his bread from him and run off with it and eat it him self.

Mr. Noel was sent from Detroyt to Montreal. And after James Trabue and the other men had made their escape and the Indeans Returned that had followed them and gave their account that they could not ketch or track them, the ballace of the prisoners was all put in a prisonship and treated bad and crewel. The british officers would go to the ship and tell them if either of them would be a waiting man for an officer he might come out of the ship. Several Men Did consent and Did come out on them Terms, but Mr. Noel said he could not stomach it. They further offered if any one would inlist in the british servise they might come out.

Mr. Noel got very tyerd of his birth. At length a french man came in the Ship and asked mr. Noel if he could write and keep books. He answered he could. He then told Mr. Noel he was a tavirn keeper or kind of a Merchant that sold and bought Rum, etc., and if he would keep his books for him he would git him out of that place. Mr. Noel agreed to it and went and kept his books for which he was very capible. This Frenchman used Mr. Noel very well and paid him some thing for his servises. Mr. Noel Remained at Montreal until the war was over. He then was exchanged and sent home in a ship to

James Trabue Returned to kentucky that same winter [1780-81], told the people in Kentucky of several men that was alive—one Man in perticular that told him he made no Doubt that his wife thought he was Dead. The circum[stance] was, he said, a little company of them was out a hunting and in the night the indeans fired on them. And as he run off an Indian fired at him and as the gun fired his foot caught in a Grapevine and he fell. And the Indians Jumped on him and made a prisoner of him. And he said their was one of his company that was close by at the time that would say he was killd and that he had a right to think so.

When James Trabue told Col. Logan that circumstance Logan said this man's wife thought he was Dead, and She was to be Married the next Day to a nother man. And he (Logan) said he would go and inform her of it and Did go and gave her the information about 2 hours before she was to be Marryed. She then Declined it, and after that her husband came to her and her children again.

7
Militia Service in Old Virginia

In January 1781 the british[1] came to Richmond,[2] 15 Miles from where we lived. Brother William and my self Got on our horses and went Down to Manchester,[3] the oppeset side of the River from Richmond. All our county men also meet their. We remained their until the neighbouring countys also came.[4] And when the Britsh found out so many Militia a gethering[5] they burned the ware houses of Tobaco and some other houses and went Down the River and got in their ships and went of[f] again.[6] Col. Robert Haskins[7] Commanded this army. We was soon Discharged.[8]

And in a few weeks the british was come to Richmond again.[9] We went Down again[10] and then british marchd up the River on the North side[11] and our men Marched up on the south side—often in sight of each other. The britech went up a bout 15 Mile to a foundery and burned it up.[12] The enemy encamed on the River on the North side and our army on the other side.

I perposed to Brother William that we could go over the River in the night and steel horses, and if we could not git them imediately a cross the River we might go a Distance up the river on the other side, that in Kentucky men would go 2 or 3 hundred Miles and have the Ohio and other Rivers to cross to steel horses from the Indians. Brother William and Frank Meryman agreed to go with me and to try the experryment.

Now all the boats, Canoes, and skifts was gethered along the River and a guard over them. We applyed to Col. Davis, who was the Commander.[13] He a greed we might go and gave us an order to the officer of the boats for us to take such a craft as we chose. We got our horses taken care of. We got a boat and mooved her Down the river a little Distance.

It was now Giting Dark and we was Just ready to move off when Col. Davis sent to us to cume to him. We went and when we got to him he told us that we must go with Major Crump[14] up the river about 10 Mile and sink some boats or hide them so that nobody Could Cross from either side.[15] We insited other waise but nothing elce would Do him. So we went and Did as he Directed. The last boat we hid in a gut and hid the Ores and we Got in the road a gain.

Two men meet with us and told us they wanted to go across the River, that they weare Merchants and their business was urgent as they wanted to go to Richmond, and the boats was all put out of the way near richmon. Major Crump informed them they could not cross hear. They concluded to go with us Down the River road to our Camp and then Down the River to Manchester oppisite Richmond. So these men went on with us and these men asked many questions. Major Crump some times give avasive answers, some times answers that which was not true. He said privately to me our orders was not to let our left hand know what our right hand Did.

When we Got near our camp on the river we left the main road. These men enquired of us whether our army extended to the road. The answer was, "No," and we Did not know that it Did.

So these 2 Jentlemen kept the big road, and as they went on their was a guard and a centry on the road. They was haild, "Who comes their?"

They answered, "Friends."

They was ordered to advance and halt. These 2 Men when they got close to the centry man which was on the side of the road, they Dashed off in a strain. The centry fired and killed one, and when his papers was examined he was a british offecer and a spy. The other got off unhurt.

We heard the gun but Did not know until morning what it ment. We had the counter sighn and passed the guard the way we went to camp and went to sleep at a late hour of the night. We understood after wards if we had went over the river that night we might have had a fine chance that night to have got horses as the british had a number of their horses in a large wheate pach next the River and out side of the centrys.

I had a good horse and road as a Valenteer on with several others, some times alone, some times with a few, and somes 40 or 50. We would go reconighting Down the river and up the river, and some times moveing our Magezene a way to some private place. The Militia began to gether from other countys again hear.

Gorge M. Smith came to us. He commanded a large fine Company and Gorge S. Smith was his Lieut. I was very Glad to see these smiths hear against the British.

Whin the British found that the Militia was gathering again, they moved Down the River again and went to their shiping. The British army lay in their shiping near about Norfork and would come on land at times and piledge the country.

The Militia was called on to go a 3 Months' Tour, and I was summond to go as one.[16] My nearest Neighbour, Capt. Edward Mosley, was our Capt.[17] He was a Wilthy Man. He told me he must have my horse to ride. He was a first-rate camp horse. He told me any price I put on him he would give me. I told him I had some Notion of rideing him my self, perhaps I could git some employ that would require a horse; but finally concluded to let Capt. Mosley have him and he got him.

We was Mustered about the first of March 1781 and started Down on the south side of James River. We went near the Dismal swam[18] and encamed in Babs' Old Field. Our army was about 3,000, all Militia Except the Artilera which consisted in about 40 Men Rank and file. We was commanded by General Mulinburgh.[19] We had not been their long before we heard the Drum beat the "general"—that is to say, "Strike your tents and March." All the soldiers and waiters in the army knows the sound of this beat. If it was at midnight every thing Moves:

> Don't you hear the general say,
> "Strik your tents and march away"?

We understood the britesh was coming on us with a superier forse.

After we had started I saw Mosley and his waiter boath on foot. It was very common for the Capt. to be on foot at the head of his company and his waiter on his horse, but when I saw neither on his horse I said to his waiter, "Where is 'ball'?" as that was the horse's name. He told me he got away from him last night and he had been a looking for him all the morning and could not find him and was a going to leave him. The bridle and saddle was in the bggage Waggon. I went to Capt. Mosley and told him I would stay behind and git his horse for him. He said he Did not request any such thing, I might be caught. I told him their was no Danger or but little about these swomps. He said Do as I plese.

As I had his consent to be absent from my place, I took the bridle and went around the camp some Distance. I saw his track and knew it. He had a large foot for Old Virginia. I tracked him a cross a swomp and going about 2 1/2 Miles I found him, and "ball" was Glad to see me. He was at a man's house where their was nothing for a horse to eat. The man said the horse was their when he first got up in the morning and kept a whikiring[20] at him and would not go away. This man told me the waey to go for a nigh cut to meet with the army, and I soon come up with them. The enemy persued us. And if I had not went after the horse, no Doubt but the enemy would have got him. Capt. Mosley Asked me how and where I found him. I told him. He said he thought I was entitled to the horse. I said, "No."

Not long after that, William Wooldridge,[21] who drove his own teme in the army to cary the bagage for our company,[22] lost his wagon horses. He had hunted for them and could not find them, and the knews was the enemy was a coming. The "general" was beating. Mr. Wooldridge was going on with the army and leave his horses and wagon behind for the enemy. Capt. Mosley called on me to know of me what was to be Done. I told him I would go with Mr. Wooldride and try to git the horses, but he must leave two men with the wagan to guard it. He agreed to it. I told the 2 Men they could see a great way off, and if they saw the enemy a coming to take to the woods, but if the enemy Did not come to stay their until we returned.

Mr. Wooldridge and my self took around the Camp and soon struck their trail. Ingoing 3 or 4 mile we got them and Returnd to the wagon in a Gallop. When we got to the waggon, they said if we had not come so soon they was Just agoing to leave the wagon. They understood the british was a coming. They thought we was gone 2 hours and that was Just the time they intended to stay and no longer. The horses was hiched to the wagon and we was gone I think in 5 Minuts. We went in a long trot and over took the army in a hurry.

This army went on a piece further—perhaps another day—and was meet by several companys, some of them from the back woods with Riffils. We then turned our cource to meet the enemy, and they retreated and went to thir shiping. We encamed near them and kept out scouting parties to keep the enemy from pelidgeing [pillaging] the country.

These Rifle men came from Rockbridge and Agusta.[23] I knw several of these men. I had seen them in kentuckey. They and the 2 Gorge Smiths and my self Did often talk about wanting to have the chance of shooting the britesh. Their fingers seem to Itch to be pulling a way at them.

A number of the men Did grumble about their provision but I thought we was well off. Some times the flour was a little spoiled, but I Did not care much a bout that for I could eat meet without any bread very well. And if the meet was a little spoiled, we could git Fish and Oisters a plenty by ketching them ourselves. And their was often cart and wagon loads of white shad brought to our Camp and sold for a very moderate price.

We had been laying Idle some time doing nothing, and their was a man that wanted to hire himself as a substitute.[24] I asked him what he would take. He told me. I agreed I would give it if Capt. Mosly would take him. I took him to Capt. Mosley and asked him if he would take him. He asked me what was my reason for wanting to leave them.

I told him as we was Doing nothing only lying by I was tyrd of it. "If we had any chance to shoot the britesh I would like it, but it seems we have no chance of ever giting a fight and I think I will go to Kentucky again."

He said, "I would not have you leave us under no consederations. If it was not for you I would have lost my horse, and wagon horses and wagon and baggage would all have been lost and in the hands of the britesh." And said he, "You have had bad luck in Kentuckey and I have been thinking of you. And why cannot you turn in and speculate in camp, buoy Rum, brandy, and cyder and sell it? And you may make a great speck. I will let you ride my horse. I will let you have Mony and will Do any thing for you I can. I Do earnestly insest on you not to lave us."

I concluded not leave this army. This man substituted him self to another man. I road the Capt. horse in the country and bought first a barrel of sider and then 2 Barrils, and sold it at a handsome profit. I had mony of my own and Did not borrow any from Capt. Mosley.

The[25] British Army moved up the River.[26] We then had to march Day and night. I took Capt. Mosley's horse and went a head and bought a cask of brandy and had it brought to where we encamped. And I sold some of it at a hansome profit. Next morning after selling some I got it put in our baggage Waggon, and when ever we stoped I would sell some. Some of the soldiers was very glad to have brandy so handy, but others Grumbled and scolded about it because it was carried in a publick wagon. And when I was not their they did steel some. When that was out I quit it for the present; however, I made a good turn out of it.

As Darke a night as I ever had seen we had to march all night and it a raining. When morning would come the word was General Phillups[27] and Arnold[28] was in the River a head of us. The army would halt a bout one hour for the soldiers to coock and then go again. Their was patrolers and spies alwaise out a waching and bring us word where they weare.

When we Got in one mile of petersburg[29] we halted, and took up Camp for the night [Tuesday, April 24], streached our tents. We was on a beutyful branch for water and wood, the soldirs all a cooking. Some few was eating and some their victuals half Done, when of a sudden the Drum beat the "General." The tents [were] Jirked down and they with the cooking tools throwed in the wagon, and in a few minuts a marching to petersburgh, which is on appermattock River[30] 10 or 12 Miles from its mouth, where the britesh landed at city pint.[31] They marched on foot and some of their smaller vessils went up in appermatack river. This river is too small for vessels of any size.

Previous to this time Capt. M.G. Smith and Lieut. G.S. Smith and Myself and the backwoods Rifle men had been Grumbling and scolding about so much Retreating and no shooting. The Militia now began to complain very Much also. They would say they would rather fight than run so much. Our captains began to talk the same way and the field officers too. But our commander General Mullenburg was afraid to risk it, as General Gates had been Defeeted the year before and at Gelford the melitia did run in confution.[32]

We Marched through Petersburgh. As the super or Diner of our mess was not Done we lost it, and as we passed through town I got leave of absence. I went to a baker's shop who I knew and got some Good loaves of bred and ginder cakes and took them to our Mess. We saved some of our bred for the next morning and put in each man's napsack.[33] We cross the river at the town—wagons, artilery and all—and took up the plank of the bridge[34] and lay on our arms all night. We was now in chesterfield county, whire I was born and raised.

Some of our county men heard of the approch of the enemy and in the night had come to us—perhaps 1 or 2 hundred, some of them light horse[35] and others on foot.[36] Their was Great counciling that night with our general and field officers. The conclusion was to fight and try the Militia.

When Morning [April 25] came at Day light the reveley beat, a Morning gun fired, the plank of the bridge laid Down, and a hogshead of Rum rooled out to every Ridgment of Men, the head nockd out. "Now, boys, drink and fill your canteens," was the word. "But Don't Drink too much. We are a going to fight to Day."[37] It was said the enemy was 6,000, our army upward of 3,00[0], nearly 2 to 1.[38]

Our cannon was not took over the river but kept on a hill[39] on chesterfield side near the bridge, and it was before sun rise the army was over the bridge. Several patroling little companys was sint out a reconetering. They weare light horse from our county Just come as Vallenteers. Our advance guard meet the enemy a bout 1 Mile from town. This advance was only a sergant and 12 Men. His orders was when he meet them to fire when they came in 200 paces of them, and then retreat to where they would meet with a larger squad. They Did so and meet about 100 which had the same orders. This 100 Men fired when the enemy was fully 200 yards Distant and fired several Times until they Got in about 100 Ditto and then Retreated to where their was about 500. They also fired several times. The bretish fired their cannon but our men was so scattered that they did not receeve much Damage, while the enemy's loss was considerable. At length the british charge on them. They thin Retreated to whear the main army was.[40]

Our men was behind a wear house, a hedge, and Diches, and fences, etc. And we fired on the britesh as they advanced.[41] We took good aim and killed a number of them. A party of our men had been sent to charge on their left flank. This seemed to halt the enemy and our people a fireing away. The britesh had no light horse and our men ventured very much with a superiour force. Our Army retrated further in the town,[42] and it was one hour or two before the Enemy advanced on our men.[43]

And while we was their waiting Colo[nel] Forkner[44] called out for volenteers to go with him to take a britesh vessil that was 1/2 mile below and a ground. He said he wanted a Capt. and subaltons and a bout 60 Men. He wanted brave men and them that could swim. A Capt. Epperson, who I was well acquainted with, run out and said, "Come out, boys." It was perhaps one or two menuts before any one turned out. One of my mess—to wit, Gabril Vest[45]—said to me if I would go he would. All the hesitation I had I thought we was needed where we was and perhaps taking the Vessil was not Much of an object. However, I told vest I woud and out we went. We weare the first that followed Capt. Epperson. The company was made up and started in 5 Menuts.

We went in a run, and before we got to them they fired on us. We went on the bank oppersit the vessil within 60 or 70 yards and fired on them as fast as we could load and shoot. They fired several times at us. When Capt. Epperson saw them puting their Mach to their canon he would cry out, "Shot!" All of us would fall Down and the cannon ball generally went over our heads. We would Jump up and fire again at the men we could see on Deck and Did actuly kill the most of them. As we now could see no other to shoot at and they had quit shooting at us Capt. Epperson sayed, "Boys, we will board her." All things was now still.

When Col. Forkner was off at a Distance of 200 yards a waching at the head of a swomp for fear some of the enemy might souround us when we did not expect it, Col. Forkner came riding as fast as he could, hollowing, "Retreat! Retreat! Retreat!" We started and when he Meet us he told us their was several hundred of the enemy a sourounding us. We run a long up the river. And when we got up to the head of the swomp where Col. Forkner had been a waching the enemy, a bout 250 me[n] was oppeseset to us a bout 200 yards off to our right. We could out run them. When they Discovered that they Could not ketch us, they turned and went to their Vessil and I suppose found the most of their men dead. We had 2 Men badly wounded with grape shot and had gone away previously. One ball went in the bank under us and knocked so much of Dirt on sveral of us that we was stuned for a little while.

We went to our redgement. They had been skrimishing while we was Gone. We meet them Retreating over the bridge. We then was before in the Retreat. As soon as we Got over the bridge we went above and below the bridge on the edge of the water to save the Retreat over the bridge.

When the enemy Discovered our men acrossing the bridge they rushed after them. Our cannon had been fireing on them the most of the Day but at the begining of their fireing they was at a Great Distance, but Now when they came near they (the enemy) was much Damaged by our cannon. The bridge was not wide enough for the men to get over fast enough. The enemy came Rushing Down to cut off our rear.

Where I stood we had a fine view of them and they weare very fair to us and we made good use of it. The enemy at the foot of the bridge was in solid Colums and was some little time combating with our men, chargeing with their bayonets. And our men resisted and Definded themselves some little, but at last they took off about 40 or 50 of our men before our faces within 60 or 70 yards of us but they paid Dear for these men. Our redgiment at the bridge fired 10 or 12 times each. I fired 13 very fair shoots, and the most of the shoots when they were nigh a plenty the wind blowed of[f] the smook. And when I fired I looked whire I shot at and I could see them tilt over. And when they Retreated up the hill from the bridge they run, as our men would keep on fireing at their flanks so as not to hurt our men who was Just made prisoners.

We lost that Day killd 40, wounded 60, prisoners 50. The enemy's loss was 6 or 800.[46] Near about the bridge after the enemy retreated the ground was covered with red coats as we could see them plain.[47]

The fireing first began a little after sun rise and continud until two hours of the sun in the evening. Their was some time on that Day when you could not hear a gun but not long at a time. Several times that day my gun was so hot that I could hardley hold it. If I would spit on it, it would fize.

Our Militia that Day was very brave. We was ordered to fire when they was some Distance from us, and when they came up nigh the men Had got a litle use to it.

At one time of that Day a redgiment Joined our Redgiment that had not been engaged as yet. And a young man in this new Redgiment, only one man betwen us, said he was very sick. He lay Down in the rear of his platoon and roold on the ground, the enemy a coming on before us. Maj. Boyse,[48] Brigader Major, Rideing along in the rear giveing orders, this sick man attempted to run away. The Major road after him, sweareing he would cut of[f] his head as he was a Coward. This young man tryed to Jump over a Gulley and fell back in the Gulley. The Major's horse Jumped over the Gulley. The young man run back to his place and stood in his place. The major Turned his horse and come back, and as the young man was in his place said nothing more. Orders was emediately give for to fire. I cast my Eye to this young man. He fired and kept on a fireing as well as any of us. I make no Doubt but this young man was sick, but it was fear that was the cause of it and Major Boyse cured him.

Their was some of my near neighbours on horse back equipt as light horse—to wit, Robert Wooldredge and 5 others—sent out in the morning to go a round the enemy, and go Down to their shiping to bring information and pick up straglers if they could. They returned about the middle of the day with 5 prisoners who was on cappital good horses. These men had some of the Generals' baggage comeing on behind, had Just come on from their shiping, and they were well armed. The way they took them: they saw them at a Distance and hid themsilves in ambush until they came close by, and on a sudden ordered them to surrender and they yealded emediately. When they brought them to our camp it did very much Revive us to see these red coats and to think our undisiplined men Did take old vetorns. Mr. Wooldredge and these 5 Men was Vallenteers and had Just came to us in the night.

Some of our wounded which was slitly [slightly] wounded could Travil on foot and 2 wagons halled the ballance. We left Petersburgh when the sun was nearly 2 hours high in the evening. I was now 25 Miles from home. We marched towards whire I lived up towards our court house. We went about 7 Miles that night, and encamed at Dark where theire was a plenty of wood and water, and all went to cooking and eating. That Day their was but few of this army that Did eat one Mouthful. For my part I Did eat a small piece of a light loaf that I had got the over night.

I Did never in my life before nor since Drink as much nor half as much rum or other sperrits in one Day as I Did that Day. I filled my canteen in the morning which held near one quart, and once in a while take a Dram out from the canteen. I Drank no water nor had no chance to git any. And I had never been used to Drink sperrits much without water; but that day when I wanted water, when I had time I wood take a Dram, and at night my rum was out and I was Duly sober. And the rest of the men Did about the same.

When morning [April 26] came we went on to chesterfield court house,[49] which was about 5 Mile. And about 2 hours of the sun in the evining Capt. Mosley told me the army would leave that place that night and he expected we would go towards where we lived. He said Corn Wallis[50] and Col. Talton[51] was also come from the south and was at Petersburgh with the other britesh army. And he further said, "I wish you would go home and go to my house and give my wife the knews and see my overseer and tell thim Thus and so, and you come to us to Morrow. I know you can and will." And said he, "Don't say one word to one of the soldiers of this, as a vast number wants to go home and some of them in sight of their homes as we March along." And said he, "Take your Mother's Waggon and load it with Brady and bring it to camp. If she has not got it, go to my Seller [cellar]. Their is plenty." Capt. Mosley was very unesey about his Negros for fear they might flee to the enemy.[52] I told him I would go.

At this chesterfield court house was Barren Stuben[53] with new recruets of soldiers and a vast number of young officers, that he was tutering for the army and publick stoors also. I had no thought of our army leaving that place without contending for it. So it was, they left it the same night after I was gone. And they Did not have wagons sufficient to remove the stoors and they left them behind.

I had 12 Miles to go and I started about 1 1/2 hours before sun set alone on foot. When I was 4 Mile from home in the Dark night I heard some body a meeting me like a heavy footed negro. I suposed he was runing a way going to the british. I halted untill he got in a bout 20 yards. I then hailed him, "Who comes their?" He stopt. I then said, "Don't run or you will be shot. Who are you?" He broake and run. I fired at him. The blaze semed to go almost to the fellow. It was a loud Report. The Fellow run off. I never heard who I shot at, but their was a number of negros run away that night.

When I got home all was well and our negros all at home. I went to Capt. Mosley's emediately and his negros was all at home. A few nights after that some [of] Capt. Mosley's did run off and one of mine. I ate and slept well that night. When morning [April 27] came my mother's Wagon was made ready and loaded with Brandy. She was very glad for me to have it. She said she was afraid the british would hear she had it when they weare in the neighbourhood and come after it, or if the negros would rise they would come after it. Now the poor woman was almost as afraid of the negros as of the british. My Mother's nigro Drove the wagon. Brother Stephen was about 14 years old. He went along with us to help to retail it.

We meet with the army at Falling creek church about 4 or 5 Miles from our home.[54] They had been Marching almost all night. Our army was perraded in a large green wheat Field and Commanded by Barren Stuben. He had some of his soldiers and officers with him. They expected the enemy every menut. They [the enemy] did on this day Come to the court house and took what they wanted and burned all the ballance. Evin the court house they burned,[55] and Talton was seen coming this way. The army marched this same evening and stopt at the cole pits near where we lived.[56]

In 2 or 3 Days I sold out my brandy and went and got Capt. Mosley's and sold it and made a handsom profit on it. When I was oblidge to Do Duty Brother Stephen was Tapster with the assistance of the negro Driver, but I was mostly their my self and would hire a man to go on Guard in my place.

Our army[57] at this time was 25 Miles from Petersburgh, and they moved back towards Petersburgh 12 Miles—not fair from Chesterfield court house at Sutberry's Old Field.[58] They weare now about 13 M[iles] from Petersburgh, and on a rainey Day [May 23] the men in their Tents, some in a barn, some a cooking, some out of camp (I was out of camp myself by permission), when Talton with 500 horse, and ivery horse one of the Infentrey behind. So their was 1,000 came up on them on the backside.[59] The men broake and run. Some of the officers hollowed to the Men to perade but all in vain. Lewis Subblit[60] (my brother-in-law) run in the barn, took his gun and catritge box, waked his brother James (but he was taken a prisoner), and run out. They told him to stop, a D[amned] Rebel, and one horseman came up with him. He Defended himself with his bayonet, Jumped over the fence in a swomp, and made his escape very narrowly. This swomp saved a bundence of the men. They took 40 odd prisoners and the most of the guns, all the cannon and all the waggons with the baggege and publick stores that they had with them.[61]

These 40 odd men was taken Down the river in a prison ship and took sick and Died—every man except 3. They weare Martain Rayley,[62] John Bowman, and Gabril Vest. All the rest did actully Die by Hard yousage. They weare plundered of their cloaths, kept in a prison ship, and nothing good to eat, not even good water. These 3 Men told me so.

Mr. Bowmer, I said, came home alive; but he was sick when he was exchanged for, and his people fetched him home and he Died. He lay as a skilitan for months previous to his Death. This Mr. Railey was a cousin of Tom Jefferson [and] a neighbour of mine, a very young man, but a man of sence. This Gabril Vest was also my neigbour and as Great a heroe as any. I saw Bowmon before he Died. They all told me the main Reason of their hard Treatment was because they would not inlist in the service of his Gracious Majesty king G[eorge] III. Mr. Vest told me he thought he would make his escape from them, but he had not the least chance as they kept them in a ship well guarded.

These men that was supprised at sutberry's Old Field was Dispersed in such a Manner, was never got to gether again. Some few was colected and went on to the north where they Meet General Fayatte[63] and General Wayn[64] on the Rappey Dan River at the Rackoon Ford.[65] My time of servise was now Out.

The britesh army was Destessing our cuntry very much and had no oppisition. Corn Wallis had his head quarters at Petersburgh,[66] and Col. Taltern roaving about the country Just where he plesed.

The people in chesterfield was mostly hid in the swomps. These swomps in the wenter is wet and poonds of water, but in the summer is Dry and very bushey—almost equil to cain breaks. Almost all our young Women left their homes and went up the cuntry. When the britesh would go to a house they would compel the negros and children to go and shew wher the meet[67] or brandy or flour was hid out.

My Mother's house was weather boarded and lathed and plastered inside; and I went on the back side and Drawd a plank or two, and put the most of the Cloathing and plate and the like, and nailed it up again. No one knew of it but me and my Mother. Some of our meet we hid out, and only some negros know where it was but those we could confide in. My sisters went to an unkil's where it was thought was a very private place. What arms and ammonition we had we hid out.

Brother William and my self when we was at home slept out. Brother Stephen (a boy) and my Mother stayed at home.

Capt. Mosley, Brother Wiliam, and my self took several tours on the enemie's line in the night. Corn Wallis and Talton left the south side of the river and went on the North side to Richmond.[68]

8

Wartime Stress on Civilian Life

Col. Good,[1] the Commander of the Militia in our county, wanted some body to go with Despaches to General Layfatte. Our Goviner Tom Jefferson was at this time up the River at charlottsvil with our Legislator.[2]

I agreed to go for Col. Good and started on sunday Morning [June 3, 1781]. I crossed James River at the Manekin town ferry[3] and in Gochland county about 18 Miles from home. As I was a going on I meet people the roadfull a runing and was rideing. The cry was, "British! British!"[4]

"Where are they at?"

"Col. Dandridge's."[5]

I went one Mile to Squire Garrand's.[6] He lived off the road. He was my relation. I road up, was afraid to alight. His son John[7] told me if I would go with him we would go and see. I said I would go. I got Down, and went in the porch, Drank some grog, eat some victuls in the porch. My horse was fed at the Door in a tub and a boy to hold him.

Cozin John and me mounted our horses and went on the back side of Col. Dandridge's on a high hill in the woods and we saw them. They appeared to be several thousand.[8] This Cousin John was a Major and but a young man. He Got to be a general after that time. We talked some time, Did not know what to say or Do. We bid fair well to each other.

I Did not think that any of Talton's horse could ketch me as I had a first-rate horse.[9] I went on that day, and at night took off the road and stayed at a private house, got my supper and slept in a little house in a field, my horse in the same house with me. When Morning came I persued my Jurney and went on only a few Miles, and crossing a big road I saw thousands of Fresh horse tracks.

Their was a tavern (to wit, Brow's Tavern)[10] about 100 yards from me on this cross road to my right hand. I road to it and enquired what tracks these ware. The Jentleman in his Doore said, "Talton.[11] Did not you see them?"

I told him, "I came the other road and Did not see them."

He said they was hardly out of sight.

I said, "Hend me some rum for a Dram and be quick!" He fetched me a case bottle and I took a Dram and said, "What is to pay?"

He said, "Never mind that. You are welcome to that little." He said he was afraid they would ketch me as he did not think the rear was yet past.

I told him, "I have got a good horse and I am not easy to ketch."

He asked me when I first road up where I was going, and I had told him I was going to our army commanded by General Fayatte. I had pistols and a sword. I Did not stop their more than one Minut and I bid him fare well, and he wished me sucksess and said, "Don't be ketched!"

I went on my Jurney a few miles and stoped and took breackfast but kept a wach at the Doore. I went on again and in a few miles I meet about 12 of The British light horse. When I first saw them they was perhaps 1/4 of a mile from me in a slow trot. I at first was not satisfyed who they weare and I kept on a meeting them. I Discovered 2 or 3 of them had common hats. And when they got neigher I stoped, and got to beleave the red coats was british and the others with the common hats was their pilats. When they Got about 150 yards of me I turned my horse, and they started after me in full speed, saying, "Stop, you D[amned] rebel!" I kipt the road about 1/2 Mile. I was no waise alarmed as I thought I could out go them in the woods. I left the road and they Did not follow me in the woods fair.

I took my road again, and the first house I came to I inquired of the lady about these men. She told me her husband was from home, they plundered her house.

And she said, "Look at the corn house Doore at the corn on the ground! They made our negros fling all that corn out, and let their horses eat what they wanted.[12] They abuesed us as rebels." I told her to make her negros through the corn in the crib again. She said she would Do that, but they had robed them of many things.

I went on until I meet with my county men who was with General Faytte and General Wayn. I was Glad to see our men, and they was glad to see me and hear from their familyes.

I Delivered the Despaches to General Fayatte. He read the contents and asked me many questians. I applyed to him for a permit to be a sutle [sutler] to his army. He said he would Do it with cheerfullness and was Determined to impress all the wagons and spirrits that Did not have permits, as every one that was in the army Ought to be in subordination to the commander. He imedeately had one wrote. He sighned it and gave it to me.

I went through the camps looking at the Different men that was selling spirrits. I Saw a Duchman that had Just come in camp. He had a fine teame and a good load of Brandy and Whiskey and two very large sacks of sweet bred. I said to this Duchman, "Have you a permit to sell your spirrits?"

He answered, "No."

I told him I heard the General Say he would Impress all wagons and spirrits that would sell with out a permit. I told him I had a permit, and I was willing to go halfs with him in his load, and we to count up the value at holesale rates, and I would assist him in selling, and we would Devide the overplus. He made me no answer and I stayed their with him a while and soon saw that these yankey Soldiers would impose on him.

After a very little while, hear comes the Ajatent and says, "Whoes waggon and spirits is this?"

The Duchman said, "It is mine, Sir."

The adjatent said, "Impress the wagon and spirrits for the youse of the army. Don't sell any more here. Guard, take possession," said the adjatant.

This Duchmon looked very much alarmed. I said to this Duchman in a whisper, "Will you agree to my proposition with you? I can save you."

He said, "Yes, yes, yes."

I said to the Adjatint, "Look at this my permit. You won't take our spirrits and wagon."

The Adjatent read it and said, "No, we won't trouble you." And the officer and guard turned off.

The Duchman said, "I am so Glad I sees you."

We examined the quanity and fixed the prices in a very few minuts. The other waggons with sperrits was all Impressed, and we had a Great run of custom and soon sold out, and we made a very handsom profit.

And we made a further bargan that we would go and git a nother load and we started to the country. And when we once got out of reach of the army, the Duchmon told me he was afraid to go with his wagon in Camp any More, that he would take his wagon home and pull of[f] the wheels. And all I could say to him Did not avail any thing. He said, "General Fayette might alter his notion." I road all around in that section of the country and could git no wagon, all afraid of Impresments. And after a few Days I told General Fayette how it was, I would go home and meet with him again in a few Days. He wrote by me to Col. Good near Richmond.[13] I went home which it was about 80 Miles as I went home. I several times heard of the britesh not being far off, but I Did not see any; but I knew it was not safe to go with a wagon back at that time.[14]

I went home and bought a good wagon and Team, and procured a plenty of Brandy and rum; but at this time their was Great Distress in the country, Corn Wallis and Talton going where ever they pleased.[15]

Several of our Meletial [militia] men was caught as they was returning from Fayette's Army as their Times was out. Lewis Subblitt (my Brother-in-law) and Mr. D. Morrisit and a Mr. Thermon[16] was a coming home. And as they heard the british was plenty they was afraid to go along the road through plantations, but when in the woods if they at a Distance could see the enemy they would have a chance to make their escape. But one Day late in the evining they concluded they would call at a house, Git something to eat, and then they could walk almost all night.

So they ventered up to the house and their was 5 British red coats in the house. They run out and ordered these 3 Men to surrender. Morrisit and Thurmon surrendered, but Sublitt Jumed the fence and run through a field. Some of them Jumped on horses and took after Sublitt, but before they over took him he was in the woods and the bushes was so thick they could not find him. The british compelled Mr. Thurmon and Mr. Morrisit to go with them a head and hollow for Sublitt but he Did not hear them. They all stayed at this house all night and kept the landlady a cooking for them and giving them as much brandy as they could Drink.

The land lord was hid out and he in the night would come home and view these fellows and he was a resulute man. He had guns hid out with him and at Day he came to a window and fired on them. They run out at the Doore and made their escape, and he fired as they run a nother time which caused them to keep on. Mr. Thurmon and Mr. Morrisit run out of the house but took a Different rout. They kept the road home and before night fell in with Mr. Sublitt again. Mr. Sublitt had not kept the road much. These men all come home to gether.

Capt. Mosley[17] and a nother Meletia captain (I Don't wish to name him) came to our house. Brother William and myself at home. They said they came to talk about the times. This other captain said he now plainly saw that it was out of the question that we could succeed in our liberty, that he thought we ought to urge our men, he said, that was at the helm of our affairs to submit to his gracious Majesty and make as good a piece as we could git.

Wil[liam] T[rabue] told him that when the seat of war was in the north and when he—W.T.—was going to the south as they Marched through this county you then told us to be brave, their was no Danger, our cause was good, and we some Day would be certain to gain our liberty. "But, now as the seat of war is hear, the main British army is hear, and we Do suffer much, our court house and our publick stoors burnt and Destroyed, and bullocks taken, great many fences and fields Gone to wast, you are for giveing up our riteous [righteous] cause. But you are rong, Capt. The storm will blow over, And if the times is Deficult, let us not back out but Do the best we can."[18]

We at this time Did not know what minut we would see Talton's horse approching. The fact was no body a stiring. We could git no knews. These two Captains and us two brothers, all had the very best of horses. Concluded we would set out and see how the times weare.

We went Down on the south side of James river near Richmond and up the appermattock river to Petersburgh and chesterfield court house, etc., was traviling two Days and nights and got home. Strange it is to say what few people we saw, hardly a man or woman or negro to be seen but some old man or woman or an Old negro at a house and very often not a soul. Very often we would see a man at a Distance but when we would Git where we saw him he woud be gone and hid himself.

We was Determined if we saw a few of the enemy we would take them. And on the first night we meet Col. William Smith and 3 others; and they had concluded, as we had, to take a few prisoners if it was in their power. And this was a Dark night. We thought they weare british and they thought we weare british. We ordered them to surrender and they ordered us to surrender. We was well armed on boath sides. We was Just a going to fire on boath sides. The guns was cocked. I thought I knew Colonel Smith's voice, who lived 10 Miles from us, and I named him. And then they knew us and we went all together that night reconetering. The british was gone over on the north side of James river, but Corn Wallis and Col. Talton had skeard the people almost to Death.

General Fayette had ogmented his army[19] and was coming to wards Corn wallace, who was at Richmond.[20] Our Melitia was called for and the other countys' also and Joined Fayette; and as he marched near Richmond, Corn Wollis left the city in the evening.[21] The next morning a little after sun rise Fayette Marched through the town with his army[22] with Green bushes[23] in each man's hat. I then thought it was the beautyfullest sight that I had ever seen. Corn wollis had retreated and our army advanceing after them.[24] Our army passed through the city some Distance—perhaps 3 or 4 miles—and then halted on the river road.[25]

I that Day had business on the left-hand road that goes by Chikehomeney bridge,[26] and after I had went 8 or 10 Miles I saw 40 bullocks sloughtered—some skined and quartered, and some only skined, and some only half-skined—and a bout 50 More in a bullock pen. Their was nobody to be seen but an Old woman. She said their was a large army of the british their about two hours ago, and all at once they went off in the greatest hurry emajinable and left their beef. And she did not know the reason. This was about the middle of the day. I think in July.[27] I went and informed Fayette of it.[28] The sloughtered beef was spoiled but the bullocks he got.

On this same Day I had my wagon and spirrits in camp and selling brisk at a good price but it was paper money. When I sold out my wagon load I quicly got a nother one in camp.

Our army never lay long at one place. They did move Down the river after corn Wallis and then some times they would move up the river again.

Our army was encamed about 8 or 10 Miles below Richmon on the river when Capt. Stratton sailed up to us in the river in a british Vessil which he had taken the night before. This Capt. Stratton was a sea Captain, and the british previous to that time had took his Vessil from him and he was now broak. His Aunt lived on the River and he was at his Aunt's when this britesh Vessil stoped and Anchored out in sight.

This Capt. Straton knowing the british Vessels was all below this, also Corn Wallis and his army was below, he was now Determined to try to take this Vessel by some stratigim. He got some of his Aunt's negro men and some free Malatters, and went Down to the River, and made a Old negro hollow to the vessel and ask them if they would buoy chickin and sweet t tateer. The answer was, "Yes." Capt. Stratton had some Guns but the most of his weapons was axxes. He got in a small pleasure boat that the seats goes all round. They (the men) lay concealed under the seats while the Old negro was on Dek seeling his chickin and sweet T taters. All at Once Capt. Stratton sprung up and his negros with him, and one shut Down the hach way, and the rest run up with thur Guns and axxes on those on the Dek. They cryed out for quarters and surrenderd.

Capt. Stratton and some of these Negros was well acquanted with the channel of this river. Whin the tide arose he hoisted sail. Capt. stratton took hold of the Cabel and give it a little pull. The officer said to him, "Sir, I can call up some of my men to help you take up the Anker." Stratton told him he was a fool. When Stratton was ready for sailing he took a axx and cut the Cabel, and off he went up the river with the tide and came to us.

When he opined the hachway he found he had 9 or 10 british prisoners and about as many negro men and some other propety. They had a great many large looking Glasses, etc. We suppose they had pelledged them. Stratton sold the negros and other propety for his own use and give some little to his Aunt's negros and the Melatters. These negros and propety was sold in our camp at the highest bidder. Capt. Statton now got in good circumstances again.

General Fayette still Augmented his Army and persued Down the river after Corn Wallis. Brother Edward T[rabue] came home from the Suthern army. He told us[29] how he was in the battle at Gelford and that he was at Gates' Defeat in the battle and as they all broak and run. As he run on some Distance thur waggoner Jumed of[f] his horse and run and left it. Edward took out the saddle horse and mounted him. He looked back and no light horse a coming and the Bri[tish] Infintry close by, but he thought he would take as much time as he would save something out of the wagon. He road around the wagon and took his Col. Forkner Port mantue and a pair of saddle bags, but the british had got close to him and ordered him to stop, but he asked no favours now as he was on a horse. Col. Forkner has Frequently told me of the exploit of Edward Trabue in saveing his Things for him.

Brother Edward agreed to go with me to sell my spirrits.[30] We went on now very well in selling our spirrits; and one of the times when we had sold out we went down on Raperhannock[31] to git salt, as it was very scirce with us. We bought our load from a widow woman. Her name was Hackney.[32] She was rich and had a number of negros and made mony fast by boiling salt t water from the river, as it was near the bay. It was tolerable salt.

Thur was great quanitys of sheep in this section of the country. I Inquired if any one had wool to sell. Mistress Hackney told me that a mr. Morgan[33] two miles below had a plenty. I went to his house. He lived on the point[34] between Rapperhannock and Peyankeytank Rivers.[35] Each of these rivers is about 3 Miles wide. Mr. Morgan was a looking through a spy Glass at a british vessil coming up. He said they would be now plundered of their sheep, etc.

The vessil sailed very fast. It took up the river. I was a going back. I went in a gallop. I had a clear view of them all the way.[36] It out went me and landed some of their men at the bush pint. My road went near them. They hollowed at me, wanted me to stop, but I knew they Could not ketch me. I was on a good horse.

After I had passed them they fired their cannon. I Don't know whether they fired at me or not, but when I came to Mistress Hackney's she run out and inquired what cannon that was. I told her the british was at the bush pint (a landing thir men) which was about a half mile. I told Edward and the Driver to start instantly and they Did start in 4 or 5 Minuts. This lady said she was ruined, they would break her up. Some times she was on her knees praying and thin run to us and say, "What shall I Do?" I indeavourd to comfort her by saying they would not hurt her as she was a widow. She requested us to take her Daughter. She was a beautyfull young lady. I told her we could not take her. I thought she was skeared out of her sencis. We had no time for chating.

The road was Dry and good and a Dead leavil. The wagon went in a Gallop and I road behind to wach. I Did not know but by chance they might have light horse that I Did not see or might take Mistress Hackney's Horses. And so it was we kept in a Gallop for several Miles. Brother Edward and the other man blamed me very much for not bringing off the young lady. We took our salt home which it was greatly needed in the neighbourhood. We quickly Returned to the army with another load of Sperrits.

About this time all and every one of our Militia was called for to go to help to take Corn Wallis. Count De Grass,[37] the commander of The French Fleet, had blocked up Corn Wallis, and he [Cornwallis] was at yorktown[38] fortyfying him self their.[39] Corn Wallis had many Thousand of Negro men and Torrys a working at his fortyfications, while he himself and vetorns was contending with Fayette for every Inch of ground. Corn Wallece was at Old Williamsburg[40] 12 Mils from yorketown, and new ridgements and Bergades a Joining Fayette every Day.[41] I was called on also. And although my permit as a sutler would clear me, yet I chose to hire a substitute and Did so. Brother William was a bergade Major in these last troops that came from our county.

We now began to think that corn wallece would be taken sure enough. Fayette was avanceing on corn wallece and they meet at a old Field Called old James Town near Williamsburgh. They had their a severe engagement.[42] The cannon Did roare Dreadfully on boath sides and the Infintory was much ingaged also. Fayette kept the Field.[43] I was in sight of this battle looking at them but was not engaged in the battle. Neither was half the men we had in it. Corn Wallace left the old town and went to Williamsburgh and went Dow[n] the River.[44]

Fayette Marched our army through the town and encamped in the Old Fields below Williamsburg. The French Infentry Joined us hear.[45] We was Glad to see them come. And I was Glad every Day as they brought silver with them—yes, French crowns—and I got many of them. They also brought Gold and we got a good sheare of that too. And we in a few Days would sell out our spirrits and could not git any more nearer than Petersburgh, which was 60 Miles; but we would go to Petersburgh and back again 3 days. The road was leavil all the way, and with the empty wagon we would go upwards of 50 Miles in the Day and a little in the night, and with our load we went over 30 Miles. We had good horses and took good care of them. We had a nigro that was a good horseler.

General Fayette allowed me a guard of a sergent and 12 Men. And I got the adjutent that ordered them out to let me chuse them, and as the adjutent was my perteceler friend and I had good rum to treat him he Did so. The men was very ancious to come to guard us as they all got something to Drink on free cost, and they weare assistence to us many a time in selling and fixing our camp, etc.

9
Yorktown and War's End

There is now a Great Difference in seeing people plenty stiring about in the country and at their homes. When Corn Wallis and Talton was roveing about I could hardly see any person. Although the Militia is all called on to go to camp,[1] now you may often see people—old men and boys, Old woman and girles, and negros—and Don't offer to run and hide as formerly; but would run to us for the knews, sending letters and other things to their men in camp—like a little coffey, chockelitt, or cloathing—and enquereing and saying, "Do you think Corn Wallace will be taken?"

"O yes, and now we are sure to have company along the road that is going to camp."

Fayett's army encreases every Day and he Advances nearer little york on Corn Wallice, and corn wallace contends for every Inch of ground and they often have skremishes.[2] General Washington is come to camp and troops from new york,[3] etc., and they fetched a number of yoakes of Oxxen[4] to hall their Waggons, the largest I had ever seen. A great many of our men ordered out on feteauge [fatigue], like sawing plank for their batterys, etc. Corn Wallis and Talton, Tories and negros, all gone in their Fortyfycation[5] but they kept possion of some of their Ridouts [redoubts] on Pigeon hill for a day or two, but they was Drove from them Works.[6] A number of our men was in the woods making [gabions][7] while some was halling plank.

They halled cannon and Morters[8] from James river to yorktown which was 7 Miles, and the French men halled one very large one and they Tryed horses two in a brest. I now Don't know how many—perhaps a hundred—but they could not make them all pull together and would be all Day and would get but a little Distance. They Then tryed these yankey Oxens and they could not git them all to work to gether. And at last the men Did pull it as they could all pull together. And it was then and their I assertained that men can pull more than horses as they can all pull together, when they could not make so large a quanity of horses all pull together at the same time.

Some times the officers would call at our Tent[9] and say to me, "Come. Go with me to the woods where Our men is making [gabions]." I had a good horse and did often go to the Different placis to see what was going on. Brother Edward and I had a wonderfull chance to see every thing that was going on, as one could stay and the other ride out to see. And the officers was apt to call at our Camp to git a Dram, and then they would give us the knews what was a going on.

One afternoon [Saturday, October 6] their came wagons loaded with spades and they weare laid out in piles. It was a sight to me. I Did not know where they could git so many from. Their was other tools[10] also laid out their too and a great many [gabions]. And now to look and see a plain leavil old Field exposed to the enemy's Fire. How will it be tomorrow morning?[11]

After dark these spades was served out and a number of men took these [gabions] and set them on end tuching each other, and the spaids was for to fell these [gabions] with Dirt and hen go on making a Ditch and through out the dirt in front.[12]

When morning came their was a Ditc all round About 10 feet wide—I meen, on the south side of the ri , where the fort was. This fort was on the bank of the River, and on the other side is called Glauster.[13] I understood they had a Ditch Dug on that side on the same night this ditch was Dug, and when morning came it was a grand sight indeed. This ditch[14] was nearly half mile from the fort and then the two ends run to the river.[15] The length of this ditch that was cut in one night was nearly 2 1/2 Miles long,[16] and in this ditch you could walk all round and could not be seen by the enemy, and in this Detch about every 25 yards they Made a battery[17] for a cannon or a morter to fling bums.[18]

When our men was working at these batterys the enemy fired on them heavy. But they kept a man on the wach, and when they saw the mach agoing to their cannon the wach would cry, "Shot!" and then they (our men) would fall Down in the Detch and you might hear the ball go by. Sometimes the ball would strike before it come to the Ditch and would skip along, and sometimes would knock the Dirt in the Ditch and bury some men. But they in Jeneral would not be hurt much. I was very often in this Ditch wher they was working at their batterys and the next night cannons or Morters carryed to every battery.[19]

I recolect one Morning I was their and several of them told me their batterys would be opined by 10 of the clock and it was true. About 10 o'clock some of our cannon began to rore and some of the morters throwing their bum shels.[20] This shell would go in a blaze. When it come out of the morter it would go up, turning over summersets as it went, and then fall Down in the fort. The report was as loud when it struck the Ground as when it come out, and the same when it bursted. The bombs aflying the cercle is much like a rain bow. O what rejoiceing their was with our men. And the rest of the batterys that wa'n't ready was working with all their might to begin, but before night come on the most of the morters and small cannon was fireing.

I Don't think thur was one Minut that night but thur was bumb shels in the aire, some times 10 or 15 at the same time. It was entirely light the whole night. Some Did say it was light enough to pick up a pin. Their was Great rejoicing in the camps. The shells over the river was als[o] seen a flying over in the enemy's fort. I felt glad and solemn too.

It looked like we had Got in a new world to see these shells flying all a round and lighting in the fort and every shell making three Reports—when it come out, when it fell, and when it bursted. It was truly awfull. These shells would go in a cirled rout, would rise up in the aire—appeard to be 1/4 of a mile high—and circle Down, and fall in the fort. When the shell would first come out you could see it turning over like a summer set, making a noise. It would go "T-wich, t-wich, t-wich," and we could see it with a great blaze all the way and hear it a going all the way "t-wich" until it would fall. And then the report was Dreadfull and emediately it would burst and then another Dreadful Report.

These shells is made of pot metel like a Jug and 1/2 Inch thick, without a handle, with a big mouth; and filled with powder and other combustibles in such a manner that the blaze Comes out of the mouth and keeps on a burning until it gits to the body,[21] where their is a big quanity of powder.[22] And when the fire gits to that big body it bursts, and the piecis flyes every way and wounds or kills who ever it hits.

We was told that it is common that when a bumb falls for some one to throw on a buckit of water, and that would put it out, and then no Damage would accrue. But we took notice that some of these bumbs would burst as quck as they would light, and we could hear the most of them burst. Their was so many a flying and falling and falling in the fort contenully we had no Doubt but we was paying them nisely for their mischief to us. When a man runs up to a bumb shell with a buckit of water and Don't put it out and it bursts he is Destoyed.

Brother William was taken sick and went home. Brother Edward and my self was busy in selling our rum; but as we had a guard mostly of our neighbours and friends who did help us, one of us could be away. And we was often out at the batterys and other places to see the great curiossities a going on.

One morning [Wednesday, October 17] Mr. Merryman, an officer in the staff, came to me and said, "That great big and mighty cannon will be ready for fireing by 10 O'clock on the bank of the river below the Fort.[23] Come, let us go Down and see the sight." We mounted our horses and started and went a circuatous rout for fear of the enemy's cannon. When we got to the place it was a sight to see such a big gun. A number of officers and soldiers their, I suppose 2 or 3 hundred besides spectators their.

We Did bhold and see a vast number of Drowned horses that the enemy had Drowned. The tide was down and we could see them. I Don't know how many, but I expect upwards of a thousand and perhaps several Thousand.[24] We all cryed out, "A sin and shame."

Just before they fired they put wool in their ears to stop them. Mr. Merrymon and I Did the same. They fired on the fort. We could all see where the ball hit and it did make a bundence of timber fly of[f] from the Fort. The earth where we stood Did shake Dreadfully and it Defined [deafened] me very much. I wanted to go Instantly but Mr. Meryman said, "Let us see a nother shot to see what effect on the wall." They soon fired again and we seen the timber and Dirt fly Dreadfully. It looked like they would soon beat Down that wall at that place.

All at once we saw a boat with a white flag from the fort coming Down the river to us.[25] The flag was received by the officer of this place, and the officer that fetched the flag said he had a letter to General Washington.[26] The officer that commanded hear sent one of his officers with the officer that fetched the flag to General Washington, which was about a mile from hear at head quarters near the center of our line. As quick as they weare gone this big cannon fired again and still continued to beat Down the wall. The conclusion among us all was that Corn Wallace was about to Surrender.

We started back and went back strait through the field as the enemy had stopt fireing. We went a little back of our Ditch and their we Did see a nother sight. The Old field was Tore up with the balls from the enemy's cannon. It looked like large bar-sheer ploughs [bar-share plows] had been runing their, only as they did skip in places and then begin a furrer again.

When we got to our Waggon and Tent we told about the Flag. The officers and soldiers said they expected it. They did not know how the enemy could stand so much fire as we had give them.

About this time the flag had reached General Washington. And in a very few Minutes the fire ceased near head quarters and continued along the line each way to cease, and as quick as the Orders could go over the River it ceased their also. So in about one hour all was still and calm and the storm over. A great many hands makes light work.

Washington and Wallis sent several Dispaces [dispatches] to each other before they concluded finally on the capitulation.[27] I think it was the second Day they finished the matter and agreed on a certain Day they would march out and ground their Arms. The day agreed on I think was two Days hince.[28]

The knews went fair and near, and a vast number of people from the Different towns and the country came forward to see the Great and mighty sight. The british had a very large gate on the south side of their fort, and on that side was a levil Old field. Our army was placed in a sold squair colom [solid square column] a bout a half a mile or more a round the said fort gate. It was a great sight to see. Part of our line was Continatal troops, a part was Meletia, and a part was French. And on the out side of this colmn of soldiery their was a vast many spectators mostly in carriges such as chariots, Fayatons, chairs, and giggs, and some common Waggons. The carreges was mostly full of Jentlemen and ladies and children, besids a number on horse back and some on foot. Some of them had come as fair as from the city of Richmond, which was upwards of 70 Miles. Their was many thousand of these spectators.

General Washington and some of the gineral offecers with their aids was about the center of the line a little advanced inside of this vast colomn emediately before the gate and about 1/2 or 3/4 of a mile Distant. And a bout the middle of the day[29] the big gate was opined, and the red coats marched out by plattoons in a solled colum with some of their officers in the front, our soldiers and officers and spectators saying, "Did you ever see the like?" And many words was spoken at that time but not loud.[30] It was the most Tremendeaus, the most admirable sight that I ever Did see. And the countenace of our offecers and solders all seem to claim some Credit for this great prise, and the countenace of these spectators seem to say also they claimed some credit also. It was truly a wonderfull sight to see so many red coats coming out to Ground their arms. They marched strait up to Washington, gave up their swords,[31] and grounded or stacked their arms, and thin returned to the fort from whence they came to be hearafter took to winchester.[32]

Our soldiers and officers mostly went to their tents, while some few advanced near the fort to guard them. I took notice that night that the offecers and soldiers could hardly talk for laughing, and they would hardly walk for Jumping and Dancing and singing as they went a bout.

That night their was a Col. Smith from our county, who was on perool, that said to his county men, "Now, boys, retaliate! Remember sutbiry's old Field! These is the very men that plunderd our men and used them so bad. Boys, plunder them but be cuning! Don't be ketched at it, as your officers will not sanction it." And their was a number of them plundered shore enough.

The continantal[33] officers and soldiers guarded the fort gate, and none of the militia was alowed to go in the fort. One reason was the small pox was brief[34] their. I had a relation who was a Continantal officer. He was Lieut. John Trabue.[35] The very next Day[36] I went with him all over the Fort. The fort seemed to be nearly one mile in length and nearly 1/4 mile in width. It was truly a Dreadfull shocking sight to see the Damage our bumb shells had Done. When a shell fell on the ground it would sink under the ground so Deep that when it bursted it would through up a waggon load or more of Dirt, and when it fell on a house Tore it to pieces.

The enemy had a number of holes and pits Dug all over the fort some large and some small—with timber on the top edge. And when the soldiers would see one B[omb] shell a coming near them, they would Jump in one of these pits and squat Down until it was bursted. These pits they Called Abatters.[37]

They had some large holes under the Ground where Lord Cornwallis and some of the nobles stayed.[38] They called them bum proff, but with all the caution they took, a vast number of them got killed.

I have been told by some of the soldiers since that they was always on the wach, and they could see the bum shell when it was a coming, and at times their was Dredfull skampering. Sometimes they woud come so often they was much beset.

A Mr. Jacob Phillup told me, "A while before they surrendered they lost 40 men every hour, and they throwed a number of their arms and cannon in the Deep water. When a bum shell would fall on any hard place so that it Did not go under the ground, a soldier would run to it and knock off the fiz or neck, and then the bumb shell woud not burst. A soldier then would Git one shilling for that act. The soldiers said they Did not care much about their life, that shilling would git some rum."

Their was a number of negros in the fort engaged in filling up these holes in the ground, makeing all things look smooth as posible.

The britesh officers and Torrys looked much Dejected and their Countenace sad as I saw them passing, and I hardley heard one word come out of their mouths. I thought the Inglish soldiers and the Hessions Did not seem to Care much a bout it, but every thing in the fort looked gloomy and sad. I thought lord C[orn] Wallis and his other big officers looked not only sad but ashamed, as they had lived under the Ground like ground Hogs.

The negros looked condemed. The british had promised them thur freedom but insted of freedom made them hall waggons by hand with timber to build their works and made them work with spads, etc., within a inch of their very lives.

I left their fort and went to our army and what a great Contrass—our men pert and lively and still rejoiceing. We sold our rum very fast. The britesh and french had plenty of hard mony and that night we sold all we had.

A little before Day [October 20] brother Edward and my self with our waggon started to go to Williamsburg to try our luck for rum. We took some of the Guard with us and left the ballance at our tent until we returned. We had twelve Mile to go. We went in a long trot. Before we got their I left them and told them what part of the town to go to. I went in a Gallop and I got their one hour of the sun.

I called on a rich old scoch Merchant. "Sir," said I, "can you tell me where I could buoy two hogshead of rum?"

His answer was, "None can be had in this town."

"Sir," said I, "you may suppose I am a press master but, sir, I am a sutler. I want the rum to sell a gain. I Don't offer paper Mony for it. I will give silver or gold for the article." I pulled out a purse of Gold that was in a net purce that looked beautyfull in them Days. "Now, sir," said I, "if you plese, try to tell me where I can posebly git it. I am in a great Hurry."

He said, "If I could tell you what would you Give?"

I said, "For good West India I would give 10/"; as the Old price formerly was 5/ for the very best sort by the Hogshead.

He said if I would give him 12/ he thought he could git me some. We quickly agreed on 11/ if I liked the rum. He made me promis not to tell that he had rum.

He took me to a back seller and the rum was good Old West India of the first class. I took two. The hogsheads had been on hand a long time and they were not quite full. He had them filled quick. The two was about 215 galions.

The waggon got their in a few minuts after I Did, and the Hogsheads of rum was put in the waggon very quick as we had men a plenty of our own. The wagon started in a few menuts. I Don't think when the wagon started back the sun was 1 1/2 hours high. I went in the scocthman's house, paid him in gold as he chose it. It come to nearly $400.[39] I took some Julup and breackfast with him and in a few menuts was off. The road was a dead leavel and Dry. The waggon horses went in a trot.

We got back to our tent by the Middle of the day with good rum, which was welcom knews to the officers and soldiers. We sold our rum at the first at $1 per quart,[40] and their came so many French crowns that it was troublesome to make the change when we was so much pestered. We then altered our price to a french Crown per qurt but told them we would not be perticular, $1 Dollar would Do if they Did not have a F[rench] Crown.[41] We had a large brass cock. One of us stood to that to Draw and the other to receive the mony. The british prisoners and The French army and our country men Came to us for rum that half Day and the ensueing night.

We sold one hogshead cheefly for silver and gold. We did give some away to our acquaintences, but yet we must have gained that Day and night $200 in good mony. We did lend mony to a number of our acquaintences that stood in need to buoy shoes and other nessery articles. The british soldery had shoes and other Cloathing and blankits to spair and did sell them to our men very low.

The next morning[42] preparations was made to start of[f] With the prisoners to Winchester, Va. All our soldery and French was not needed to go with the prisoners. So only a part of the Militia went with them, while some was Discharged.

A number of the back woods Rifle men wanted to sell their guns but could git no sail for them. One young man applyed to me and said, "I will sell you my Rifle for 20/ and a pint of rum, as I am sick and not able to carry her. And I live in Rockbrige County near 300 Miles, and I have no mony and Don't know what to Do." I told him I Did not want to buoy, if I Did I would not take her at so small a price.

He said he knew the gun was worth more, but if I would give him what he asked (which was 20/) I would much oblidge him. I told him, "No." He turned of[f] to go away and I saw Tears in his eys. I called him back, gave him $10 and his canteen full of rum for his gun.[43] He thanked me and cryed for Joy. After I got home I sold the gun for $15.

This morning we started off with the prisoners[44] and agoing the road near where we lived.[45] We left a number of men behind, like the French and county people that had Come after their negros, etc.[46] I was told that when all to gether at York—to wit, The French Fleet, French Infintry, the American Regulars, the Meletia, the negros, the British and spectaters, and Torys—did all exceed 100 Thousand souls.[47] It was said their was 100 thousand rations per each Day issued out.

The first Day we went 12 Miles and Got to Williamsburgh and encamped near the town on the east end of the town. The britesh encamed near a branch, their tents near each other; and our men encamed all round them and centrys about 50 yards Distant up all night. The british General and Field offecers went on horse back, the Captains and subaltons and soldiers afoot, and they had bagage Wagons to Cary their baggage along. The officers still wore their swords and went about seemingly as they pleased. Our wagon and tent was on the big road within 200 yards of the town at one end of the line of our troops. We sold our rum tolerable fast but nothing like we had Done.

The next morning a man Came to our tent and said his name was   Day, and that the horse Col. Talton was rideing did belong to Sir Paton Skipeth,[48] and he (Mr. Day) was his steward. He further stated that agreeable to the capetulation he was afraid their might be Deficulties in giting him, as the Terms was that all the horses that was taken in a action might be retained; but such as was at taken at plantations, etc., was to be restored if applyed for, and upon a Disagreement Commissinors to Determen it.[49]

He further stated that this horse was hid out in a swomp with a number of brude [brood] Mears, etc., and some guard with them to take care of them near Dan River,[50] and when Talton came near their he heard of this horse. He was Named "black and all black" and was said to be the best rideing horse in America. And he (Talton) sent some of his men in serch of him and found him and took him with some others.[51] This horse was a stalion. Mr. Day further stated that he was afraid they might say they took the horse in a action. He sayed the truth was their was a pistal or two fired when the horse was took.

And he sayed the horse was worth 500 pounds in specia, and he had come all the way from Dan river on purpose to Git him, and that he was Determend to take him by suprise but wished to Do it where none of the big offecers weare.

Their was a Captain's Tent with some Sabolten officers with in a few steps of our tent. I had been encourageing Mr. Day, and we Mentioned the thing to the said Officers, and they encouraged him also. We was all Draming of it that morning and as merry as Crickets. We had rum and loaf sugar.

Mr. Day said the Day before he had eyed the horse and Talton but said nothing. He thought it was quite likely that Talton would be apt to come along the road where we then was this morning to go in town before we marched. Their was a Marshey wet place near where we was and some bushes a growing their. Mr. Day stoped their and Cut him a sweet Gum Stick—the big end a bout as thick as a small man's rist, the little end much smaller and nearly three feet long—and said with that cudgil he would knock Talton off his horse if he Did not git off when he bid him.

It was not many Minuts before the word was, "Yonder comes the mighty Col. Talton with his servant with him, boath in high style and well mounted."

Mr. Day observed, "Yes, their is 'black and all black.' Now I will have him. The Mighty Col. Talton is on him." We at this time was at this officer's tent which was on the side of the road.

Mr. Day put his cudgil under his big coat and went on the other side of the road. When Talton came a long Mr. Day was on his left and this tent was on his right. Mr. Day was near the road and said, "Good Morning, Col. Talton," and took the horse by the Bridle and said, "This is my horse. Dismount!" Col. Talton said, "Have you got a permit to take him?"

Mr. Day said, "Did you have a permit when you stole him?" and at the same time took out his cudgil, but holding the horse at the same time, he Drawed back his cudgil as if to strike.

Col. Talton Jumed off quicker than I ever saw a man in my life. Mr. Day ungearted the saddle and throwed it of[f] seeming with Disdain. Mr. Day had a man with him that he called his overseer. He Jumed on the horse and as he road off Col. Talton said, "Are you agoing to keep my bridle and halter?"

Mr. Day replyed, "When you stole him he had a better bridle and halter then [than] he now has." I think Mr. Day perhaps was a little incorrect, for I thought the bridle and halter was as eligant as I ever beheld.

This overseer went off in a very long trot through wiliamsburgh. Col. Talton went on foot about 100 yards. When he Got to the first tavern in the town he went in, and his servant came back and took the saddle and went to the tavern and put it on the servant's horse. And Col. Talton got on the horse and road by us and went back to head quarters.

And in a few minuts this Tavern keeper came to us and sayed, "You had fine fun hear a little while ago."

Mr. Day replyed, "How?"

The tavern keeper sayed, "In takeing away the horse from Col. Taltern."

Mr. Day said, "Was that Col. Talton?"

He sayed, "Yes."

Day said, "We did not know him."

The tavern keeper said, "Who was it that took the horse?"

Mr. Day said, "None of us knew either of the men." The tavern keeper went away.

Mr. Day said he was certain that the tavern keeper came on purpose to find out who it was that took the horse in order for information for Co[lonel] Talton. Mr. Day said his man was to go to a certain house and wait for him to meet him. Mr. Day told us he expected their would be a fus a bout it and we must say, "We did not know the man that took the horse." He said he would travil with us that Day on purpose to know about it.

O how we Did laugh after it was all over, to think How that mighty man that had caused so much Terror and alarm in Virginia and other places, now that a common little chenkey [chunky] man should make him Jump off on the rong side of his horse so quick with nothing but a stick against him, when Talton had a fine sword by his side! We concluded he was not Spunk [spunky], he Jumped off the rong side so quick. We laughed about it many times and all agreed that Col. Talton was a very Piart [pert], active man equil to a cat. I have laughed to my self above a thousand times about it. Mr. Day was a little chunk of a man. Col. Talton was a tall, large, likely man.

We moved on after breackfast, I supose by 8 O'clock. We heard nothing more about it. As we pased through the town, the windows and Doors was full of spectators. I frequntly heard some of the people say, "The british officers Don't look as saucy as they did." And as we passed along the road almost every house on the road was crowded with spectators. And at some plantations where the houses was at a Destance their was crowds of people come out to the road and was on the fences and big gate, etc., all to see Corn Walles and Co[lonel] Talton and their soldiers.

Some would say, "You Don't look so haughty as you Did when you had the upper hand."

I heard several Ladies say, "When you," speaking of the bretish, "come a long by hear before, we run off and hid from you, but thank the lord![52] We are Glad to see you in this cituation you are in."

When we had sold out our rum we was oppesit wher we lived and we went home. We had gained part of that summer and part of that fall $1,000 in specia, 163,000 pounds in paper Mony, one waggon, one Cart, several Waches, 7 Valuable horses. The paper money was worth about $550 specia; the horses, waggon, and cart, about $600. We would have made more if it had not have been that the paper mony Depreceated so fast that summr and fall. As well as I can Recolect in may it was 500 for one, in June 600 for one, July 700, August 800, September 900, October 1,000 for one.[53]

Our men, some went home, some went to Winchester with the prisoners. After a little when all was at home all was peace. When I passed a long the road and at other places I could see people a plenty stiring about, not like it was in the spring and summer.

The ensuing winter their was more feasts, more Weddings, more frollicks than I had ever seen or heard of before. When the people was to gether how they would be chitchating about the Deficulties, Troubles, and trials they had seen and felt, laughing and telling how they hid out in the swomps, and some times some of them would be alarmed in the night and what skampering they had with the woman and children! And the men that had been out in the army telling about the battles that they was in and the Great hazord, Dangers, and Meraculos escapes they had experienced and some wounded, some one hand off, some one leg off, some lame, etc.! And then to hear some telling about the loss of their Relatives who was killed in battle and Died in camp. And some telling about how the enemy had starved the prisoners to Death because they would not inlist with his good and Gracious Majesty to help to fight his battles against thsse wicked Rebils.

But upon the hole their was a General Rejoiceing among our people that we had taken Lord Corn Wallis and Talton, and their seemed to exzist a perticular friendship one to another. All seem to be like brothers one to a nother.

July the 4th, 1782, I was Marryed to Mary Haskins,[54] Doughter of Col. Robert Haskins of chesterfield County. And on that Day was the first time I ever heard of that Day being celebrated. Their was a fireing of canon at the city of Richmond, and but few people knew what was the meaning of this fireing, as we could hear it from Col. Haskins' which was 24 Miles. In June 30th, 1783, we had a son born and named him Robert.[55]

In 1785 we concluded to move to Kentucky. Early in the spring I started to kentucky. Took a negro man with me to raise a crop of corn and to move out in the next fall. Brother James Trabue, myself, and this Negro set out in about the last of March to come through the wilderness and some few of the Virginians with us.

When we got on the fronteers the knews was the Indeans was very Troublesome, and but few people was agoing the wilderness road.[56] These Old Virginians turnd back and home they went. My Brother and me and my negro went on to Powels Valley and Tarryed several Days, waiting for company.

Capt. Thomas Gest[57] from Ky. and a Mr. Bramblit from Va. (bedford County) and a Frenchman and one more Man concluded we would set Out and we would Travel in the night in the most Dangerous places. So we set out and got to cumberland Gap about Dark, expecting we could git by Day light to the big lick[58] which is above 20 Miles. And we thought then we would take the woods, or if we kept the Trace we was not in so much Danger after we past the big lick. But the Darkness of the night and the Dreadfull bad mud holes and sleppery banks and Cain breaks and some logs which was across the road and great Defecultys we meet with, Day overtook us much sooner than we wished; and it was so that we could not leave the trace in that section of the country.

In respect of the River, Mountains, and cain breaks we was now, we thought, in great Jeoperday but we had to run the risk and Trust to providence. I was going before. I stopt and pulld out of my saddle bags a bottle of rum and every one took a good Dram. Not one knew I had it and they weare all mighty gld of it, as a spir [spear] in the head is worth two in the heal.

We went on the trace brisk and bravely until we got past the big lick, whear the Indian War road leveas the Ky. road. We lift the trace a little Distance, let our horses eat grass a little while, and eat our selves, and went on again.

That evining we meet a large company of men from Ky.—about 100. They informed us their was Indian sighn a plenty a head of us at about the place we intended to camp that night. Our calculation was these indeans would try to supprise Either us or that big company that night.

When it was Dark my brother told me to take off the road and go straight to a large stair [star] which he shewed me and said he, "Go about 1 1/2 or 2 Miles. Git at water if you can." Said he, "I will wait hear about 1/2 hour to see if any Indians is following us." So I went on and the men followed me. And we went nearly 2 Miles and found water, hoppled out our horses; and in about 1/2 hour he came to us. We had a small fire. After we was Done eating we let the fire go out. One of us kept a wake all night.

Next Morning we started again. And when we got to the road again we looked sharp for indian tracks but could see none. My brother said, "I think the Indeans followed the big company last night. I think we are now safe." And I thought we was now prety well out of Danger but it was best to look sharp.

Bro. James or my self Jenerally went a little a head. And I was now before and I saw an Indian on our left a bout 100 yards before. He was by the side of a tree looking at me. He went behind the tree. He was near the road as we had to pass. I stoped. The men came up. I told them I saw an Indian and where. Capt. Gist said he had himself been Mistaken. He expected it was a Deer. And the same Indean or a nother one came walking out nearly at the same place and stoped and looked at us and run off, appeared to be skeared.

All the men saw him and Mr. Bramblit said, "Lit us take after him and kill him."

James Trabue said, "He is not their by him self. Indins Don't go to war 300 Miles unless they are prpared for it." He further said, "If we stay hear a nother Minut we will see a plenty of them."

Capt. Gest said, "What shall we Do?"

James Trabue said, "Dash off in the woods with all our might."

Capt. Gest told him to go before. Capt. Gist was an Old Indian fighter. He also obsered that this Indian run off that fashion on purpose to git us to run after him as they might Decoy us.

James Went a head and the rest of us followed in a long trot or Gallop for some little Disttance. We kept the woods nearly all that Day and Did see a bundence of Indeans' sighn. So we found out their was a large quanity of Indians in that sectinon of the country. We felt very wild and skittish. I then thought this would be the last time I would ever travil this wilderness with so little company. We was only 6 Men and one Negro. Yet we was all will-armed [well-armed] and Determined to Do our best if Compelled. We thought that it was probible we might come a cross some straggling little parties a hunting, and we concluded to kill them if we could. We did see wheare they had killed Deer, etc., in the woods. Thur sighn was plenty. We was expecting a body of them was waching the road, so we kept the woods, stoped a while, and let our horses eat grass, and looked sharp, holding our horses in our hands and eating our selves at the same time.

Just before night we came to the road near Rockcastle.[59] We then kept the road. We had to go up scagses creek and crossed it many times.[60] Dark overtook us. It was cloudey and I Did think it was as Dark a night as I ever Did see. We was all very ancious to go along, as we Did all conclude we was in emenent Danger; and concluded we would travel in the night and keep on to the Crab Orched to a station.

And as we went on, the frenchman's horse fell with him Down a steep bank several feet; and we was a long time a trying to git him out, but at last we was compeled to make a light to git him out. We went on again and soon meet with some other Dificultyes, at last had to conclude to stop. We turned our horses out to eat grass but hoppled them. Some of us kept a wake while the others slept a little while. I for one Did not sleep any. As the horses was alarmed at somthing we apprehended it was Indians. I waked up the men, told them it was not so Dark as it was, and the horses was alarmed at something, we had best git up and start, to which they all consented. And we was very lucky and got our horses and Did start again.

We got to the Crab Orched in the morning about 9 o'clock and ordered breackfast and our horses feed. The land lord agreed to it. I went in the house almost a sleep, laid by my saddle bags and gun, and went to the bed to lay Down and go to sleep. Afterwards I Did remember that I did go to the bed but could not remember of laying Down. I think I was a sleep before I was Down. It was some time before our breackfast was ready and I had some sleep, and as soon as I was Done eating I went to sleep again.

That after noon brother James and I and my Negro went on to Gilberts creek where G.S. Smith lived and from their to woodford[61] to where I intended to move to. My Brother James went back to Virginia and left me. I made some arrangements for the reseption of my family and in July I set out for home again.

When we went through the wilderness this time we had above 100 Men in company and they voated me in as their Capt. to commad said Company.[62] We kept out strong centrys every night. We got through the wilderness very safe and all well. I soon got back to chesterfield to my family[63] and made arrangements to move to Kentucky by the way of Fort pit.

10
The Separate Baptists of Revolutionary Virginia

I had sold my land and Mill to Col. Fleming[1] for which he was to pay me a goodly sum of mony but Failed in the payment of the mony.[2] His credit with the Merchants of Richmond was Good, and I took up the most of it in Merchandise. I got the goods at holesale prices so that I thought I could advance on them. I also turned other Debts to Merchandise so that I thought I had a pirty good assortment of Merchandise[3] and I could trade of[f] the Goods to a good advantage in Ky.

This was in August 1785 and all of a sudden I got Convected for my sins and got, as I thougt, a pardon for them. I will now relate my experience.

My parrnts was very Morril and was Members of the Episcopel[4] church, which was the established church of Ingland, also the established church in Virginia. And in December the 7th day, 1770, William Webber and Joseph Anthony,[5] two baptist preachers, preached in the neighbourhood in our county (chesterfield) and they was taken up and put in Jail by Col. Cary[6] as Disturbers of the peace.[7] They weare held in contempt by the most of the people.

And one evining in the same winter uncle John Dupuy[8] and John Waller[9] and Mr. Waffer[10] Came to my father's and Told Father and Mother that this Waller was a baptist preacher and they weare a going to the Gail to visit the prisoners in Jail—to wit, Webber and Anthony.[11] Uncle further stated that he expected the family and neighbours would be glad to hear the baptist preach and the neighbours might be notified of it, and as they came by the skoolhouse uncle told the children to tell their famelys of it.

Father told uncle he would not suffer him to preach in his house as he Did not have a favourable oppenion of these Annabaptist—as they weare called in that Day.[12] My father stated that he beleaved these people weare false teachers, and we ought not to be Dreven about with every wind of Doctrain, and at this time we had a good establishment and a good parson and all at peace, and their was a wo prounanced against them that was the cause of offencis.[13]

A number of people some how heard of this meeting and Came to our house and insested on father to let him [Waller] preach, as they might hear him and prove all things and hold fast that which was good. Father Refused. He said he would not give offence to Col. Carry and the church.

Uncle John Dupuy then said, "Let him sing and pray, read the screpture and give his vieus on it"; as the people was so Deserous of hearing him.

My father then told Mr. Waller he might sing his hymns and plalms [psalms] and read, and pray, and give his vieus on the scripturs, siting in his cheer; but he must not stand up and take a text and preach,[14] to which Mr. Waller agreed.

Mr. Waller and Mr. Waffer sung several psalms and hyms, and kneeld Down and prayed very earnestly that god would be with them and Derect them aright. He then read the 3 chapter of John through out and gave his views on the chapter. He Dwelt some time on this new birth, insisting we was all sinners and if not born again we could not enter into the kingdom of heaven. He also Dwelt some time about the wind blowing where it listed, etc., and you could not tell from whince it came and wheather it goeth, so was the power of the lord. He also told us that the gosple of christ would be persecuted, etc.

And before he was Done I got to beleave he was one of christ's Minesters and he was preaching the true Doctrain. I was nearly Elevin years Old. I emedeately betoock myself to praying to god to Direct me.

Uncle John Dupuy soon got baptised [June 16, 1771]. And the preachers from a fair would come by our house to go to the prison and did often preach at our house. My Mother, sister Magdelun, and Sister Jane, and after a while Brother John, all Got to profess they had religin and was baptised.[15] The baptist preachers from the North, south, and west, all came to visit the prisoners and would preach in the county as they passed and repassed. Col. Carry, when he would hear of it, would send the Sheriff with a warrent[16] and put them in Jail unless they would give bond and security not to preach in the county for one year.[17] He had 7 preachers in at one time.[18]

These preachers would preach in the prison so loud that they could be heard and great congregations flocked to hear them and numbers got convicted and converted. Col. Carry, as he was the leading Man in the county, had a brick wall built around the prison, and the preachers would preach so loud they could be heard by the people out side.[19] These preachers got so many people on their side that after a while they got a mijorety of the court to give them the bounds.[20] They then preached so much and so many people administered to their nesseties in Mony and provisions they weare all turned out and let go home.[21] Persicuteing these people was a real benifit to thur cause, as the people thought it was for righteousness' sake that they weare persecuted.[22]

I was very much convicted for 3 o 4 years and prayed and read the scripture and other good books. I was fond of reading bunjan's *Pilgrim's Progress*. I heard a great many Precious sermons prached but I found no comfort for my poor soul. At length I got careless and hardened and give Out[23] praying and put of[f] religion for the present time.

When I was 17 years Old I was taken sick with a severe fever. It was thought I was Dangerously sick. I was in a Dreadfull rack of Misery and had Dreadfull Dreams and awfull apprehensions. The horrow I felt was great. I was awfully afraid of Judgement. My friends mentiond these things to me. I told them I was too sick and my misery was too great to think about Religeon or prepair for Death now.

I Did pray to god to spear my life at this time, and if he would raise me up again I would serve him my life out and would never Do as I had Done. And I Did really think I would perform to my Vows.

I Recovered my health and went out into the army and soon niglected to pray and became a Deist[24] and would frolick, courouse, and Dance, and curse and swear at times. Some times my concience checked me but after a while I got hardened so that I could laugh and make Deversion of the relligous people. My father Died [October 1775] a beleaver in Jeesus a little while before I went in the Army. My Mother and uncles Did not know how bad I was.

In august 1785 uncle James Dupuy[25] told me that at a meeting, he said, last night the power of the lord was with the people. He said he was in hops they would have a revival of religion about him, which was 9 miles from my Mother's. I thought but little about it.

I went to the city of rechmond—15 Miles from my Mother's—and was at richmond 2 or 3 Days fixing my business to start to Kentucky. And in the evening as I was going home I was thinking and further planing my business and was thinking my affairs was so aranged that I was Doing very well, I would now move my family to Ky., etc. This was a bout sun set Thirsday night, and all of a sudden these words came in my mind, "Thou fool, this night thy soul shall be required of the." It almost seemed to me that I heard a voiece. I was by my self. I looked around to see if I could see any thing.

I could not tell exzactly how the words came but I thought I would go emediately to Judgement. I thought of trying to pray. The next thought was who to pray to—to that god I had promised when sick if he would raise me from my sick bid I would serve him the rest of my Days? I emediately thought of my vows being broake and my wicked Doings, and in perticular in laughing at the profissers of Jesus christ and saying their was nothing in religion.

These words came to my mind, "I will laugh at your calimity and mock when your fear cometh." I trembled. I was much alarmed and said to my self, "What shall I Do?" I felt condemned and Did not know what to Do.

I went home and went to bed. My wife enquired of me what was the matter. I told her I was not well. She asked me what made me tremble. I told her of my case. I slept none. When Morning came I got up and went to the woods and thought of praying but Did not know what to pray for, as I thought it would be prosumtian to ask god to have mercy on me. I went home Just as I was.

My Mother told me that my cousin Ben Watkins[26] was to preach their that night, and he Did come and preach and he in his preaching condemnd me. He was a great preacher. I told him my condition and what a rebel I had been and Did now think the Day of grace was past and their was no mercy for me. He told me to try to submit to soveraighn grace, that Jesus came to save the lost and helpless. I asked him to pray for me. He said he would.

I realy thought I had acted so foolish and so wicked that it was a wonder how the almeghty had boare with me so long. I thought, "O, if I had my time back again when I had a soft heart, when I was a penitent, when the lord Did knock for entrence, but now it is too late. The Doore of Mercy is shut against me and I am condemned."

The next night, which was sunday night, their was to be a meeting at uncle James Dupuy's where this revival was. I concluded I would go and see, but would not—I could not—make any promis what poor wreached me ever would Do hearafter. I could not think of asking the lord to have mercy on me but was often a breathing thus, "O, lord god, Direct and guide me. I am a wicked Rebel."

I went to the meeting and their was a number of people their, a number convicted, some Giting converted; and while I would look at some of these penetents, I Did wish I was as they weare. They seemed to have soft penetent hearts. They could cry. They were tender, etc., but poore wreached me has a hard wicked heart.

I went home and on Munday I was with one of my neighbour—a religous man. He told me what to Do. He said I must pray to god to shew me mercy, I must pray often and very much, and their was no Doubt but I would obtain mercy. He said, "He that seeketh findeth, and knock and it shall be opined unto you." He said their was no Danger, if I would persever, but I would find forgiveniss.

I felt very much encourraged, concluded I would make the tryal. I went a way in the woods to a private place. "I will now begin with my petetion to ask the lord to have mercy on me." A thought struck me: how would it Do to ask god to Do an unjust act as to have mercy and save such a wicked creature as I was? I thought it was a wonder he bore with me to think of such a thing.

I turned back and went a little way and stoped and prayed to god to[27] Direct me what to Do. It seemed to me that god was angry with me and would condemn me. I thought I was already Condemned and I could see no way for my escape, and I thought it was Just that I should be condemned.[28]

I went to bed but slept but little. I studied and thought and at last had to conclude the same thing: I was already condemed and this sentence was Just. I said, "O, lord, thy will be Done. It is my fault. Thou art Just and I am guilty, guilty." I got out of bed after it was day. It was tuesday Morning, and from Thirsday night to this time I had neither eat nor slept any of consequnce.

I went a way of[f], a going to the woods, but beforore I got to the woods these words came into my mind, "Stand still and see the salvation of god." The words came with power, and in my emagination I saw the great salvation of Jesus christ to save a lost world. I fancied I saw it in streams, in ocions of love and mearcy. It is emposible to Describe it. It was unspeacable and full of Gl[ory]. I was so Delighted to view this great and mighty sight. I thought it was no wonder that saints, Angles, and all the heavenly Hosts praised him, worshiped and adored him, that he was king of kings, lord of lords, he was Alphia [and] omega, the begining and end, the first and last, the almighty.

I stood a while in this field and moved on towards the woods, and every thing I saw, like the Field, the herbage, and Trees, looked to me more beautyfull than I had ever beheld them. They all seem to be adding glorry and praise to the lamb of God that wrought out this great and mighty salvation. I felt light and Delighted in vewing this great sight. I thought to myself, "Glory to christ Jesus."

I thought emediately I had better be thinking about my poor condemned soul but I could not think of it much. I had to vew and admire this wondrous salvation, and when I was returning to the house These words Came to my mind, "Christ came to save poor lost sinners." Thought I, "I am a poore lost wicked sinner, but it is not possible it is for me. I am to big a sinner." And these words came to me, "He is a great saviour and saves to the utmost."[29] All that Day I was thinking of these things and would try to look for my guelty burden of sins but could not find it. These words came to me:

    I need not go abroad for Joys.
    I have a feast at home.

I went to a meeting that night between my Mother's and whire the revival was. The meeting was at R. Mosley's.[30] Reverend G.S. Smith and some other preachers was their. I thought I heard the beautyfulest singing by the preachers and brethren I had ever heard. I looked at a poor old man and a poor old woman and they sung so Melodeous. I thought I could see something like the Image of the savour in them. They was very Old and it looked like they would soon be in heavin. I had such a love for them that I had never had befor. These words came to me, "We know that we have passed from Death unto life because we love the breathren."

The preachers preached and I was built up. I thought I had an interest in this great salvation and it was without money or price. It was free grace. And I then cryed out Oloud, "Free grace!" I Did not intentinally hollow it out a loud but I was constraind to Do so. I hollowd it out, "Free grace"; etc. "Glory, glory"; etc. I called on the people to praise the lord. I wondered why the people was not all praising and gloryfying the lord. I could see the plan of salvaseon in my view so plain that I wanted every body to come to chist and be saved.[31]

I went to my Mother's and told my brothers and sisters of this great salvation, etc., and also to my wife's father's and told them the same, and many of each family soon professed to have religion. In a few Days I was baptised by The Reverend G.M. Smith, and more than 20 others was baptised at the same time. Thur was a great revival in the several neighbourhoods, and a great many of my relations and neighbours professed religion and was baptised. My wife got a hope but was not baptised until she got to Kentucky. She was baptised by the Reverend John Taylor[32] at Clear creek meeting house.

11

Postwar Conditions in Trans-Appalachia

We Did intend to start to Kentucky the first of september [1785] but we Did not git off so soon. Capt. John Watkins and his family and his son-in-law James lockit[1] went with us.

When we first started when Sunday came we lay by and would not travil. But on one sunday when we was between winchester and Red stone[2] we concluded to travel, as we thought we ought to hurry on for fear the cold weather might ketch us. And as we passed by one of the Squers he sent two young men to his big gate on the side of the road as we passed by, and ordered us all to stop and the head of the families to go to the Squer's house to him to answer for a breach of the law in breaking the Sabbath.[3]

Capt. Watkins and my self was concludeing to go when one of our negro men said to one of these young men, "I spose you is sich good fokes hear you will let us all stay hear and find us[4] and won't charge any thing for it."

This young man cursed the negro and talked of knocking him in the head.

I said to Capt. Watkins in a lowe voice, "Let us go on and not obay the Squere as the young man made use of such profane language, and they Did not shew any warrent to us, and it is quite likely we can git out of this Squer's Juressdection by the time he can git his warrent and constible, etc."

Capt. Watkins said to me, "I will leave the matter to you. Do as you plese."

I said to these young men, "We was Just a going to the house, but when we heard that young man make use of such wicked and profane language we cannot think of stoping at any such house." I hollowd out to the negros to Drive on. They cracked their whips and Jumed and skiped and broake out in laughter and Drove on.

These young men was Dressed very fine as if they had on their sermon-sunday cloaths. They walked very brisk and went back to the house. They looked angry and confused. We had 5 or 6 white men and 12 or 15 negro men in company. Our Company all to gether was above 70 souls. We did not see or hear any more from the Squre or young men.

We went on to red stone and got a large boat[5] and put in all our horses and all our carriges and goods and our people. Our boat was heavy loaded.

Uncle Bartholumy Dupuy with 3 of his sons and a number of his Negros and several other famelies—all started Down the river at the same time. I think their was 5 boats. I think in all their was 2 or 300 souls all set out to gether to Desind the river.

It was thought their was great Danger of the Indians Molisting of us, but as we had many guns and agreed to stick close all together we thought we might go in safety. We thought the water was suffecently high for our boats, but after we had left the settlement our boats would run aground at the riffles and we had to git out and with hand sticks had to shove of[f] our boats.

Our boat was loaded very heavy and was more apt to run aground than any of the boats. But we had many Negro Men and we was all very resolute, so that we got a long as well as the rest of the boats until we came to a riffle some Distance belowe the Conawha at an Island that is called the Dead man's Island.[6]

It was agreed by Mr. Lockit and myself that he would steer the boat and I would be in the front of the boat and wave my hand and Derect him which way to steer. And we kept exzactly after a nother boat that was before, and on a sudden our boat stove against an End of a log that was under the water. The boat made a sudden stop, and all the horses and all the people fell Down.

I observed the boat was still and the water run as [s]wift a[s] a mill tail. I saw their was a plank bursted at my end and the water coming in very rapid. We was about 40 or 50 feet from shore.

I hollowed out to Mr. Lockit and waved my hand for him to turn his end to the shore. He Did so and it took several stroacks with the assistance of a nother hand before they could turn it. And after it Did turn I hollowed out to Jump out when it got near shore and hold it. And by the time that end got to the shore—as the boat was now squair across the river—the end that was stove at first was fast, but when it was turned got intirely loose. The men (some of them) was out and held the boot in good time. I hollowed out for the woman and children to go to the end and Jump out, and the men (black and white) to through out the things. My end began to sink very soon, and I and another man cut the ropes that tyed the horses, and as the boat sunk the horses swom out. I think from the time the boat struck the log until it sunk was not longer than three Minuts.

The people was all saved but we lost a considerable part of our goods. If the hind end had turned the other way it was thought the most of the woman and children would have been Drowned. We was very thankful that kind provedence had saved us. Although we saw a great many of our things a swiming off, their appeared to be not a murmer or regreat but thankfull it was no worse than it was.

The reason that the other boats escaped and ours struck the log was because our boat was a great Deal the heaviest loaded and sunk Deeper in the water. The Other boats stoped and came to our assistance with their canoes as quick as they coud. They did ketch some few of our things thas was a sweming.

We apprehended very Great Danger of Indians. We moved the women and children in canoes emediately in the Iseland. We moved all our things also in the Iseland. The same Night the other boats and us all encamed together. The next morning we went to our boat and took out all our Iron things, and she than swom; but she was so much Injured we could not mend her. The Owners of the other boats agreed with us that our horses and their horses should all be sent by land and we then might have room in their boats. We did so.

We was 21 days on the river—three times as long as we expected—so that our provision was scirce and we often went a shore with our canoes and killed turkeys. They wear very plenty. It was thought their was great Danger of Indians, but nessity compelled us to go ashore and kill Turkeys. Mr. Lockitt and I killed turkeys for our familys, and some others off their men killed for thur families.

We had a hearty laugh at one of Capt. Watkins' negros. He (watkins) told his negros they must eat Turkeys and save the bread and bacon. The negro said, "That will Do very well, master. If we have a plenty of Turkeys we will never Die; but if we have bread and bacon too, we would live a heap longer."

We got all safe to limestone[7] and landed and waited several Days previous to the arival of the horses, and when the horses came the men brought bad news with them. The Indians had fired on them and we lost a number of our horses.

So we went on with part of our families and goods and sent back for the ballace. We all settled in Faytte (now Woodford). I settled on Grears creek[8] near the Kentucky river. We thought that was a safe place from the Indians as several people lived over the river and we thought it would soon be better settled.

The next year [1786] Brother Edward Trabue and his family came out. He settled on the cleft of Kentucky river. My Mother, uncle John Dupuy, uncle Bartholomey Dupuy, and uncle James Dupuy, all settled in the same neighbourhood.

The indians soon got very Troublesome, and the people that lived over the river broak up and moved on our side of the river. The Indians not only kill people on the other side of the river but came over the river in our neighbourhood and killed several people. We persued the Indians many times but could not succeed in overtaking them. The Indeans was too cuning for us.

One time they killed Mistres Scercey[9] about 2 Mile from us. The indeans went Down to the river where they had a raft, and it was thought they crossed the river at that place as the sighn went into the water. This was Just at night when this was assertained.

Early next Morning a company of us went up to Steel's ferry[10] and crossed the river and went Down to the same place, expecting to strike their Trail, but no sighn of their coming out of the river at that place. We thought that perhaps they might have been beat Down the current. So we went Down the river several Miles but could not make any Decovery. So we returned home. I suppose we traveled that Day through rough ground above 30 Miles. We got home at night. And it had been assertaind the same Morning that the Indians had kept Down in the river and had come out on the same side; and another company of men persued them several Days, but they was so hard to trail they could not ketch up with them.

Their was but one instence in where the indeans was overtaken that had come to our neighbourhood; and that was because a unexpected snow had fallen, so they could be tracked. The company that persued them had no officer with them. The indians went with all their might. Our men als Did their best. The men got tired and night over took them. The men stoped and took up camp.

Jacob stucker insisted to go on but the men refused. After they had made a fire and ate something, this same Jacob stucker went himself alone the cource the Indians went, and about 2 Miles he Discovered the Indians' Fire. He went close up to them and made what Descoverys he could and returned to the company and told them the knews. They then fixed up and went to the Indians' camp and fired on them and killed and wounded several of them and got consederable plunder. Mr. Stucker picked up one of the best of the Indians' blankits and roped it around himself and said, "This will keep me worm this winter." This J. Stucker was a poore Duchman. He was soon made a captain and he made a good officer.[11]

Their was several campaighns went against the Indians.[12] And they was not so troublesome as they had been, and the people went back to their homes.

And when we thought all was peace and safety, in the year 1792 we heard the Indians had killed some people near Frankfort.[13] I had two sisters lived near their—To wit, John Major's and Tom Major's wives.[14] Brother Stephen Trabue and myself went their early the next morning after the mischief was Done. As we was agoing we meet a number of people a moveing away, and a number of Familys had got together. We went to our Brothir law's. They had flocked together.

We got in company with a large company that was Determined to persue the Indians, but all in vain. We could not strike their Trail, and at the same time we was hunting these Indeans they was further in the settlement, lying in ambush. We lived about 12 Mile from where this Meschuf was Done, and the Indeans was about half way between our house and where the meschief was Done. They was so crafty that after a few Days—when the people had quit hunting them—they slipt off undiscovered.

The mischuf was as follows. Two men by the name of Cooks[15] with their wifes lived in one house with a Cabbin rough and the weight pools [poles] pined on fast. These Mr. Cooks was boath together a shearing their sheep with their Riffles by their sides. The Indians fired on them and killed one in the spot. The other one run in the house and slamed too the Door. The women helpt him to make the Doore fast. He then feel [fell] Down in the floor and Expired with the wound he had got. He left his gun where he was shot, so the Indians got boath of thir guns.

The Indeans ordered them to opin the Doore, and as the woman Did not opin the Door they tryed to break the Doore shutter. But as the Doore shutter was made of thick strong timber they Did not break it. The Indians then went on the top of the house and tryed to pull it Down but faild. They then made a fire on the top of the house, and the woman put it out with water and milk and hens' eggs. And at lenghth the Indiand thretned them very severely and ordered them to opin the Door.

One of the woman replyed, "We are afraid to opin it."

The other woman Replyed, "I am not afraid. You may Do your worst."

The Indians answered, "What can you Do as you have no gun?"

This woman then remembered that their was a nother gun in the house. She then took it and fired at one Indian through a crack of the Door and killed one, and emedeatly the Indians Dispersed and carryd off their Dead indian with them.

These woman remained in the house about 2 hours, and Col. Finney[16] with a company of men Came to their assistance. These woman was so badly skcared that they had not wept at the Death of their husbands, but so soon as the company came to them they then wept sorely for thur husbands. The Mr. Cooks was buryed and the woman was moved off to a neighbou's house about 2 Miles.

We was the next Day at the house. We saw the blood where they was shot, saw the blood in the house and the blood where the Indian was killd, and saw the whole where the house was burned on the top, etc. We also saw these woman a washing off their husbands' bloody cloaths. We talked some with these woman. It was they that related this naritive to us. Also Col. Finney Related the same.

These Indians took a man presoner by the name of Dement[17] and kept him with them while they lay concealed. It appeard they had got so fair in the settlement that they was afraid to go home. So they stayed 2 or 3 Days and hid them selves in the bushes. Mr. Dement says they saw a large company of white men pass in sight of them, and when they left the settlement Mr. Dement got away from them and came home. And the people was very much alarmed when they heard the indians had been lurking in the settlement.

In the summer of 1794[18] I was with general Wayn at Greensvil at the Indian Treaty.[19] General Wayn did hire some of the first Indeans that came to the treaty to go to other towns and git the Indians to come to the Treaty.[20]

Wayn had a large army and very well Disipblind and a number of cannon and Did often Muster and perrade his men. And they fired their Muskits[21] and Riffles and cannon when on perrade to the astoneshment of the Indians.[22] Wayn's army cut a Marshal appearrince.

The indeans was hard to persuaid to bring in the presoners and treat, but they graduly come in and brought at last a number of prisoners. A number of men and women that came to this treaty that had been taken when cheldren that Did look like Indians.

I was at Fort Jefferson about 6 Miles from Greensvil.[23] And at a Distance in the pearae [prairie] we saw an Indian a rideing up towards the fort, and when he got in a bout 200 Yards he halted. Capt. McColester becconed to him and told him to advance. He came up some nigher and stoped. Capt. McColester went out to meet him and I went with him. We took no arms with us, and this Indian told us he was a chief and he was willing to talk a little about this Traty. He could speak broken Inglish.

When he told us What nation of Indians he belonged to, Capt. McC[olester] asked him if he knew Stephen Riddle and Abram Riddle.[24] He said he Did. Capt. Mc[Colester] told this Indian that the father of these Riddles was then at Grensvil and wanted very much to see his children, and that he (Old capt. Riddle) had give many presents to other Indians to go with presents to his cheldren and persuaed them to come in.[25]

Capt. Mc[Colester] invited this Indean when he first came up to alight and come in the fort, Drink some Whiskey. He refused and after talking some time and asking him more perticular about the Riddles, he said, "Me," and striking his hand on his brest said, "Me Stephen Liddle."

The Capt. and I emedeately shook hands with him and told him we was mighty Glad, we was mighty well acquaintd with his father, and he must get Down and take a little whiskey. He refused but the capt. had a little brought to him. He Drank one Dram and then told us that Abram was not far off with some other Indians. The Capt. told this Indian that if he would come in the fort he would send after his father, and he (Capt. Mc[Colester]) would go whear Abram and the other Indians weare, and they would all come to the fort Together. It was agreed to.

The capt. sent off a Messinger after Old Capt. Riddle and Capt. Mc[Colester] went with this Indean Chief to where these indians weare. I was realy afraid for Capt. Mc[Colester] to go with this Indian for fear he was a counterfit, as he Did not look like any thing elce but a full-blooded Indean. However, in a little time they came to the fort. They was all on horse back—to wit, Stephen Reddle and his squagh, Abram Riddle, and Abram's Adopted brother.[26] They all alighted and came in the fort and all had the appearrence of Indians. They weare all painted and very Dirty and shabby. However, as they had some silver trenkits hanging about thir necks and brests, and some broaches in their brechcloaths, and beeds in their leggans and Moxckersons, I suppose they thought themselvs fine; yet they weare all Dirty looking creaturs. They all Drank Whiskey and ate very hearty.

None could speake Inglish but stephen, and he in a very broken manner. He was taken a prisoner at his father's fort on Lecking in June 1780. When the fort was taken he was then about 9 or 10 years old,[27] and a Ductch boy Abram was taken at the same time. He was then about 4 or 5 years Old. He could not speake Inglish. Stephen's squagh was a Old, ugly, black looking, Dirty wench of a creature.

In this fort their was several of the soldiers had their wifes with them, and a number of the soldiers and these white woman had gathered together in the house where these Indians weare when old Capt. Reddle came. Capt. Mc[Colester] Conducted Old Capt. Riddle to his children and Intreduced them to each other.

Emedeately Old Reddle cryed out aloud and fell Down on the floore, Crying and bewailing his condition. Said he, "My cheldrin is Indians!"

Stephen took hold of his father and said, "Holt your heart, fatter. Holt your heart, fater."

These Indeans, the white woman, and some of the soldiers, all cryed and several cryed aloud. The Old Capt. Riddle continued some time crying. When ever he would look at his children he would renew his crying. This was after night. The next morning O[ld] Capt. Riddle gave his sons clean Cloathing and got them to wash of[f] the paint and put on these clean cloaths.[28] I gave Abram's adopted Brother a shirt, and he was very Glad of it. We told Old Riddle he ought to give stephen's wife something. He refused. Their was a stoore in this fort. Some of the officers got some calleco for her and the white woman in a little time run it up. Now this old squaw looked very sower and Dejected when she saw the rest have new cloaths, and she an Old smoked blankit over her sholders and some Dirty old cloath tyed around her waste. She was seting Down by her self, her head hung Down, when her cloathing was Gave to her.[29] She put them on and was[30] highly pleased.

Amongst the Indians they have Defferent grades of chiefs. Some is captain of 50, some of 100, etc. This Capt. stephen was a captain. He commaned a company and it was said he was resolute in battle. He told me he was in the battle when Harmer was Defeated, also when senclear was Defeated.[31] He also told us he was in the battle when Wayn Defeated them on the Mommea.[32] He said the british had told them previous to the battle that if they got Defeated they might run in their fort, but when the pench come they told a Lie.[33]

Now the way that this battle was brought on: their was about 250 men called spies who was commanded by col. Price, who marched in advance about half mile a head of the Army Down the Momea river.[34] Their line extended from the river squaer off, so that their line was a half mile in wedth. Col. Price's orders was that when ever he meet the Indians after fireing to Retreat to the main army. This was to give the main Army time to form the army for battle.

Now says this Capt. Stephen Reddle, "I Did Realy beleave when we meet this advance party we meet the main army; and we persued them with all our might, thinking we had Defeated them. And when we," said he, "meet the big army we tryed to out flank them and souround them, but to our astonishment the whites out flanked us and all of a sudden made a charge on us.[35] And the indeans all run as they was over powed by a much Greater forse of men."

And sayd stephen, he and his men all run to the British fort gate for entrance; but the british, sayd stephen, Lied. They would not opin the gate but Ded refuse them.[36] Capt. Stephen sayd they was nearly Exhusted, and several of his men killed, and the whites a rushing hard on them; and it was with Defeculty he made his escape. So he was willing to make peace with Ky. and the Americans, but the britesh he would never like again as they had told a lye and Decived the Indians.

The next Day Old Capt. Riddle and his children and the indians that was with them, all went to greensvile. And after 2 o 3 Days Old Riddle told me he knew that I could be of benefit to him. He sayed his son Stephen thought a great Deal of me and he wished me to talk to Stephen and persuaid him to quit his old squagh and go home with his father.

The fact was Stephen Did profess to think much of me. I talked to him about it. Stephen said he would not give up his squagh. He was willing to go home with father but he would take her with him. He would not give her for no woman in the world; for, said he, she was mighty good to him. She would Do any thing for him. She would git up in the night and fetch him a Drink of water. But Old Reddle Did mislike very much to let her go home with him.[37] I had several conversations with them. Stephen asked me if I thought it was wright for him to quit her. I told him it was very Desagreeable to his father, and I had nothing to say or advise him about it.

The fact was I [di]d not know what to say; but I thought Old Riddle was in fault for giveing up the fort to the British and Indeans when he Did, when Brother James Trabue and Capt. Hingston and others was much opposed to it and adviseed otherwase. But he put too much confidence in the British.[38]

One night at Greensvil, Stephen and his company's horses all run away from them. I asked him if he was not a going to hunt them.

He said, "No"; his squagh was gone after them.

I said, "Who went with her?"

He said, "No one. She could go by her self."

She was gone two or three Days and brought all their horses (5 in number) and she by her self. She found the horses at the Distance of 40 Miles. I then thought she was worth all the rest of their company together, as the men might have gone themselves or at any rates one or two Might have gone with her. I seen many such cercumstances of the kind.

A number of prisoners was fetched in and gave up to their families and was taken home. Brother James Trabue had a very likely young negro Woman taken at Riddle's fort. I heard where she was but could not git any Indians to fetch her. General Wayn told them they must fetch her and all the rest of the presoners to this Treaty. This nigro woman had at that time 2 or 3 children. Her name was Selah. She was at, as I understood, near the mouth of St. Duskey[39] but some of the Indeans Denied it. It was stated that an half-breed Indin by the name of Joe Scott had her as his serant. The Indians Did not bring in all the presoners.[40]

I saw Many men their that came from the Fronteers of New York, Pensilvanah, Virgenia, and kentucky, who came for the Express purpose of trying to git their Reletives who was Prisoners. Many Got and many did not git. Their was Great Joy with some and Grief with others. The Indians had killed many Prisoners, as I understood.

Their was Many lemantable tales told me. Their was One in perticular I well Relate as well as I can recolect. A Col. Crofferd was Defeated some Whiare above Siotea and many of his men made presoners.[41] The Indians Burnt many of them.[42]

One man—I have forgot his name—was Tied to a stake, and wood for fuel put all around him.[43] He now thought it was his time to Die. He had seen many of his fellow creatures burnt at such a place as they had him fixed at. This was in the afternoon. They had that same morning burnt one or two. This poor creature was in great Destress when they put fire to the wood. But before the wood got sufficiently on fire their a rose a black cloud and came on a very hasty rain and continued for some time, so that the fire was put out.

The Indians then untyed this poore man from this stake and took him in to one of their camps and tyed him very fast, so that the ropes or tugs hurt him Much. His hands, arms, thighs, legs, and feet was all made fast. The Indians went all to sleep. This poore Man thought the next Day he would be burnt, but he would try to git loose from his fetters and git away from these savagies. So he tryed to pull out his hands, but they was tyed so tight he could not. He pulled and pulled with all his might but could not git his hands loose. He tryed all night but could not git loose.

He saw Day breaking. He had been praying all night but now he thought all was over with him, he was gone. He said, "Lord, have mercy on me. What shall I Do?" He thought he would Try one more time to pull out his hands. He pulled with all his might and got out one of his hands and then the other, and then he quickly untyed him self or got a knife and got his fetters all off. He slipt off from the Indians and left them all asleep. He took a bridle or a halter and got one of the best of their horses and left them while it was yet Dark but could see Day a coming. He road fast and Did make his escape.

I had considerable talk with many of the Indean chiefs. One in perticular I will Mention. He was an Old Man. We had talked a few words together at Defferent times. We agreed to walk out some Distance and set Down and talk about the Despute between the Indeans and white people.

This chief said to me, "You big Captain. Me big Capt. too. What Do you want to take Indian land from them for?"

Answer: we Did not want to take their land. Who told them we did?

He said the british told thim so and the britesh told them they ought to fight for their land and kill the whites.

I told him we alwaise bought their land and paid them for it and if any body had Ever been in the fought [fault] it was the british king. It was them that first made a settlement in America on their land—if it was their land. But said I, "How come it to be your land? Who maid it and who give it to you?"

He laughed and said the britesh told them it was their land and the Great spirret had made it for them.

I asked him if he beleaved that storry.

He told me he would now tell me how he thought it was. He said he beleaved the Great Spirret made all the people—the Indean and the white people. He made all the land and it was the Great sperrit's land. And it was rong for Indian or white man to say it was his land. This was a lie. "Now," said he, "if Indian make house it is Indean's house. If he make corn field it is his, but the land is the Great Sperrit's. But," said he, "the white man he marke of[f] land in the woods and say it is his land." Said he, "This is a lie. It is not his land. It is the Great Sperrit's land."

I said to him, "Don't you think the great sperrit made the land for the white people as well as the Indian?"

He said, "Yes, but," said he, "he must not come too nigh to the Indean towns."

I said to him, "We buoy your land and come so nigh you, you Come to see us and we let you have gun powder and lead and blankit. You got land enough left, and as the Great sperrit made the land for white folks as well as Indean, what make you Mad about it?"

He said the truth was the british give them Rum and tell them the white people will never stop untell they take all the land from them.

I told him the britesh tell lie; the white people want to make corn, and as their was a great many white people they could seell some more land.

He said, "Yes"; he was willing. He said he had been to Philledelphia and he saw much people and he knew it was best to make peace. He said he had lost a number of his people who was killed in the war. He was now Determined to use his best influence to make peace.

A very Remarkable accurence happened to two men that landed at the falls of Ohia now Lewisvile. It was said they thought themselves interpriseing men and they had left their former place of Residence, which was some where in the Mongahela country,[44] on the account of their thinking they had boath been Slighted in some offices they wanted. They sold their possessions in that country and with their families Removed to Kentucky. And in the fall of 1[7]79 they landed at Lewisvil with their families.

Some little time after, Col. R. G. [sic] Cark[45] proposed a settlement Down on the Misssippi at or near the Chickesaw bluffs.[46] Squire Boon,[47] these two men with their Families, and many others embarked in this skiem.[48] They Got in flat bottom fammely boats and Decinded the Ohio and built a fort[49] at the Checkesaw bluffs. And the Indeans was so much Displased about it[50] and some other cercumstance that happened, that the conclusion was to abandon this settlement.[51] And as they had but few horses some came back on them and some on foot, while others went Down the River to Knaches, which at that time belonged to the Spanesh Government.[52]

This place at the Checkesaw bluffs proved very seckly, and several of this company Died. I will Return to these two Men and their families.

One of these min Died and left his wife a widow. The other Man's wife Died and left him a Widower. And as they was Obledged to go a way they got in a flat bottom boat—this man and his children and this widow woman and her children, all in one boat—and Decended the Massepee [Mississippi] with an intent to go to knaches.

They had but a scant allowence of provision, and it intirely give out. And they run their boat on a log and could not git it off. The boat was near the shore so that they could go on shore. They cut hand sticks and tryed to shove off the boat but could not. This man had a Good Gun and Amonition and went several times a hunting for something to eat but all without suckceess. And they weare all nearly starved to Death, and in those Days it was but seldom any boats passed up or Down.

This man proposed to this widow that they should cast lots with their children and kill one to eat to save the rest of their lives. She objected and said she had rather all Die together and advised him to hunt again. He Did but with out suckcees.

This man said he would kill one of his own children and Did cast lots. And the lot fell on a small Girl. And this Girl knew of the plan and she walked up and Down on the shore a crying, while this widow woman insisted it must not be Done and told this man they must make a nother attempt to get of[f] their boat. But he refused to help. And this woman encouraged all the children to help and Do their very best, and they shoved off the boat. This woman thinks the water had raised a little.

And all went along together, but this man had got very fractery and peevish. And the woman and children Managed the boat mostly themselves. And as they was moving, it appeared their was some hopes. And this little girl's life was spared from Day to Day.

And at length they meet a French Man in a Ceel boat a going to the Elenoy [Illinois] at Caskasey [Kaskaskia] and they petetiond him for food. And he said he was scarce but he would give them some. This woman informed the Frenchman that they ware not all one family and to Give her and her children's portion to themselves. And he Did so. And she give her children a little at a time and eat but little her self at one time, while this Man eat so much at once he actuly Died.

And this widow and boath sets of children all did arive at knaches. And some of her friends some time after that heard of her Destress and went to her and took her and her children around to Baltimore and then to her own people again.[53]

12

Violence on the Kentucky Frontier

And on the day[1] appointed they[2] come. I Furnished them with Mony for their expences and ammonition, etc., and they set out. They persued Down the River[3] and often heard of them [the Harpes], and when they was in the Checkeesaw Nation[4] 2 of the McFarlins was took with the Ague and fever. Remained their some time and in the fall they Returned but had Done nothing. The legislater passed a law in their favour[5] and gave them $[150], which sum nearly satisfyed them includeing what I gave them at ther start.

    Account of the Harps. It is sayed these Harps—to wit, Micajor Harp[6] and Wiley Harp[7]—was Natives of North Carolineer. Micajor was a large   Daring looking man. They had   [far]med in N. Caroliner or Tenesee[8] for   . [Mica]jer had two sisters.[9]   wife also. They   .[10]

    a log they hid him.[11] They had not traveled much Further before a Jentlemon Fell in company with them on the Road by the name of Lankford.[12] Mr. Lankford saw them at some house on the Road.[13] They found out Mr. Lankford had Mony and a very likely horse, etc. At a convenient place in the woods they killed him and thowed him out of the road and covered him with logs. Some cow Drovers found the Dead Men.[14]

    And these Harps was Judged for the Murder and the knews reached Kentucky. And Mr. Joseph Balengor,[15] a noted Valient Man in time of Danger, living at Stanford, with some others, knowing that they [the Harpes] had gone the road towards the Rolling fork of salt River,[16] persued them. And about the head of the Rolling fork they over took them[17] enc[amped]   company road up to   them to surrender

    Jail[18] when th[e]   .

    Negro had stole it. They[19] went Down the River[20] in serch of it. When they found the conoe they hunted the bushes near to it And came on these Harps, who Jumed up. They had 2 guns, which they took from the guard at Danville,[21] and cursed these pursuers who Retreated.

    These pursuers went to Henry scaggs,[22] who went with them, who was a valient man in battle and a great Hunter and had good Dogs. When they came to the place the murderes was gone. They pursued them with their Dogs for some Distance; but as night came on and the cain very thick they give out the persuit, went home, and went to sleep.

The next morning the said scaggs went to a log rooling. Major James Blain[23] was their. And when Scaggs told this knews and at the same time told that the two men that was hunting the negro said the Harps had broak Jail and these was the very men, Major Blain perposed that they should quit the log rolling and git Dogs and go and persue these Dredfull, wreached Murderers. But the company said the cain was so thick that they thought it was a bad chance. What a pity it was that they did not go after them. If they Had little John Trabue might not have been killed.[24] Major Blain, Henry Scaggs, and the rest of the men Reflected very much on themselves for their negligence. This ought to be a warning to others hearafter to always to Do their Duty. These Murderers came nearly by my house—to wit, D[aniel] Trabue's—where they got my son John.

They went on towards the south west 12 or 15 Mile from hear. They killed a Calf in a remote part of the Nobs[25] on the east fork of little Baren,[26] left their Old Mockersons, and made New ones with the calf skin.[27] From thence they went on and came across a man by the name of Mr. Stump,[28] who had a good gun; and when Stump had shot a turkey they went to him, killed him, and took his gun, which was a very Good rifle. They went from thence to big Barren River, stole a Canoe, and went Down the River, killed one or two more men going Down Barren River.[29] I Don't Recolect their names.

They went to the yallow Banks,[30] and kept themselvs very private, hid their mony and some other things under a cleft of Rocks.[31] They went from their towards the Chickeysaw Nation, and went to stones River, from thence to Knoxville.

Near knoxvile they killed a man by the name of Ballard.[32] They cut opin his belly, put stones in it, and sunk him in the river. They then started for kentucky again. They did not go fair before they killed a young man by the name of Coffey, son to Chesley Coffy.[33] He was arideing along the road one evining to git a fiddle. They smeared a tree with his brains, making out his horse had run him against the tree.

The next account was that Robert Brassel and James Brassel was coming from knoxvil to Kentucky.[34] James was on foot carrying a gun. Robert was on a horse and had no Gun. The said Harps over took them, appeared to be in great Hast, and sayed when they Come up, "Jentlemen, what is the knews?"[35]

The Brassils Replyed, "I suppose you heard about the Murder of Ballard and Coffey," and went on to relate the perticulars. These Murderers asked who was it thought had Done the mischief. The Brassels Replyed it was thought it was the Harps.

These Harps said that they was in persuete of the Murderers and they suspected that, "You are the men that has Done this Murder. And we have more men behind a coming, and you must stop until they come up." The Brassils agreed to stop. The big Harpe Mecager sayed to James, "Hend me your Gun." To which he Did. He took the gun and set it up by a tree. He then pulled out a large string and said, "Hold your hand together while I tye you."

Robert sayed, "James, Don't be tyed!"

The little Harpe said to Robert, "Dam you! I will kill you in a minuet if you Resist."

As Robert thought and believed that these men was the Murderers, he Jumped off his horse and tryed to git James' gun that was by the tree. But the Murderers interfered so that he Did not get it. But he run off leaving the big one (Mecager) a tying of his brother. The little man run after him and tryed to shoot, but he Got away from them, leaving his brother and horse behind.

He (Robert B[rassel]) some times left the road and some times kept the road, but after a while he meet a company of 6 men and a woman. Robert Brassel informed this company of what had happened. Robert B. also told them he would go back with them, if in case they meet with these Murderers that they would fight for life and kill and take them. It was Mutally agreed to.

A man by the name of dale was one of this Company. He had his wife with him and a good rifle Gun. He promised very positive he would shoot the big Man; and the rest promised to Jump at the little man, let the event be what it might.

They went on. And when they came to the place where Robert left James, a little in the woods they found James Dreadfully Buchered[36] and the gun broake to pieces. They Descovered the track of the Murderers gone to wards knoxvil. And after goeing a few Miles they saw them a comeing meeting them, the big Man rideing a gray horse (as Robert had preveously told them he was rideing a gray horse). They was all convinsed they weare the same men. Where they meet them, these Murderers was Just a riseing a hill.

Robert B[rassel], expecting they (his coppany) would perform what they said, he rather halted when he got oppesite to them, but the company passed on. Robert ran to mr. Dale and sayd, "Hand me the Gun," and laid hold of it; but Dale refused to let him have it, stateing his wife would be Terrified.

They say the Murderers looked very awfull at them. Some of the men observed, "If they will let us alone we will let them alone." So they passed on.

It was Descovered that the Murderers was heavy packed with cloathing previous to their overtakeing these Brassils. They laid off their luggage and roade fast to overtake these Brassils, and after they had killed James they went back for their plunder. And when this company meet them they had a great Deal of luggage, more than when Robert B[rassel] first saw them.

Robert was Much Destressed and complained to them very Greviously, but this company was skeared and Glad to Get off them selves. Robert B[rassel] would have persued them if he on[ly] could have got a gun. Robert B. went with this company several Miles when he meet another company a coming to Kentucky. He turned about with them. And they all agreed if they come up with the Harps they would kill them, and went on by where his Dead brother lay. And they all w[ent] on to Kentucky.

When they came to the ferst settlement in stocton's Valley[37] they saw a company of men hunting a Mr. Tully,[38] who they sayed was strangly lost, and they could not imagin what was gone with him.[39] They looked near thir road and[40] found him killed and hid by a log and coverd with logs.[41]

While the company was a burying Mr. Tully some of the men agreed they would persue these Murderers in Deffrent routs. Wil. woods, Esquir, was at that time a young Man and bold and couragious, set off emedeately with another young Man by the name of Nat Stocton.[42] These young men Did not take time to git their horses as they was out in the Range.[43] They concluded they would go emedeately on foot to my house—to wit, D[aniel] Trabue's—expecting the murderers would go their, as I had a stoore and had been active in haveing them hunted. They (Mr. Wood and Mr. stocton) got to my house,[44] which was 40 Mile. They told me the knews.

I sent out that night for some of the neighbours and made arangements that night. Sent one man off by sun rise the next morning to Frankfort to the Governor, as he might have it published in the knews papers. Mr. Wood's and Mr. Stockton's statement I rote Down, and I swore them to it of What they knew of their own knoledge and what Robert Brassil had told them. At the same time I sent a nother man Down to the yeller banks to General Sam Hopkins[45] with the same knews and statement. Derected the men to go as fast as they could and spread the knews as they went. This knews was emedeately put in the knews papers.[46]

The man I sent to General Hopkins was by the name of John Ellis.[47] As he went on he spred the knews and he happened to go the same rout that the Harps went. And they (the Harps) heared of him and persued Ellis and endeavoured to overtake him. They sayed to one man at a house they was in persuete of the Murderers and was trying to ketch up with Ellis to go with him. And they weare in two hours of overtakeing him at one time not fair from General Hopkins'. They would have ketched up with him if he had went moderately, but he (Ellis) had a good horse and went 60 or 70 Miles per Day.

The whole state got in a Great uprore as it was uncertain which rout they (the Murderors) would go. In a number of instancis people got alarmed, and when men would go to a house the people was afraid to opin their Doors and was afraid to travel.

The next night after they (the Murderers) left stockton valley I suppose[48] these Murderers was a going up Marrow bone Creek[49] about 25 Mile south from my house. They called on a old man by the name of Mr. Graves who had a son, a young man. They killed Mr. Graves and his son and hid them in some brush.[50] Mr. Graves and his son was a making a crop at a new place in order to move ther family when they Got Ready for it.

It may be remembered these Harps had been Down to the yallow banks the year before,[51] and some where near their they had built a cabin to move to; and when they broak out of the Danvil jail they left their Woman behind, and after a laps of time these woman went to this cabin. No Doubt but Tully had enformed them wheare their woman weare as he was accqunted with them, but Ellis was before them in their neighbourhood. And General Hopkins had men a waching their house emedeately the same Day. So the Harps was afraid to venter up. Hopkins had the Cabbin wached for about 10 Days. And after they quit waching the cabbin the murderers ventured up and got their woman and cleared off.

The Harps went to mr. Stegall's, now in Christian county.[52] Mr. Stegall was gone from home to git a horse for Major Love,[53] who was to stay at stegall's until he returned. The next morning when stegal got home he found his wife and child was killed and house burnt up and also Major Love was killed and burnt up.[54]

Mr. Stegall alarmed the neighbours and about 10 or 12 Men set out to persue them.[55] They easey tracked them as they had several Horses.[56] The first Day they did not come up with them. They encamped in the woods and early in the Morning—perhaps by sunrise—they over took these Harps and women at the head of a branch.[57] When they came to the camp their was no one their but the 3 woman. On inquerry about the men they was told they was gone Down the branch. They went Down the branch and descovered 3 Men and fired on them and wounded an innocent Man—to wit, Gorg Smith[58]—who was out a hunting a horse. And the Harps was talking with him and was Just agoing to kill him, as it is supposed. When the persuers came on them the Harps run off. They was persued but soon lost them.

When the persuers went to the women theire was but one their. The Pusuers inquered where the other two woman was, and she appeard to be loath to tell them. One man run to her and said he would kill her instantly if she did not tell any thing they asked her. She then stated the Big man Mecager had run round and came to the camp and was gone with his two women. They weare all on fleet horses. They made her shew the track they started on. The men went with all speed. Some horses tired.

In going a bout 7 Mile they came in sight and fired on the big man Mecager. He road very fast with his woman with him. They shot several times. This big man cursed them and told them, "Fire away!" They had not hit him as yet.

Capt. Christian[59] fired at him and wounded him, but he road on with all his might. At last a Mr. Leeper[60] road up close to him and Jumped of[f] his horse and took a true aim at him and give him a mortal wound. He Droped his gun, bled like a beef, and road off rather slowly.[61] The woman,[62] when they saw his gun fall and see the blood, they stoped.[63]

Memorandom: I, Daniel Trabue, in November 1780 started to Virginia from Logan's Fort, Ky., and previous to my Departure I was at the cabins that was erecting on near the head of Green River,[64] that was a building for Old Mr. William Mongomery[65] and his sons and Mr. Russil.[66] I was very well acquaented with them all,[67] as I lived in Logan's fort where they lived.

Memorandom of the settlement of the Mongemerys and the indeans' Attacking their cabbens and killing some of Them.
About the 25 of December 1780 Old Mr. William Montgomery, his son William Montgomery,[68] his son John Montgomry,[69] and his son-in-law Joseph Russel settled them selves on the head waters of Green River. They had built 4 Cabins and was a liveing in them. It was thought at this time their was no Danger of indians at this place as they had never been about their. And they was not very well fixed for them. Their Doors was not made very strong and no stockeading around their cabbins.[70]

And on the 27 of Febuary 1781 the Indeans[71] paid them a visit. Tom Montgomery,[72] who lived with his father, was gone to lexington with his gun on Guard, and then their was no gun in Old Mr. Mungomery house.[73] Mr. Ressil's Gun was out of Order. And at Day light the indeans attacked all the cabbins nearly at the same time.[74]

Old Mr. Montgomery and a Negro Man went out of his Door, and the Indians shot them boath Dead. Old Mr. Montgomery was shot with 7 bullits. He fell in the yard. The Negro fell in the Door. The Old Man's Daughter Jean[75] Moved the negro out of the Door and shut the Door and fastened it. The Indians broak opin John Montgomery Door, and as he Got up out of his bed they shot him Dead and took his wife and Nego Girl Prisoners. They also broke open Mr. Russel's house and took them all prisoners Except Mr. Russil. He made his escape. William

Montgomery, who was after Col. W. Montgomery,[76] Jumed to his Door when the indeans was trying to opin it and put a large Trough against it and then shot at 2 endeans at once and Mortally wounded one and broak the other one's thigh.

The Indeans emedeately Fled and carryed off the 2 wounded indeans. They took John Montgomery wife[77] prisoner and skelped their Negro Girl and lift her behind. She lived. They Also took Mr. Russel's wife and 4 children.[78]

Old Mr. Montgomery's Doughter Betcy[79] inquerd of her sister Jean where was Tom's Gun, and she told her Tom had it with him. Thire is no Doubt but if she had a Gun but what she would have made use of it. The indeans was a screming and hollowing and shooting. These young woman could see that the indeans had possession of thur brother John's house. And then Betcy got out of the house and attempted to run off, and one Indian Run after her. She run Back and the indin after her.[80] She run to her Brother John's house and went in it. The indian Did not follow her in the house. She then Run out and made her escape.

After a little while one Indian got up on a log, appeared to be scolding about something; and William shot him Down Dead. The rest of the Indeans was gone, so he lay their in the yard.

And after a little while William Montgomery opened his Door and went to his father's Door and told his sister Jean and sister Flory[81] and little his brother Robert to come out. And they with William and his wife and 3 of William's children, and a lad that lived with him—all went to Pettet's Fort.[82] Betcy got their first and had already gave the knews.

William Cassey, who was after Col. Cassey,[83] went with speed to Col. Ben Logan's, and give him the knews, which was 12 Miles. And after a while Logan and Cassey and several othes came to Pettet's fort. And Logan, Cassey, and William Montgomery, and others to the number of 25 Men started after these Indeans with a Determination to follow them until they over took them if it should be near to thur towns.

The indeans made litters to carry the wouned Indeans on. The number of Indeans and presoner made Much sine. They was easy to follow. 2 of logan's men went on a head on foot in a run and the rest on horse back.[84] So they went very fast. These Men that was before would be Releaved by others. And going about 15 Miles they over took the Indians and Prisoners.[85]

One Indean was behind as a spy. He Descovered the persuers. He then throwed Down his pack and Run to the other Indians, geving them the knews. When Logan's men saw the Indean's pack on the trail they understood it and Rushed with all their Might. The Indeans killed Mr. Russel's Doughter Flory—she was about 8 years[86] Old—and then Run off with all their might and got in a cain break, so that our men Did not shoot at them. The indeans made so little sighn in this cain brak and scattered in such a manner that our men persued no further after them. The prisoners was all Recovered Except Florey Russil. She was emediately Burryed by puting logs on her.

The indians left the Indian with his broken thigh on his litter. Logan's Men soon fineshed him and let him lie their for the wolves and[87] fowls of the air to eat. They said this was a remarkable large indian. It took 4 indians at a time to pack him.

The prisoners said their was 25 indeans which made their escape. So thur was in all 28. Flory Russil told her mother as She was traveling along that she had counted the Indeans and thur was 25 besids [the] wounded ones. She also told her Mother she wished that she had run under the bed. She thought they would not have found her as they was hurryed off so quick.

They all got to Pettit's fort that night. Some of the men Traveled that Day 54 Miles. The same Day they put the Dead bodys in one of the housis and the next Day they buryed them all Deacntly.

The prisoners gave account that they saw the indeans packing the 2 wounded Indians, and after a while some Indians was left behind with one of the wounded Indians. And they kept on with the indean with the broken thigh, and after a while the indians that was left behind came up. They said something that our presoners Did not understand; however, the indeans all cryeed very much. So the presoners concluded that the woended Indian was Dead.

Jean Montgomry says she was looking at the Indean on the log when her Brother William shot him. She seen him fall and she was glad. She thinks this indian had been Runing after Mr. Russel and Did not know all that had happened. She further states that she Did not know that her Brother William had shot the other 2 Indeans. The indian that was shot from the log lay their, and the hogs and other   eat him.

Thomas Montgomery,[88] a son of William Montgomery, was then 6 years Old. He is now known by the name of Judge Montgomery. He says the first thing that suppresed [surprised] him he was a wakined by the guns and screming of the indians and runing of the cattle with their bells ringing. It was very alarming. His father fastend his Door very quick by puting a large trough against it, which appeared to be Imposible for one man to Do it so quick.

Jean Montgomery after this got Marryed to William Cassey,[89] after this was col. Cassey.[90] Elizebeth or betey Montgomery was after this Marryed to her cousin William Montgomery,[91] who was after known by the name of Col. Wi[ll] Montgomery.[92]

Notes

Introduction

1. Ella Trabue Smith to Lyman C. Draper, Witcherville, Ark., April 17, (?), Draper MSS (State Historical Society of Wisconsin), 57J150(2).
2. James Trabue to Draper, Louisville, June 25, 1844, ibid., 57J148(a); Draper to William Martin, Pikesville, Md., July 18, 1844, ibid., 3XX30(2).
3. Draper MSS, 32S395-473.
4. Croghan to Draper, Locust Grove, Feb. 23, 1845, July 13, 30, 1846, ibid., 10J225, 227, 228; Josephine L. Harper to Chester R. Young, Madison, Wis., Nov. 28, 1956, Oct. 8, 1971.
5. Ella Trabue Smith to Draper, Witcherville, Ark., April 17, (?), Draper MSS, 57J150(1-2).
6. James Rood Robertson, *Petitions of the Early Inhabitants of Kentucky to the General Assembly of Virginia, 1769 to 1792*, Filson Club, *Publications*, no. 27 (Louisville, 1914; reprint ed., New York, 1971), pp. 114-16.
7. William Waller Hening, ed., *The Statutes at Large: Being a Collection of All the Laws of Virginia, from the First Session of the Legislature, in the Year 1619*, 13 vols. (New York, 1819-1823; reprint ed., Charlottesville, Va., 1969), 12:663-64 (hereafter cited as Hening, *Statutes*).
8. Reuben Gold Thwaites and Louise Phelps Kellogg, eds., *Documentary History of Dunmore's War, 1774* (Madison, Wis., 1905), pp. 239, 374.
9. Lewis Collins, *History of Kentucky*, 2 vols., rev. ed. (Covington, Ky., 1874; reprint ed., Louisville, Ky., 1924), 2:418.
10. Daniel Trabue to Johns[t]on, Woodford County, Aug. 21, 1796, Zachariah Johnston Papers (Photostats, Virginia State Library); Craig to Johnston, Richmond, April 21, 1795, ibid.
11. Trabue to Johns[t]on, Woodford County, Aug. 21, Sept. 24, 1796, ibid.
12. Executive Journal, 1796-1799, Gov. James Garrard (MS, Kentucky Historical Society, Frankfort), p. 86; Militia Report, [Woodford County, Ky.], "Strength of the 11th regt. before the division 1797," Governors' Papers (MS, Kentucky Historical Society, Frankfort), Jacket 16; "A return of the Strength of the Eleventh Regiment . . .," Nov. 5, 1796, ibid.; G. Glenn Clift, *The "Corn Stalk" Militia of Kentucky, 1792-1811* (Frankfort, Ky., 1957), pp. 14, 27, 53.
13. Trabue's memory played tricks on him in 1832 when he applied for a pension as a veteran of the Revolutionary War. Then he declared that he had moved to Green County in 1795. Daniel Trabue, Pension Declaration, Adair County, Ky., Aug. 6, 1832, p. 5, in Pension File S14727, records of the Veterans' Administration, Record Group 15, National Archives; also Adair County (Ky.) Court Order Book E (MS, Courthouse, Columbia, Ky.), pp. 345-47, 355-57.
14. Lillie DuPuy VanCulin Harper, *Colonial Men and Times: Containing the Journal*

of Col. Daniel Trabue . . . (Philadelphia, 1916), p. 222; William Littell, ed., *The Statute Law of Kentucky; with Notes, Praelections, and Observations on the Public Acts*, 5 vols. (Frankfort, Ky., 1809-1819), 2:242.

15. Lyman C. Draper, Interview with Zachariah Holliday, Adair County, Ky., Oct. 1844, Draper MSS, 9J230-30(1).

16. John Avroe Steele [Rollin M. Hurt], "Notes on Adair County," *Adair County News* (Columbia, Ky.), May 28, 1919 (hereafter cited as [Hurt], "Adair County"); William B. Allen, *A History of Kentucky* . . . (Louisville, Ky., 1872), p. 383 (hereafter cited as William B. Allen, *Kentucky*).

17. "Military Appointments . . . Commencing in the year 1799," bound with Executive Journal, 1800-1804, Gov. Garrard (MS, Kentucky Historical Society, Frankfort), July 20, Sept. 18, 1799, pp. 2, 7; Blane et al. to Garrard, Dec. 21, 1799, Governors' Papers, Jacket 15; Blane to Garrard, Dec. 28, 1799, ibid., Jacket 15; Trabue to Wilm. Barnet, May 16, 1800, ibid., Jacket 19.

18. The date of its constitution, though unknown, may have been a year or two earlier. In view of the fact that none of the ten churches listed (Russell's Creek being one) in the minutes of the Green River Association of Baptists for November 1800 is designated as having entered the fellowship at that session, it is assumed that all of them had participated in organizing the union five months earlier. John Henderson Spencer, *A History of Kentucky Baptists from 1769 to 1885*, 2 vols. (Cincinnati, 1885), 2:105 (hereafter cited as Spencer, *Kentucky Baptists*); John Wilson Townsend, ed., *Supplemental Check List of Kentucky Imprints, 1788-1820*, no. 38, Historical Records Survey, *American Imprints Inventory* (Louisville, Ky., 1942; reprint ed., New York, 1964), pp. 11-13 (hereafter cited as Townsend, *Kentucky Imprints, 1788-1820*).

19. The principal nineteenth-century Kentucky Baptist historian mistakenly conjectures that Elijah Summers was the organizer of the Skinhouse church. Spencer, *Kentucky Baptists*, 1:308.

20. *Acts Passed at a Session of the Tenth General Assembly for the Commonwealth of Kentucky* (Frankfort, Ky., 1802), pp. 68-71. This dwelling was situated on the hundred-acre plantation which he had acquired from William Skaggs and which lay along the southwestern edge of the land he had bought from Johnston. Adair County (Ky.) Deed Book A (MS, Courthouse, Columbia, Ky.), pp. 186-87; Deed Book C (MS, Courthouse, Columbia, Ky.), pp. 67-69.

21. Ruth Paull Burdette, *Early Columbia: The Beginnings of a Small Kentucky Town* ([Columbia, Ky., 1974]), pp. 4-5.

22. Executive Journal, 1800-1804, Gov. Garrard, Dec. 19, 1801, part 2, p. 45.

23. Adair County (Ky.) Court Order Book A (MS, Courthouse, Columbia, Ky.), p. 9.

24. For examples of this process see Columbia (Ky.) Board of Trustees, Book of Proceedings, 1811-1839 (MS, Office of County Court Clerk, Courthouse, Columbia, Ky.), March 9, 1811, Feb. 28, 1812, Feb. 5, 1814, Jan. 5, 1815, Oct. 14, 1816, Feb. 1, May 3, Aug. 12, 1817, Nov. 4, 1819, April 1, 1822.

25. Nathan Montgomery, Certificate, Dec. 31, 1810, in Census of 1810, Kentucky, I, 17, records of the Bureau of the Census, Record Group 29, National Archives.

26. Trabue did not attend the five annual sessions for which rolls of messengers are extant in the period 1820-1830. *Minutes of the Eighteenth Russell's Creek Association of United Baptists*, 1822 (n.p., n.d.), p. 2; Columbia (Ky.) Baptist Church, Minute Book No. 3 (MS, Church Office, Columbia, Ky.), Aug. 17, 1895, p. 2.

27. "A Baptist Minister Visits Kentucky: The Journal of Andrew Broaddus I," Oct. 28-29, 1817, ed. John L. Blair, *Register of the Kentucky Historical Society* 71 (Oct. 1973): 411 (hereafter cited as "Journal of Broaddus").

28. Townsend, *Kentucky Imprints, 1788-1820*, pp. 37, 41, 45, 47, 49, 51, 63, 69, 77, 83; B.W. Penick, "History of Russell's Creek Association, Continued from 1810 to 1820,"

NOTES TO PAGES 15-24

Minutes of the Russell's Creek Association of United Baptists, 1895 (Louisville, Ky., 1895), pp. 8, 9, 11, 12, 13; *Minutes of the Russell Creek Association of Kentucky Baptists,* 1955 (Hawesville, Ky., 1955), p. 54.

29. Townsend, *Kentucky Imprints, 1788-1820,* pp. 87, 91, 93.
30. Ira M. Allen, ed., *The United States Baptist Annual Register for 1832* (Philadelphia, 1833), p. 189.
31. Spencer, *Kentucky Baptists,* 1:243.
32. *Minutes of the Russell's Creek Association of Baptists,* 1813 (n.p., n.d.), p. 2.
33. Penick, "History of Russell's Creek Association," pp. 9, 10. Townsend erroneously identifies the 1815 offering as the first taken in a Kentucky association for such a purpose. *Kentucky Imprints, 1788-1820,* pp. ix, 63.
34. John Augustus Williams, *Life of Elder John Smith with Some Account of the Rise and Progress of the Current Reformation* (Cincinnati, 1870), p. 119 (hereafter cited as Williams, *John Smith*).
35. Adair County (Ky.) Court Order Book A, p. 21.
36. Adair County (Ky.) Court Order Book B (MS, Courthouse, Columbia, Ky.), p. 34.
37. Adair County (Ky.) Deed Book B (MS, Courthouse, Columbia, Ky.), pp. 42-43.
38. Trabue, Pension Declaration, Adair County, Ky., Aug. 6, 1832, p. 5.
39. *Acts Passed at the First Session of the Twenty-ninth General Assembly for the Commonwealth of Kentucky* (Frankfort, Ky., 1821), pp. 212-13; *Acts Passed at the First Session of the Thirtieth General Assembly for the Commonwealth of Kentucky* (Frankfort, Ky., 1821), p. 302; *Acts Passed at the Second Session of the Thirtieth, and the First Session of the Thirty-first General Assembly for the Commonwealth of Kentucky* (Frankfort, Ky., 1823), p. 173.
40. *Acts Passed at the First Session of the Thirty-second General Assembly for the Commonwealth of Kentucky* (Frankfort, Ky., 1824), p. 408.
41. Ibid., p. 407.
42. John James Marshall, ed., *Reports of Cases at Law and in Equity, Argued and Decided in the Court of Appeals of the Commonwealth of Kentucky, [1829-1832],* 7 vols. (Frankfort, Ky., 1831-1834), 3:598.
43. "Journal of Broaddus," Oct. 28, 1817, p. 410.
44. Census of 1820, Kentucky, I, 26, records of the Bureau of the Census, Record Group 29, National Archives.
45. Adair County (Ky.) Deed Book G (MS, Courthouse, Columbia, Ky.), p. 70.
46. Even though the Replevin Act of 1820 had been revoked on June 1, 1824, Trabue's case was not affected because his debt had originated before the repeal and because the change in the law restored a three-month replevy.
47. Adair County (Ky.) Deed Book G, p. 70.
48. Thomas C. Brown to Chester R. Young, Hodgenville, Ky., Aug. 10, 1974.
49. H[erschel] C[lay] Baker, "Sketches of Adair County," *Adair County News* (Columbia, Ky.), March 27, 1918 (hereafter cited as Baker, "Adair County").
50. Elder Craig was licensed on July 2, 1827, to celebrate the rites of matrimony. Adair County (Ky.) Court Order Book E, p. 125.
51. Baker, "Adair County," *Adair County News,* March 27, 1918.
52. *A Compendium of Church Discipline, Shewing the Qualifications and Duties of the Officers and Members of a Gospel Church, To Which Are Prefixed the Constitution and Principles of Union of the Russell's Creek Association* (Bardstown, Ky., 1825), pp. v-vi; James Garnett, [Jr.], *History of the Columbia Baptist Church* (Columbia, Ky., 1927), p. 2.
53. Williams, *John Smith,* pp. 29, 35, 38.
54. *Minutes of the Twenty-sixth Russell's Creek Association of United Baptists,* 1830 (Bardstown, Ky., 1830), p. 6.
55. *Minutes of the Twenty-seventh Russell's Creek Association of United Baptists,* 1831

(n.p., n.d.), pp. 4-7; Alonzo Willard Fortune, *The Disciples in Kentucky* ([Lexington, Ky.], 1932), p. 107.

56. *Minutes of the Thirtieth Russell's Creek Association of United Baptists*, 1834 (n.p., n.d.), p. 7.

57. Williams, *John Smith*, p. 395.

58. Ibid., p. 396.

59. In 1830 the Mount Gilead Baptist Church reported the exclusion of nine persons. *Minutes of the Twenty-sixth Russell's Creek Association of United Baptists*, 1830, p. 2.

60. Williams, *John Smith*, pp. 397-99. The Mount Pleasant Baptist Church excluded twelve members that year. *Minutes of the Twenty-sixth Russell's Creek Association of United Baptists*, 1830, p. 2.

61. *Minutes of the Twenty-sixth Russell's Creek Association of United Baptists*, 1830, pp. 2-3; Williams, *John Smith*, p. 394.

62. *Minutes of the Twenty-sixth Russell's Creek Association of United Baptists*, 1830, p. 4.

63. [Hurt], "Adair County," *Adair County News*, May 21, 1919.

64. In 1832, when President Andrew Jackson was reelected, Trabue voted for Henry Clay, who lost to Old Hickory. Clay carried Kentucky but not Columbia or Adair County. Poll Book, Columbia Precinct, Nov. [5-7], 1832, in *Adair County News*, Nov. 7, 1972.

65. Adair County (Ky.) Court Order Book E, front flyleaf.

66. Ibid., front flyleaf and pp. 273, 372, 393.

67. Richard Peters, ed., *Public Statutes at Large of the United States of America, 1789-1873*, 17 vols. (Boston, 1850-1873), 4:529-30 (hereafter cited as Peters, *Statutes at Large of the United States*).

68. Trabue to [James L. Edwards], Columbia, Ky., Dec. 6, 1832, in Daniel Trabue, Pension File.

69. Adair County (Ky.) Court Order Book E, pp. 345-47, 355-57.

70. Trabue to [James L. Edwards], Columbia, Ky., Dec. 6, 1832, in Daniel Trabue, Pension File.

71. Peters, *Statutes at Large of the United States*, 4:563-64.

72. Daniel Trabue to Robert Trabue, Columbia, [Ky.], March 21, 1833, Durrett Collection, University of Chicago Library.

73. Trabue to the Congress of the United States, [Jan. 1836], in Daniel Trabue, Pension File.

74. Ely McClellan, "An Account of the Epidemic of Cholera, during the Summer of 1873 in Eighteen Counties of the State of Kentucky," in *Public Health: Reports and Papers Presented at the Meetings of the American Public Health Association in the Year 1873* (New York, 1875), p. 218.

75. Thomas C. Brown to Chester R. Young, Hodgenville, Ky., June 17, 1974.

76. Trabue to the Congress of the United States, [Jan. 1836], in Daniel Trabue, Pension File.

77. 24th Congress, 1st Session, *House Report*, No. 510, March 26, 1836, p. 2, ibid.

78. 24th Congress, 1st Session, Bill H.R. No. 507, March 26, 1836, ibid.

79. 24th Congress, 1st Session, *Congressional Globe*, pp. 263, 437, 441, 467.

80. Peters, *Statutes at Large of the United States*, 6:654.

81. Daniel Trabue, Jr., to J.L. Edwards, Burk[e]sville, Ky., Nov. 20, 1837, in Daniel Trabue, Pension File.

82. Daniel Trabue, Jr., to J.L. Edwards, Nov. 20, 1837, ibid.

83. S.F.J. Trabue to unknown attorney, Frankfort, Ky., ca. Sept. 17, 1850, ibid. Stephen FitzJames Trabue, a grandson of Daniel's brother Stephen and a Kentucky lawyer, uncovered in the Auditor's Office in Richmond, Virginia, during the winter of 1849-1850 a

NOTES TO PAGES 32-39

ledger labeled "Expenditures in the County of Kentucky." In this record book he found a payment of £500 made to Daniel Trabue on March 1, 1781, as an issuing commissary in Kentucky County.

84. Daniel Trabue, Jr., to Joseph Ficklin, Burk[e]sville, Jan, 29, 1838, ibid.

85. Two years after Trabue's death, the twenty-dollar pension was paid to his estate for the period from March 4, 1837, to the day of his demise. Albion K. Parris to J.L. Edwards, Second Comptroller's Office, Aug. 18, 1842, ibid. In March 1851 the first annuity was readjusted by the Pension Office on the petition of Daniel Trabue, Jr., and set at the rate of $470. An amount based on this increased rate for the period from March 4, 1831, to Trabue's death date, less $1,630.38 previously paid, was turned over to this estate. File wrappers, Jan. 23, March 20, 1851, ibid.

86. Census of 1840, Kentucky, Green County, p. 177, records of the Bureau of the Census, Record Group 29, National Archives.

87. *Baptist Banner and Western Pioneer* (Louisville, Ky.), Jan. 21, 1841.

1. The Huguenot Heritage

1. Note by Trabue on the flyleaf opposite page 1: James Trabue—Commissary in Ky. in 1780—Captured in June of that year (Martin's and Riddell's Stations). Journal of fall session Va. H[ouse] of Delegates 1781, pp. 50, 64.

2. This date agrees with the one Daniel Trabue gives in his pension declaration. His tombstone erroneously records his birthdate as March 17, 1760.

3. Anthony Trabue, Sr., (1667-1723/4) was a native of Montauban, a river town in southern France on a tributary of the Garonne. His parents had reared him in the Reformed or Calvinistic communion. On September 15, 1687, a former pastor from Montauban furnished Anthony with a certificate of good character with the purpose of encouraging Reformed believers to aid him in his flight to safety.

4. When Louis XIV entered upon his active rule in 1661, he set in motion an intensive campaign against toleration of Huguenots. He resolved to convert the heretics, to constrict further their religious rights, and to root up heresy once and for all. In 1685 he revoked the Edict of Nantes by promulgating the Edict of Fontainebleau, which prohibited Huguenot worship and education. All meetinghouses were to be destroyed or used as Catholic churches.

5. Trabue grossly underestimates the ratio of those who escaped to those who suffered torture, death, or the confiscation of property. A true proportion is one emigrant to every three dissenters who remained in France.

6. The edict of 1685 rewarded informers with half of the estates of lay emigrants.

7. Trabue's mother, Olympia Dupuy (1729-1822), married John James Trabue in 1744. John James Dupuy (1698?-1775) was the third child of Bartholomew Dupuy (1653-1743). Both father and son had wives named Susanne Lavillain. Bartholomew Dupuy served eleven years in the French military and attained the position of captain of the Household Guard of Louis XIV.

8. Susanne Lavillain (1663-1737) married Bartholomew Dupuy in 1682.

9. The bracketed portion is canceled in the original but is included here as necessary in delineating the actions of the paternal grandfather of Trabue's mother.

10. Other sources indicate that Dupuy was a Huguenot.

11. *Diabolical craft* is a substitute for the word *church,* which Trabue cancels. The confiscated property of an emigrant Huguenot was generally given to a Catholic kinsman.

12. By a letter dated March 18, 1699/1700, King William III ordered Governor Francis Nicholson of Virginia to make grants of land to a group of French refugees and to help settle them.

13. Magdelaine, the daughter of Jacob Flournoy, was born in France about 1671. She died in Henrico County, Virginia, in 1731.

14. The Board of Trade intended the first company of refugees to settle in Norfolk County, Virginia. Since no vacant, undisputed lands existed there, the Virginia Council decided on August 8, 1700, that the newcomers should be seated in Henrico (now Powhatan) County at Manakin Town, a site some twenty miles beyond "World's End"—the common designation for the Falls of the James River.

15. For this purpose the Virginia Council reserved ten thousand acres of fertile land in the Piedmont region of the James River. Each family was entitled to receive 133 acres. During the first ten years of settlement only about half of the tract was apportioned among the refugees.

16. The first pastor at Manakin Town was Benjamin de Joux, who had been ordained by the bishop of London for the purpose of ministering among the Huguenots in Virginia. De Joux, formerly a minister of the Reformed Church at Lyon, arrived in the Old Dominion in October 1700 with the second Huguenot company.

17. Early Huguenot polity had been more presbyterial than congregational. After 1661, however, Protestant synods were outlawed in France; in time the churches became more and more independent.

18. The Church of England was established in Virginia throughout the colonial period.

19. In December 1700 the Virginia Assembly formed Manakin Town and its environs into King William parish. The refugees were accordingly exempted from the church levy in any other parish. In addition they were excused from all public and county levies for seven years. A statute of 1706 provided that the French were "left at their own liberty to agree with and pay their minister as their circumstances will admit." Hening, *Statutes*, 3:201, 478-79.

20. On October 25, 1700, the French settlers at Manakin Town and the emigrants who had arrived at Jamestown a few days earlier were described as being "destitute of all meanes of support and subsistence." Robert A. Brock, ed., *Documents . . . Relating to the Huguenot Emigration to Virginia . . .*, Virginia Historical Society, *Collections*, n.s., 5 (Richmond, Va., 1886; reprint ed., Baltimore, 1966): 49.

21. William Byrd I (1652-1704) had previously lived near the Falls of the James at Belvidere, but in 1688 he purchased Westover, an estate some twenty miles down the river in Charles City County. Byrd's grist mill was located on Falling Creek, which flows into the James River on the south side a few miles below the Falls.

22. For a contrary view of this economic progress in Virginia, see John Lawson, *A New Voyage to Carolina*, ed. Hugh Talmage Lefler (rev. 1709 ed., Chapel Hill, N.C., 1967), pp. 90, 119.

23. Byrd was indeed an influential gentleman at the time the Huguenots settled at Manakin Town. Politically, he was a member of the Virginia Council, the auditor of public accounts, and the receiver general of the colony. Commercially, he was the principal Indian trader in Virginia, an importer of white indentured servants and black slaves, and an exporter of furs, pelts, and tobacco. The oral tradition that Trabue here records pertains not only to the elder Byrd but to his son William II (1674-1744) as well. Soon after the death of the elder in 1704, the son returned from England, where he had lived most of the time since the age of seven, and virtually assumed the role of his deceased father.

24. Daniel Trabue's grandfather received his first Virginia land grant on March 23, 1715/6, in the name of Anthony Tribue for 163 acres on the south side of the James River; the second, on March 18, 1717/8, in the name of Anthony Trabue for 522 acres on the

Great Fork of Swift Creek. Virginia Land Office, County Abstracts No. 17 (Microfilm, Virginia State Library), pp. 39, 43.

25. This parchment, measuring about five by eight inches, survived until 1889, when the residence of Anthony Edward Trabue of Hannibal, Missouri, was destroyed by fire. About seven years earlier this great-great-grandson of the French exile had received it from Macon Trabue, a Virginia cousin.

26. Anthony Trabue, Jr., (b. ca. 1702) married a daughter of Moyse Vermeil. Jacob Trabue (b. ca. 1705) headed a family of five children. John James Trabue (1722-1775) was born at Manakin Town.

27. John James Trabue (1745/6-1802) married Jane E. Porter in 1782. John Trabue (1754-1788), who was the husband of Margaret Pearce, died in Kentucky. William Trabue (1756-1786) married Elizabeth Haskins on February 12, 1783. Her father, Robert Haskins, gave three other of his daughters to be wives of three of William's brothers. Daniel Trabue (1760-1840), the author of this narrative, was the first of this family to marry a Haskins woman. Edward Trabue (1762-1814) and Martha Haskins were joined in matrimony on August 18, 1786. After her death Edward married Jane, a daughter of Eleazar Clay, the famed Baptist preacher of Chesterfield County and an uncle of Henry Clay of Kentucky. Stephen Trabue (1766-1833) and Jane Haskins became husband and wife on July 24, 1788. Samuel Trabue (1770-1777). Magdelaine Trabue (1748-1815) was the wife of Edwin C. Clay, an uncle of Henry Clay of Kentucky. Phoebe Trabue (1750-1767). Jane Trabue (1752-1802) and Joseph Minter were the parents of fourteen children. Mary Trabue (1758-1792) became the wife of Lewis Sublett in 1779. Martha Trabue (b. 1762) and Josiah Wooldridge were married on February 18, 1785. Elizabeth Trabue (1768-1835) was the wife of Fenelon Wilson, a native of England. Judith Trabue (b. 1774) was married to John Major. Susannah Trabue (1772-1862) and Oliver Thomas Major were married in 1793.

28. Heavy rains caused unprecedented flooding of the James and the Potomac rivers in May 1771. Large quantities of tobacco were damaged at public warehouses in Chesterfield, Henrico, King George, and Prince William counties. Hening, *Statutes,* 8:493, 494, 496, 501.

29. On page 128 Trabue sets December 7, 1770, as the date on which Joseph Anthony and William Webber preached in his neighborhood.

30. Wesley M. Gewehr gives a sevenfold basis for the concerted opposition to Separate Baptists in colonial Virginia: 1) the opinion of many officials that they were lawbreakers deserving punishment, 2) the fear of the decline of the Establishment in case of their success, 3) a regard toward them as a threat to society, 4) a view of their preachers as false prophets, 5) Baptists' rash attacks on the Anglican Church, 6) the belief that their extended meetings resulted in idleness and lost labor, and 7) their reputation as social outcasts.

31. For various periods of time, beginning in December 1770 and continuing through May 1774, seven Separate Baptist preachers—Joseph Anthony, William Webber, Augustine Eastin, John Tanner, John Weatherford, Jeremiah Walker, and David Tinsley—served sentences in the Chesterfield prison, having been convicted of breaching the peace because they had preached in unapproved meeting places or without licenses as dissenting ministers. No more than three of them were in the jail at any one time; the longest period of confinement of any inmate was five months.

32. In 1771 Virginia Separate Baptists, who were persecuted more rigorously than were Regular Baptists in the colony, had fourteen churches with 1,335 members. Three years later they had fifty-one churches with 3,954 members.

33. Imprisonment of Separate preachers in Chesterfield ended in 1774, and only one case is on record elsewhere in Virginia after that year.

34. In Westmoreland County some wheat and rye crops were so severely hurt that they were fit only to be mowed down for fodder. In parts of the Tidewater the leaves fell from the trees and the forests appeared as if autumn had come.

35. The Shawnee, tributary to the powerful Iroquois Confederation, lived in present-day Ohio on the Scioto River, to which by stages they had removed from the Cumberland and the Savannah rivers in the South.

36. John Murray, Earl of Dunmore, (1732-1809) Virginia's last royal governor, promoted a punitive war against the Shawnee and their Ohio allies. The Virginia army was composed of two divisions—one personally commanded by Lord Dunmore, the second by Colonel Andrew Lewis of Augusta County.

37. James Trabue was a lieutenant in one of the companies in the Dunmore division.

38. In the bloody Battle of Point Pleasant the forces of Colonel Lewis contended fiercely with the Indians led by Cornstalk, the great Shawnee chief. The Virginians won the day-long battle, much of which was carried on at close range, often in hand-to-hand combat. James Trabue did not participate in this battle because after leaving Pittsburgh Dunmore had changed his plan to meet Lewis at Point Pleasant and had taken his division into the Ohio country, where later the Shawnee sued for peace.

39. The phrase "in 1775" is canceled at this point in the text.

40. The minds of Virginians were ill at ease in the summer of 1774. The blighting frost of May, the controversy with the mother country in the wake of the parliamentary "Intolerable Acts" aimed at punishing Massachusetts, the jurisdictional dispute between the governor and the House of Burgesses, and the Indian trouble on the frontier, all had uncommonly agitated public opinion.

41. At least nine merchants in Chesterfield County were natives of England or Scotland. Five of them were friendly to the patriot cause, three were anxious to return to Great Britain in 1777, and the position of one is unknown.

42. Realizing his mistake, Trabue cancels the words "to Wit, Archerbald McRobert" at this point in the text. Archibald McRoberts, the Scottish rector of one or both of the parishes in Chesterfield County, was an early dissenter against the liturgy of the Established Church. The minister became a Presbyterian in time.

43. In order to carry his argument the parson greatly exaggerated. The population of the thirteen British colonies in 1770 is estimated at 2,148,076; the people in London twenty years earlier are numbered at only 676,250.

44. A servile insurrection was Dunmore's purpose in issuing a proclamation of emancipation on November 15, 1775; however, his pronouncement only served to increase public sentiment against the governor.

45. At this point in the text the following insertion occurs: "AAA read the loose sheet." This instruction may refer to a paper with a triple A marking, once a part of the manuscript but now lost.

46. The phrase "in 1775," placed at the beginning of this sentence, is canceled in the text. In Chesterfield County at least two public meetings were held in 1774 to consider the condition of the colony. On July 14 two county representatives were chosen for Virginia's first revolutionary convention, scheduled for August 1. On November 25 a county committee of correspondence was selected by a small group of freeholders in conformity with the eleventh resolution of the First Continental Congress, which had met in Philadelphia the previous two months. This resolution had called for the forming of local groups to enforce the Association—an economic boycott against British goods, effective December 1.

47. Both organized religion and government called for days of fasting in Virginia during 1774. Separate Baptists designated two Saturdays in June as public fast days with a view to securing the release of their imprisoned preachers. The House of Burgesses set June 1, the date on which the Boston Port Act would become effective, as a day of "Fasting, Humiliation, and Prayer." In 1775 Virginia's revolutionaries specified that a solemn fast be observed on July 20, the first fast day recommended by the Continental Congress for all the colonies.

48. Apparently Trabue is referring to two different legislative actions. In December 1776 the General Assembly instructed the governor to deport natives of Great Britain who were agents or partners of British merchants, except persons sympathetic with the patriot cause. The following spring the legislature passed an act to require all free male residents of Virginia to swear allegiance to the new commonwealth, renouncing loyalty to King George III and agreeing to report to the authorities all persons suspected of treason. Recusants were to be disarmed and deprived of certain civil rights, but exile was not a penalty imposed against Virginians. Hening, *Statutes,* 9: 281-82.

49. In Virginia many English and Scottish merchants who had refused to side with the cause of freedom embarked for the British Isles early in 1777. In March the state government moved against those who lingered. They were to be arrested as prisoners of war and concentrated at two camps—one at Cumberland Courthouse, south of the James; the other at Caroline Courthouse, north of that river.

50. The following sentences are canceled at this place in the manuscript: "One of their church parsons near us was throwed Down and a Company of soldiers walked over him. Every one Trod on his body. One was tard and feathered."

51. Civil processes, including the collection of debts, came to a halt in Virginia courts on April 12, 1774, with the expiration of the Fee Act of 1745 and its amendments. Hening, *Statutes,* 5: 326-44, 8: 515-16. This law might have been renewed had not the House of Burgesses been dissolved the next month. The revolutionary convention of March 1775 recommended that the courts continue to reject civil suits (with certain exceptions). The burgesses were of the opinion that the shutting off of foreign trade required that this occlusion of the courts be maintained.

52. The capture by the British navy of commercial vessels carrying salt to Virginia had made the commodity scarce in that colony. To alleviate this shortage the revolutionary convention of December 1775 provided for the distribution of 3,600 bushels of salt, 140 of which were allotted to Chesterfield County.

53. John James Trabue died in October 1775; John James Dupuy, the preceding February.

54. An ordinance enacted by the Virginia Convention of July 1775 required most free males "above the age of sixteen, and under fifty years" to be enlisted into the militia. Five months later another law set March 1776 as the date for dividing each militia company in every county into ten equal "divisions," which would serve during emergencies according to their numerical order. Hening, *Statutes,* 9: 27, 89-90.

55. The patriots put an end to royal authority in Virginia by defeating Lord Dunmore on July 8-10, 1776, near the mouth of the Rappahannock. Trabue stated in 1832 that on his tour against Dunmore "we Started at Chesterfield Courthouse, went down the South Side of Said [James] river, did not go fare before we were halted; remained only a few days or weeks, and were discharged, for which we were credited by a tour of duty; Capt. Blackburn [Blackman] Mosely and Colo. [Robert] Goode, the officers, if I rember aright." Pension Declaration, Adair County, Ky., Aug. 6, 1832, p. 1.

56. In 1832 Trabue recorded this event as occurring in the spring or summer of 1776, when "shortly after he was 16 years of age, he was called on to guard the Magazine, that had been removed from Williamsburg to Chesterfield County . . . and continued as a guard for more than one month under the Command of Capt. Walter Scott." Ibid.

57. In the fall of 1777 Virginia authorized a maximum of eighty companies of sixty-eight volunteers each. These men were to serve in the Continental Army for six months unless released sooner. Hening, *Statutes,* 9: 345-49. By this time George Washington had already been in the North as the commander-in-chief for over two years.

58. William Trabue, who was four years older than Daniel, was discharged from the Continental Army on September 5, 1780, after a three-year term of service.

2. A Martial Introduction to the Kentucky Wilderness

1. Trabue errs in locating the home of George Rogers Clark (1752-1818) in Hanover County. He had grown up in Caroline, to which his parents had moved from Albemarle when he was five years old.
2. The Falls of the Ohio later became the site of the town of Louisville.
3. The western campaign of Clark was designed against British posts in the Illinois country.
4. Clark's appointment of James Trabue of Charlotte County as a recruiter for his western expedition violated an agreement between Governor Patrick Henry and Clark that all enlistments would be made beyond the Blue Ridge.
5. The principal road westward across Virginia led from Chesterfield County through Powhatan, Cumberland, Buckingham, and Bedford counties, crossing the Blue Ridge at Blue Ridge Gap into Botetourt County. At Big Flat Lick, where present Roanoke is located, this route intersected the Great Valley Road (sometimes called the Philadelphia Wagon Road), which ran in a northeast-southwest direction between the Blue Ridge and the Allegheny Mountains. Following the Great Valley Road southward, the Trabue party crossed the New River at Ingles' Ferry and went by Fort Chiswell before arriving on the Holston.
6. The American—sometimes called the Pennsylvania or Kentucky—rifle was a modification of the gun brought to this continent by German gunsmiths.
7. The Holston River community was begun in 1746, and by the outbreak of the Revolution a sizable populace had developed. When the Trabue party stopped there, this settlement lay in Washington County, Virginia, with part of it spilling across the undefined state border into North Carolina (now northeastern Tennessee).
8. From the Block House on the Holston River to the Cumberland Gap, the trail led over steep mountains, through gaps, and along the streams of well-watered valleys. West of the Block House the route forded the North Fork of the Holston, went through Moccasin Gap of Clinch Mountain, crossed the Clinch River, scaled up Kanes Gap of Powell Mountain, and climbed over Wallen Ridge into Powell Valley. Crossing Powell River, the trail wound through the remainder of the valley to emerge at Cumberland Gap.
9. Laurel was the common name applied by early settlers to the true rhododendron—a flowering, evergreen shrub indigenous to eastern North America.
10. Such abandoned cabins in Powell Valley evidenced the ravages of the Indian war of 1776-1777. This valley carries the name of Ambrose Powell, one of the hunters who accompanied Dr. Thomas Walker on his exploration of Kentucky in 1750.
11. This branch, which passed through a thicket of rhododendron at the foot of the hill, issues from a spring below the entrance to Cudjo's Cave on the north side of the gap.
12. This route, commonly called the Warriors' Path, was part of a system of ancient Indian trails leading from Georgia and the Carolinas through eastern Tennessee to Cumberland Gap.
13. Three years earlier when Daniel Boone laid out this road to Boonesborough, he had followed the Warriors' Path as far north as Flat Lick, located nine miles beyond the Cumberland River ford. There, branching off northwesterly on his own, he marked out the first trail in this area made by a white man. Between Laurel and Rockcastle rivers at a place which came to be known as Hazel Patch, Boone's Trace passed a path leading to the west. Called Skaggs's Trace, this path led to the site where Logan's Fort would be built. Boone's route continued from Hazel Patch almost directly north to the Kentucky River.
14. The Cherokee lived on the waters of the Tennessee and the Savannah rivers in the Appalachian Mountains behind the Carolinas. In 1776 the tribe attacked the frontier patriots from Georgia to southern Virginia but upon making peace the following year ceased to be a real threat.

NOTES TO PAGES 44-47

15. Gun flints of the Revolutionary Era were flat-sided with beveled edges.

16. The words "up the mountain we went our orders was" are canceled at this point in the text.

17. This stream was probably the Davis Branch of Yellow Creek. When the Trabue party came into Kentucky, Yellow Creek was still called Flat Creek, the name given to it by Dr. Thomas Walker in 1750.

18. In view of the fact that these red men were moving northward on the Warriors' Path and left behind considerable Indian goods, they may have been Shawnee returning home from a raid against the Cherokee.

19. At Flat Lick in present-day Knox County, Boone's Trace turned to the northwest, leaving the Warriors' Path on its northward course to the Ohio.

20. Boonesborough had been the seat of the proprietary colony of Transylvania from its settlement in April 1775 until the newly established state of Virginia asserted jurisdiction over Kentucky by creating a county government for the entire area in December of the next year.

21. Beyond Flat Lick, Boone's Trace, crossing the Laurel and the Rockcastle rivers, cut through twenty miles of "dead brush" and about thirty of canebrakes.

22. The settlement was located in Sycamore Hollow on the south side of the Kentucky River almost one mile below the mouth of Otter Creek.

23. Eight families plus an indeterminable number of Virginia military men lived at Boonesborough on March 26, 1778. [John D. Shane], Interview with Josiah Collins, Bath County, Ky., May 2, 1841, Draper MSS, 12CC64.

24. The fort, enclosing about an acre, measured approximately 180 by 240 feet with the longer side paralleling the river. Its closest corner came within some sixty feet of the stream. Blockhouses occupied two of the corners, and the exterior walls of the cabins together with palisades standing ten or twelve feet completed the perimeter of the fort.

25. The phrase "in good money" is canceled in the text.

26. Early Kentucky settlers were dependent on the buffalo to a marked degree. Its flesh was their common food; its skin when tanned provided a good grade of leather. From its thick coat of hair—at a peak in February—a coarse clothlike wool was produced.

27. Thomas and Williams Brooks both enlisted for Clark's Northwest campaign.

28. Daniel Boone (1734-1820) was then one of several militia captains in Kentucky County.

29. The Lower Blue Licks, the site of Boone's salt camp, was connected to Boonesborough by a road as early as 1779. These salt springs are located in northeastern Kentucky on Licking River.

30. Boone with about thirty men had gone out from Boonesborough early in January 1778 to make salt. On February 7 he was captured by a Shawnee war party and the following day he encouraged his salt-makers to surrender. As to the number of prisoners, Boone recalled six years later that there were twenty-eight including himself.

31. Logan's Fort, first occupied in February 1777, was located near two adjacent springs in the valley of Dix River about a half mile southwest of the present town of Stanford. This site had been named St. Asaph's by John Floyd's party of surveyors and adventurers, who camped there in May 1775.

32. When Josiah Collins of Halifax County, Virginia, arrived at Boonesborough that spring on March 26, he found "a poor, distressed, 1/2 naked, 1/2 starved people, daily surrounded by the savage, which made it so dangerous, the hunters were afraid to go out to get Buffaloe Meat." [John D. Shane], Interview with Collins, Bath County, Ky., May 2, 1841, Draper MSS, 12CC67.

33. This clause means "Before I got here that Sunday."

34. Miguel de Cervantes (1547-1616), the Spanish novelist, puts this adage in *Don Quixote*, "There's no sauce in the world like hunger." Part II, book III, chapt. 5.

35. Harrodstown, later called Harrodsburg, was the first permanent settlement in Kentucky. It was laid off by James Harrod (1742-1793) on the waters of Salt River in June 1774. During the ensuing year a fort was constructed which enclosed a spring of considerable size. This settlement was located eighteen miles from Logan's Fort.

36. Benjamin Logan (1743?-1802) was the captain of the militia company from the St. Asaph's district and the first sheriff of Kentucky County.

37. The word *Dutch* was a common colloquialism used in eighteenth-century North America to indicate German-speaking people.

38. One George Layl enlisted in the militia company of Captain Richard May on October 7, 1778.

39. The following cancellation occurs at this point in the manuscript: " 'And the cain break is too bad to go through it. And Did I not tell you that their was no indian in the nation that could hurt us?' "

40. The canebrake was a thicket of bamboolike grass, the stems of which grew so closely together that movement through it was greatly impeded. The cane reached a general height of ten or twelve feet, sometimes fifteen or sixteen. The thickness of the stem varied from two inches in diameter down to the size of a "goose-quill." Cattle and horses thrived well on the leaves and young shoots of this evergreen.

41. Joseph Lindsay, who had come to Kentucky by 1775, lived at Harrodsburg in the fall of 1777 and served as the militia commissary of Kentucky County under Colonel John Bowman. His work included sending out hunters to kill and preserve wild meat. Occasionally Lindsay went out to their hunting camps and brought the meat into the forts. Until his death at the Battle of Blue Licks in 1782, Lindsay filled various positions involving military supply.

42. Arriving at the Falls on May 27, George Rogers Clark soon erected on Corn Island blockhouses and cabins in the form of an Egyptian cross.

43. A keelboat was a "long, slender, and elegant" craft capable of transporting a cargo of fifteen to thirty tons. Its main advantage was navigability in shallow waters.

44. Having joined on October 7, 1778, the militia company commanded by Captain Richard May, James Trabue became the purchasing commissary for that unit on the following March 13. He served in that capacity until August 2, 1779. Four months and six days later James was appointed the militia commissary for Kentucky County, in which post he continued until his capture at Ruddle's Station the next June. Contemporary evidence presents an unclear picture as to whether or not Trabue replaced Lindsay as the chief commissary for Kentucky.

45. The settlement at the Falls was named Louisville in honor of Louis XVI, the first ally of the United States.

46. Succeeding Azariah Davis, Daniel became the quartermaster sergeant at Logan's Fort on July 13, 1778. From that day through October 6—a period of about twelve weeks—he bought for that garrison 84 bushels of corn, 724 pounds of pork, 2,779 pounds of "tame beef," and 2,820 pounds of buffalo beef. Joseph Lindsay, commissary for the county militia, certified Daniel's report on October 15. Draper MSS, 17J9. In 1832 Trabue recalled that his duty consisted of a "great deal of hard and dangersous labour; employing hunters, pressing cattle, buying corn etc., etc., a great deal of provisions being needed as many of Col. Clark's men were frequently passing and drawing provisions from our fort, and also as in times of immnent danger companies of men were called on from the Houlston country." Daniel Trabue, Pension Declaration, Adair County, Ky., Aug. 6, 1832, p. 2.

47. With some 175 handpicked soldiers in flatboats Clark shoved off from the Falls on June 24.

48. Philippe François Rastel, Sieur de Rocheblave, was the civil magistrate at Kaskaskia, in the ungarrisoned Illinois country. Clark's little army reached the town shortly after dark on July 4 and took it without firing a shot.

49. Rocheblave was sent under guard to Williamsburg by way of Cumberland Gap. After a period of imprisonment he was released on parole, from which he escaped on April 18, 1780, to the British lines in New York.

50. Influenced by the priest from Kaskaskia, the five hundred people of Vincennes on the Wabash River switched their allegiance from Britain to Virginia in July 1778; and Clark sent a unit to occupy the town. Lieutenant Governor Henry Hamilton of Canada marched down from Detroit and retook the Wabash village in December. His victory was undone two months later when by an epic move Clark arduously trekked overland from Kaskaskia and forced the British commander to surrender.

51. The gunpowder of Trabue's day was composed of six parts of saltpeter (potassium nitrate), one part of charcoal, and one part of sulphur by weight. The spoiled condition of the powder in the Kentucky forts may have meant that lumps had formed in it, that it had become moist, or that the saltpeter—the heaviest of the components—had separated from the other two by settling to the bottom of the kegs which contained it. The "working" of the powder may have been, accordingly, the reduction of the lumps, the elimination of the moisture, or the inversion of the kegs.

52. Trabue has exaggerated the rate at which he was compensated. While he was the quartermaster sergeant of Captain May's company he was listed with the rank and file and received the pay of a private—1s. 4d. per day.

3. Disruptive Indian Incursions

1. Samuel Coburn and his wife were living at Logan's Fort in February 1778, when their widowed daughter Ann McDonald married James Harrod there.

2. The site was the mouth of Knob Lick Creek of Hanging Fork.

3. Alexander Montgomery, a brother of the wife of Benjamin Logan, was an ensign in Logan's company.

4. Richard May, formerly from Botetourt County, became the commander of a militia company in Kentucky County on October 7, 1778. Daniel served in his unit from that date until August 2, 1779.

5. This salt vein, known as Flat Lick, was located about two miles southeast of the fort.

6. The following sentence is canceled in the text: "The woman said to me, 'Commessary, stay with us.'"

7. The world *also* is canceled in the text at this point.

8. The word *item* had the meaning of "hint" or "warning" in early Virginia.

9. The reminiscences of Benjamin Briggs, who was a thirteen-year-old member of May's unit, reveal some details that conflict with Trabue's account.

10. William Whitley (1749-1813) was serving at Logan's Fort in 1778 as a private in Captain Benjamin Logan's militia unit. In 1793 he was commissioned a lieutenant colonel in the militia regiment of Lincoln County.

11. In her edition of this narrative Lillie Harper erroneously renders this place name Holland, Kentucky. Samuel M. Wilson identifies her mistranscription with Holland or New Holland, a fort located near the Falls of the Ohio before 1784. Harper, *Colonial Men and Times*, p. 25; Wilson, *The First Land Court of Kentucky, 1779-1780* (Lexington, Ky., 1923), p. 62.

12. Trabue mistakenly identifies this session as the beginning of the Kentucky County Court. The initial meeting had been conducted at Harrodsburg on September 2, 1777.

13. After the first session of the court at Harrodsburg as provided by law, Logan's Fort became its meeting place.

14. Trabue means that the supposed halfway point was ten miles from Logan's Fort. The attack occurred near the site of present-day Danville.

15. William Poage had moved his family to Kentucky and settled at Boonesborough in 1775.

16. At this time Logan's militia unit included four officers, four sergeants, and more than twenty-four privates.

17. John Bowman (1738-1784) became the county lieutenant of Kentucky County on June 14, 1777. He was present at the opening session of the county court. Captain Isaac Ruddell commanded a military company in Kentucky County in 1779-1780. It is doubtful that he was a member of this court. Richard Calloway, a native of Bedford County, was elected in April 1777 as a member of the lower house of the Virginia legislature representing the new Kentucky County and was appointed two months later as a justice of the peace. Benjamin Logan was among the initial corps appointed to the court. In view of the fact that only three other appointees—George Rogers Clark, Isaac Hite, and Robert Todd—had qualified for the post, the opening of the court was delayed from March until September. A quorum required five justices. In addition to the justices mentioned by Trabue and those just listed, the following served in this capacity during the initial year of the new western county: Daniel Boone, John Floyd, James Harrod, Nathaniel Henderson, James Dorchester, John Kennedy, and John Todd. Levi Todd (1756-1807), a resident of Harrodsburg and a militia captain, had already been installed as the court clerk on September 2, 1777. He was the grandfather of Mary Todd Lincoln, wife of the future president. John Todd had been trained in law in Old Virginia, where he had been admitted to the bar. Residing in Kentucky since 1775, he had been a militia captain and a Kentucky County representative to the Virginia Assembly. His service as attorney for the county would have required him to vacate his seat on the court.

18. Leeper was a militiaman in the company commanded by Captain Benjamin Logan.

19. This word has here the obsolete meaning of "fearful."

20. The obsolete meaning of "a mere Marricle" is "nothing less than a miracle."

21. Archibald McKinney had arrived in Kentucky the previous year and soon became acquainted with the Green River country.

22. Two other accounts relate that the two bullets shattered his right shoulder.

23. On December 12, 1777, County Lieutenant John Bowman wrote General Edward Hand at Fort Pitt that the Indians "have left us almost without horses enough to supply the stations, so we are obliged to get all our provisions out of the wood." Draper MSS, 4B140-41.

24. William Whitley and Nehemiah Pore of Logan's Fort and four companions from Harrodsburg, all led by Andrew Johnson, one of the captives at Blue Licks the previous February who escaped from the Shawnee, had crossed the Ohio on rafts in May 1778 and captured seven horses about fourteen miles above the river. They succeeded in arriving at their homes with their booty after a journey of two weeks. Whitley, Narrative, Draper MSS, 9CC26-28.

Led by Daniel Boone, thirty men, including Simon Kenton and Alexander Montgomery, had set out from Boonesborough near the end of August on a scouting expedition beyond the Ohio. Intent on recovering stolen horses, twenty of them got as far as the Shawnee town on Paint Creek, a branch of the Scioto, where an Indian party was engaged. The Kentuckians promptly retreated homeward, leaving Kenton and Montgomery, who tarried behind, retrieved four fine mounts, and reached Logan's Fort with them on September 6. On page 57 Trabue writes about this foray, which preceded the siege of Boonesborough.

25. Simon Kenton (1755-1836) served as a secret agent in Dunmore's War and as a valued scout in Clark's campaign into the Illinois country.

26. County Lieutenant Bowman requested Kenton to go as a spy beyond the Ohio. Even though Kentuckians often referred to this expedition as a "horse stealing" foray, the recovery of stolen animals was incidental to its purpose.

27. George Clark, a sergeant in the militia company at Logan's Fort, is to be distinguished from George Rogers Clark.

28. In 1778 Chillicothe stood on the Little Miami River between present-day Xenia and Springfield, Ohio. There were at least four successive sites of this Shawnee town. During Dunmore's War and again in 1787, the village was located at the place where Trabue indicates.

29. Seven were caught and taken away.

30. Large; considerable.

31. George Rogers Clark had returned on August 20, 1779, from his expedition into the Illinois country. Trabue has dated this event by mistake in the late summer of 1778.

32. Hugh McGary had settled at Harrodsburg with his family in the fall of 1775. Later he became a lieutenant colonel in the militia of both Lincoln and Mercer counties.

33. In her old age Ann Harrod once spoke about feats with the rifle performed by several women on the frontier. She added, "But I never could do much with a gun; I have tried it often, but never could succeed. I did manage to kill a [buffalo] cow and a bear, or the girls would never have got done laughing at me." M.M. Henkle, Obituary of Ann Harrod, Harrodsburg, Ky., April 20, 1843, clipping from *Western Christian Advocate* (Cincinnati), May 12, 1843, Draper MSS, 12C25.

34. Puncheons were sometimes made by splitting in half logs that were about eighteen inches in diameter and by smoothing the face of them with a broadax. They were then laid as floorboards with the rounded side down.

35. John Bakeless mistakenly identifies the musician for this occasion as the French violinist Jean Nickle, who in fact had stopped at the Falls on his way to Kaskaskia the preceding December and had performed on Christmas Day at a housewarming in the new fort on the mainland. *Background to Glory: The Life of George Rogers Clark* (Philadelphia, 1957), p. 235.

36. The first salt works in Kentucky were located at Bullitts Lick, three miles north of Salt River. The site, discovered in 1773 by Captain Thomas Bullitt, is about three miles from present-day Shepherdsville in Bullitt County.

4. The "Big Siege" of Boonesborough

1. In the fall of 1778.

2. Under the terms of a 1777 Virginia law a militia commissary was obligated to obtain a certificate of service from his commanding officer and to present it to the governor and council in order to receive "such reward as they think fit." Hening, *Statutes*, 9: 296.

3. William Hancock, who had been among the saltmakers captured at the Lower Blue Licks, escaped from the Shawnee at Big Chillicothe on July 8 and reached Boone's fort nine days later completely exhausted and nearly naked.

4. Two Canadian officers had told Hancock that in three weeks the British and Indians would come against Boonesborough with some two hundred men whereas the red men had said that the army would be double that number.

5. Boone was already at his fort on the Kentucky River when William Hancock got there. Trabue erroneously reverses the order by which these two captives escaped and returned home. Running away from the Indians first, Boone arrived at Boonesborough on June 20 after a quick four-day journey. When Hancock showed up on July 17 he reported that Boone's abrupt departure had caused Blackfish, the Shawnee chief, to delay his attack against the fort by three weeks but that nine days of the grace had already elapsed.

6. While Boone was at Detroit, its commandant was Lieutenant Colonel Henry Hamilton, lieutenant governor of Canada.

7. The escaped captain gave his attention to strengthening the fort in general and extending it on the east side. Deteriorated posts in its stockaded walls were replaced. At its southeast and southwest corners new blockhouses were constructed with the second stories going up high enough to conceal a man when standing erect. These two bastions were left roofless because there was not time enough to complete the work.

8. This word replaces the expunged word *town*.

9. By appointment of Colonel George Rogers Clark, Major William Bailey Smith had succeeded to the command of Boonesborough after the capture of Boone, in spite of the fact that Colonel Calloway outranked him.

10. Trabue's sketch of this raid into the Ohio region is misleading. This event is referred to on page 54.

11. Boone's party returned to the fort on September 6. The red men were not far behind, because they camped on the north shore of the river that night. Crossing over the next morning, they made known their presence before Boonesborough.

12. The envoy and interpreter for the enemy was an officious black man named Pompey, who had probably been captured on an Indian foray against the whites.

13. For accounts of the complex parleying that preceded the assault on the fort, see Lyman C. Draper, Interview with Moses Boone, Draper MSS, 19C9-13(1); [John D. Shane], Interview with David Gass, Paris, Ky., ibid., 11CC12-13; John Bakeless, *Daniel Boone* (New York, 1939; reprint ed., Harrisburg, Pa., 1965), pp. 196-210.

14. Captain Daniel Boone was virtually the commander during the beguiling negotiations and the ensuing siege, even though Calloway and Smith held superior ranks. Boone later told Simon Kenton that it was he who gave the pointed order to the men in the blockhouses "to fire into the whole crowd outside if any thing happened." John H. James, Interview with Kenton, in James to Mann Butler, Urbana, Ohio, Nov. 12, 1835, Draper MSS, 11C76(1). (Trabue was not present at the siege of Boonesborough but received secondhand information.)

15. Smith put the number of defenders at thirty men and twenty boys, while a contemporary youth observed that about thirty-five men were able to bear arms in the fort. Boone calculated the number of the enemy as 444 Indians and twelve French-Canadians. For the statistics given by eleven other persons, see Lyman C. Draper, "Life of Daniel Boone," chapt. 16, Draper MSS, 4B210n (hereafter cited as Draper, "Boone").

16. Shawnee Chief Blackfish, who had adopted Boone as a son earlier that year, commanded the red army.

17. The significance of this backwoods diplomacy from the settlers' point of view lay in their hope that the passage of time might bring help from the Holston. The substantive features of the resultant treaty (the text of which has not survived), calling for the reds to withdraw beyond the Ohio and the whites to swear allegiance to the British crown, were unimportant in themselves.

18. According to a report by Simon Kenton, an Indian chief informed Boone after the treaty had been signed that "it was usual with them, in making friends, to shake hands; but when they made a long and lasting peace, they caught each other by the shoulders and brought their hearts together." John H. James, Interview with Kenton, in James to Mann Butler, Urbana, Ohio, Nov. 12, 1835, Draper MSS, 11C76(1).

19. The Indian attack that ensued was known among Kentucky pioneers as "the big siege of Boonesborough." For a list of source materials dealing with this military action, see Draper, "Boone," Draper MSS, 4B252(2)n.

20. Trabue's efforts to present Calloway in a favorable light go astray at this point. It was Squire Boone, Daniel's brother, who tried his skill as an artillerist that summer at Boonesborough. Squire, a gunsmith as well as a Baptist preacher, had a smithy situated handily in the courtyard of the fort, adjoining his cabin. Before the siege the smith had fashioned two swivels out of black gum logs and banded them with wagon-tire iron. One of

them burst when it was tested. The other, having been proved safe, was fired one foggy morning during the attack, but it was not used again because its wooden barrel had cracked.

21. Lieutenant Antoine Dagnieau DeQuindre of the Detroit militia had been sent on this expedition as an adviser to Chief Blackfish and as the leader of a squad of eleven Frenchmen.

22. The Kentuckians feared that the Indians would use this mine to introduce a large body of men into the fort, to lodge gunpowder underground and blow up the structure, or to fire its walls by placing along them the poles that they had wrapped with flax and scaly bark hickory.

23. Simon Kenton later reported that Boone informed him that he initiated this countermining, which was done under the riverside cabins of the fort. One youthful observer estimated that the settlers' ditch ran for twenty feet and was three or four feet wide and eight feet deep.

24. The year before, John Holder had married Fanny Calloway—one of the three girls kidnapped at Boonesborough in 1776. By April 6, 1779, he was the commander of a militia company in Kentucky County.

25. This unsophisticated woman was "Old Mrs. South"—wife of John South, Sr. Her statement became a byword among the men and an object of their ridicule.

26. John Gass, an early settler of Bourbon County, estimated that the Indians dug within ten feet of the fort wall. They had come so close that the Boonesborough men who were countermining inside the fort could hear "the sound of the strokes of whatever they were digging with." [John D. Shane], Interview with Gass, Paris, Ky., Draper MSS, 11CC14.

27. The Indians abandoned their mining because the continually rainy weather interfered with the excavation and caused their tunnel to collapse.

28. After diplomacy failed, the siege that ensued lasted nine days and nights.

29. Six years later Boone recalled that thirty-seven Indians were killed during the siege. On the settlers' side there were two deaths—one black man and one white man.

30. By April 1780 William Patton was living in the district of St. Asaph's, in which Logan's Fort was located.

31. Over the smaller spring near the fort a cabin had been erected. Leading from this springhouse to the fort, an underground passage was formed by covering a ditch with logs, which were in turn concealed with dirt from the excavation.

32. Roasting ears of Indian corn, still in the milky stage, were cooked by roasting or other methods.

33. Another version of this incident shows that Logan went on this errand because his two militia spies (Nehemiah Pore and a man named Clary) were reluctant to go.

34. In making his escape from the Indians, Logan held the thumb of his broken arm in his teeth to keep it from catching in the cane. This fracture had not completely healed by April of the next year.

35. Benjamin Pettit had learned from the Cherokee, among whom he had been a fur trader, the use of native herbs in the treatment of wounds. He had been living with his family at Logan's Fort since February 1777.

36. The inner bark of the slippery or red elm contains a fragrant, gelatinous substance with soothing and mollifying qualities. In this instance the bark, probably moistened, was used as a poultice to reduce pain and swelling.

37. John Martin was a militiaman in Captain Benjamin Logan's company in 1778.

38. Blockhouses that were constructed at two or more corners of a fort projected about two feet beyond the stockading and the outer walls of the cabins. The upper story was cantilevered some eighteen inches beyond the lower.

39. For the reminiscences of an old man who as a lad of thirteen years had lived in

in Logan's Fort during this alarm, see Lyman C. Draper, Interview with Benjamin Briggs, Lincoln County, Ky., fall 1844, Draper MSS, 9J186(1).

40. In response to Boone's urgent plea of July 18, the Virginia Executive Council authorized Colonel Arthur Campbell of Washington County on August 12 to send a militia unit of 100 to 150 men for "the relief of the People of Kentucky." Exceedingly tardy, eighty soldiers from the Holston arrived in Kentucky shortly after the siege was lifted, and they served at two of the distressed forts for a brief period.

41. Captain Boone's court-martial arose from several factors, including the following: 1) false rumors of his disloyalty; 2) jealousy of escaped prisoners of war (including William Hancock) who had seen the preferred treatment that the British afforded Boone during captivity; 3) Calloway's antagonism aroused by Boone's aggressive leadership and devious schemes in delaying for three days the commencement of the Indian attack and in ending it satisfactorily; 4) the captain's success as an affront to the colonel's rank and position; and 5) intercolonial rivalry between Old Virginia and North Carolina—the former places of residency of Calloway and Boone, respectively.

42. In his recent work of fiction Allan W. Eckert may have used this sentence as the basis on which he erroneously names Daniel Trabue as the president of the court-martial which tried Boone. Still beyond the realm of fact he ascribes to the youthful Trabue the rank of colonel, designates his nationality as English, and locates the proceedings at Boonesborough. *The Court-Martial of Daniel Boone: A Novel* (Boston, 1973), pp. v, 5, 13-16.

Trabue's account remains the principal evidence for the court-martial of Boone. His recalling, forty-nine years after the event, of the specific charges against the captain is remarkable in view of the fact that he witnessed this trial as an eighteen-year-old lad during his first year on the Kentucky frontier—a year that burned into his memory many startling happenings.

43. From its headwaters in Magoffin County, the Licking River moves northwesterly to join the Ohio at Covington.

44. Consonant with Boone's report, Henry Hamilton wrote General Guy Carleton on April 25, 1778, that "the people on the frontiers have been so incessantly harrassed by parties of Indians they have not been able to sow grain; and at Kentucke will not have a morsel of bread by the middle of June. Cloathing is not to be had, nor do they expect relief from the Congress. Their dilemma will probably induce them to trust to the Savages, who have shown so much humanity to their prisoners, and come to this place before Winter." Hamilton to Carleton, Detroit, Draper MSS, 11C96(3).

45. The phrase "in favour of the britesh" replaces the erasure "a Tory."

46. Boone's promotion in rank was the means by which his fellow officers on the Kentucky frontier underscored their verdict of acquittal. The new grade that they gave the captain thus appropriately recognized his indispensable leadership during the recent siege of Boonesborough.

47. The contemporaries of Boone varied considerably in their judgments about this affair. Mrs. Richard French, reflecting the adverse opinion of her father (Richard Calloway), believed that "Boon never deserved anything of the country." Samuel South, who as a boy carried water for the treating parties outside the fort, saw the captain's actions as evidence of boldness, firmness, and bravery. [John D. Shane], Interview with Jesse Daniel, Montgomery County, Ky., Draper MSS, 11CC94.

48. Trabue mistakenly dates Rogers's defeat in the fall of 1778. It occurred on October 4, 1779.

49. Colonel David Rogers had been commissioned in January 1778 by Governor Patrick Henry to secure from the Spanish at New Orleans badly needed supplies for Virginia units in the West. On his return up the Ohio the following year with a number of boats, he unwisely landed some men to attack a small Indian party seen on the Kentucky shore. The

Virginians were suddenly surrounded by a hostile party three times their size. The death of Rogers and a number of his soldiers resulted.

50. Fort Pitt had been erected by the British at the Forks of the Ohio soon after they forced the evacuation and destruction of Fort Duquesne at that site during the French and Indian War.

51. One of the boats managed to escape to the Falls but at least two were captured.

52. John Watson.

53. Captain Robert T. Benham.

54. After a few weeks of shifting for themselves in the wilderness, these men were rescued on November 27.

55. One Thomas Phelps entered the militia company of Captain Richard May on October 7, 1778—the day Daniel Trabue joined this outfit.

56. John Clary belonged to Captain John Boyle's militia company in Kentucky County in April 1780.

57. The Clinch River, rising in present-day Tazewell and Bland counties, Virginia, is a tributary of the Tennessee and runs parallel to the Clinch Mountain.

58. John Vardeman, Jr., a native of Sweden, migrated in the fall of 1779 to Kentucky County.

59. Jeremiah Vardeman (1775-1842) was celebrated in Kentucky, Tennessee, and Missouri as an accomplished Baptist preacher.

60. Ingles' Ferry was located in Montgomery County on that segment of the Great Valley Road through western Virginia which connected Fort Chiswell with Botetourt Courthouse. Authorized by the legislature in 1762, it was operated by William Ingles from his land on the eastern bank.

61. This tavern was probably the one kept by William Ingles near his ferry.

62. The path that Trabue had been traveling merged at Ingles' Ferry with the Great Valley Road, leading northeastward down the Valley of Virginia through Lexington, Staunton, and Winchester, and crossing Maryland and Pennsylvania to Philadelphia. To the south this route led into North Carolina and across the Blue Ridge to the Yadkin Valley.

63. "River Daniel" (b. 1753) was the son of Jacob Trabue, an uncle of "Kentucky Daniel."

64. On April 22, 1779, below the Rockcastle River, Calloway assumed charge of a contingent of British prisoners being sent by Clark through Kentucky County to eastern Virginia. He left this party on May 4 at Washington Courthouse and hastened on to Williamsburg, where the legislature had convened on the previous day.

65. Calloway and James Harrod were the members of the Virginia House of Delegates who represented Kentucky County in 1779.

66. The legislative session continued until June 26.

67. Located in Montgomery (now Wythe) County, these mines were owned by William Byrd III and the estates of John Robinson and John Chiswell. In the fall of 1776 the General Assembly had required the proprietors to furnish the state with one hundred tons of lead annually at the rate of £33.6.8 per ton.

68. This law, entitled "An act for establishing a Land office, and ascertaining the terms and manner of granting waste and unappropriated lands," set up the office of county surveyor, specified the requirements for militiary grants, and detailed the procedures for securing warrants, making entries, surveying lands, certifying and recording the resultant surveys, and issuing patents or grants. Hening, *Statutes*, 10:50-65. Another measure, commonly known as the Land Act of 1779, was passed at this session in an attempt to bring order out of the jungle of conflicting land claims in western Virginia.

69. Each volunteer was to furnish his own horse and to be paid two shillings per day until he returned to Old Virginia.

70. John Logan, a younger brother of Benjamin, did not attain this rank until the fall of 1779, when he assumed command of the latter's militia company.

71. On June 1, 1779, John Bowman and his avengers had crossed back into Kentucky after a four-day Ohio expedition against the Shawnee at Chillicothe. The number of Indian dead is unknown; the whites lost nine men. The Kentuckians brought home 163 horses and a considerable quantity of plunder all of which when auctioned off amounted to about £1,500. The invaders also did great damage to the Indian town by applying the firebrand. Trabue's adverse judgment of this campaign reflects a later interpretation of its significance which does not square with contemporary opinion.

5. The "Hard Winter" of 1779-1780

1. Moses McIlwain was a native of Ireland. Marginal citation by Trabue: See *Western Christian Adv[ocate,* Cincinnati, May 8, 1835], Vol. 2d, p. 5.

2. On April 17, 1779 (two months before he left for the West), Ambrose White received from his father a gift of one hundred acres of land on the waters of Little Otter River.

3. Colonel Daniel Brodhead, who was located at Fort Pitt, was the commander of the Western Department of the Continental Army from April 1779 until September 1781. This officer may have been the "Mr. Broadhead," whom Trabue identifies below as a merchant.

4. One account puts the captivity at five and a half years.

5. The following sentence has been erased in the manuscript: "As he had Dressed him self in the highest Indian style and painted like an Indian, they (the family) yelld out, not imaging what that Indian came to their house for."

6. His home was on Elkhorn Creek about five miles below Frankfort.

7. The Land Act of 1779 established a four-member commission to determine the land claims of residents in Kentucky County.

8. One newcomer estimated that nearly three thousand persons arrived in Kentucky during the fall of 1779.

9. The status of Daniel and his brother James as commissaries during 1780 is unclear, but in April they were members of the militia company in the St. Asaph's district of Kentucky County.

10. In Richmond on February 16, 1780, James Trabue, as the purchasing commissary for Kentucky County, was reimbursed the sum of £1,677.4.5 for provisions furnished the militia.

11. The following cancellation occurs in the manuscript: "as their would be a vast Many people out hear on the account of the land office being opined next spring. It was quite likely our Old neighbours and Relations—some of them—might be out hear. James Foster, who Marryed my Aunt, Moved out and stoped at Logan's Fort. George S. Smith, whose Father had maryed another of my Aunts, also came out to this Fort. Foster and Smith boath Tryed to buoy corn but could git but very little."

James Foster was the husband of Martha Dupuy, a sister of Daniel's mother. George Stokes Smith (d. 1809) was the son of Thomas Smith and Magdelaine Trabue Guerrant Smith of Powhatan County. Each of his parents had been married previously. His mother was a sister of Daniel Trabue's father. George S. Smith was among the group of Baptist preachers brought up in Dupuy's Meetinghouse in Cumberland (later Powhatan) County, Virginia. In time he would help to organize the Elkhorn Baptist Association, advocate emancipation, and sit in the Kentucky Constitutional Convention of 1792.

12. The following spring Jeffery Davies and William Maxey were living in the district of St. Asaph's, in which Logan's Fort was located.

13. Chaplin River is a tributary of Beech Fork, which in turn flows into Rolling Fork of Salt River.

14. The habit of wild turkeys to roost in flocks on the bare branches of trees made it easier for them to be discovered by hunters. Audubon reports that these birds, perched on tree roosts in the moonlight, would often endure the repetitive fire of a rifle without flight. In this way an entire flock might be readily destroyed.

15. Tuckahoe was the name applied to eastern Virginians to distinguish them from western Virginians, who were called "Quo'he's."

16. When Dr. William Fleming visited Bullitts Lick on November 13, 1779, he described it as "perhaps the best Salt Springs" in Kentucky. He found there an area of many acres excavated for twelve or so feet. Further digging produced a hole in which salt water would rise. The boiling of some three thousand gallons of this water yielded about three and a half bushels of salt.

17. Late in November salt was selling near the Falls for $200 per bushel—the wage for ten days' work.

18. A traveler from the Falls of the Ohio to Harrodsburg recorded the winter's first snow as falling during the night of November 28-29.

19. A snowstorm occurred at Harrodsburg on December 5-6. At Logan's Fort it rained on the eleventh and twelfth and snowed the next two days, the night of the fourteenth-fifteenth being excessively cold with a hard frost. A snow fell on Boonesborough during the evening of the seventeenth, and the Kentucky River froze over two days later and was solid enough to support the weight of horses by the last day of the year. Cumberland River was frozen over in eastern Kentucky from January 6 through February 13, causing Dr. Thomas Walker and his associates who were surveying the Virginia-North Carolina border to "lay still" in a riverside camp.

20. During cold, snowy seasons with the surface of the snow frozen to a crust, wild turkeys often stayed on their perches and abstained from eating for several days at a time.

21. Gilberts Creek heads up in Garrard County east of Lancaster and flows some seven miles into Dix River in Lincoln County.

22. In mid-autumn 1779 corn had sold for $30 per bushel at Harrodsburg. Four weeks later it could not be bought for $50 on Bear Grass Creek near the Falls of the Ohio, and by the middle of January 1780 the price had jumped to $165. Three and a half months later it had fallen to $30.

23. The most common illnesses observed by Dr. William Fleming during this winter in Kentucky were colds, fevers, and ulcers on the throat, tongue, and glands. Some persons were seized with pains in the head, back, and chest, accompanied with a looseness of the bowels and the elimination of green or black bilious matter. The constant diet of corn bread and smoked, unsalted buffalo meat accounted for a good deal of these disorders, the doctor argued.

24. By the first of May 1780, the supply of corn at Louisville had been replenished by the arrival that spring of almost three hundred large boats, bringing grain and additional settlers for the Kentucky stations.

25. Bartholomew Dupuy was the second child of John James Dupuy and Susanne Lavillain. His home was in Amelia County. Five years later he moved permanently to Kentucky with his family.

26. George Milpon Smith (1747-1820), the eldest son of Thomas Smith and his first wife, succeeded John Dupuy as pastor of Dupuy's Meetinghouse in Powhatan County. He moved to Kentucky in 1804. His wife was Judith Guerrant, a first cousin of Daniel Trabue.

27. Dix (then written Dicks) River begins in Rockcastle County and flows northwestward to join the Kentucky.

28. Dupuy's Meetinghouse sheltered a Separate Baptist church located on the farm of John Dupuy in the lower part of Powhatan County. Dupuy, a brother of Daniel Trabue's mother, had been the chief organizer of the congregation in 1771, when the area was part of Cumberland County. After David Tinsley, the first pastor of the church, was thrown into

the Chesterfield prison in 1774, John Dupuy was ordained as a minister and installed in that office. Ten years later, in preparation for his moving to Kentucky, Dupuy deeded to the church the acre on which the meetinghouse stood.

29. The expression "or 3" is expunged at this point.

30. Paint Lick Creek, flowing northwesterly into the Kentucky River, forms the boundary between the present-day counties of Garrard and Madison.

6. The Captivity and Escape of Two Trabue Brothers

1. Samuel Sherwin was appointed on April 23, 1778, a colonel in the militia of Amelia County.

2. John Floyd (1750-1783) had arrived on Bear Grass Creek in present Jefferson County on November 8, 1779. A former surveyor for the Transylvania Company, Floyd would become next year the county lieutenant of the newly created Jefferson County.

3. Linn's Station was located on Floyds Fork of Salt River in the region of the Falls of the Ohio.

4. John May had been appointed in 1777 surveyor of Kentucky County at the first session of its county court.

5. Wilson's Station was situated on a tributary of Salt River about two miles northwest of Harrodsburg. The county surveyor opened his office there on May 1, 1780.

6. In the procedure of securing a land patent the step of making an entry followed the purchase of a land warrant and preceded the survey of the tract by a county official.

7. By lottery on the afternoon of May 4, 1780, the order was determined by which entries could be made with the county surveyor by the three hundred persons whose land warrants bore the earliest date of issue. Then schedules were set for holders of warrants issued on each succeeding day.

8. Between this initial trip to Wilson's Station and a visit to Ruddell's Station the following month, James entered in his own name 2,600 acres on May 25 and 3,050 on June 8.

9. Not until May 9 did the surveyor begin to receive entries for land. Many people returned home because they had become impatient with the slow pace at which the land office was functioning; others left because no food could be bought at the station.

10. Under the Land Act of 1779 the Virginia Land Commission, meeting at Harrodsburg on February 4, 1780, had sanctioned Daniel's preemption of a four-hundred-acre tract on the north bank of Salt River. The youth was entitled to this option by virtue of a settlement he had made two years earlier at this site four miles from Floyds Fork in the direction of Brashears Creek. The acreage included a cabin at the head of a spring. This tract was entered at Wilson's Station on June 1, 1780; however, it was not surveyed until four years later. Daniel's additional two thousand acres cannot now be identified.

11. In December 1781, sometime after James Trabue had escaped from his captivity in Canada, he petitioned the Virginia legislature that the Kentucky people from whom he as a purchasing commissary had bought produce be "allowed the depreciation upon the certificates given by him since his releasement." Both houses resolved that his request was "reasonable" and that commissioners be appointed to settle these citizens' claims against the state. *Journal of House of Delegates of the Commonwealth of Virginia . . . Held in . . . October, in the Year of Our Lord One Thousand Seven Hundred and Eighty-one* (Richmond, Va., 1828), pp. 36, 50, 51, 64.

12. Ruddell's Station, settled in April 1779, was located on the right bank of the South Fork of Licking River. The site is about three miles below the point at which Hinkston and Stoner creeks merge to form the South Fork.

13. These Indians, commanded by Captain Alexander McKee, were an advance party.

14. Captain Henry Bird, leader of a band of some 700 Indians and 150 white men, reached the fort around noon with two pieces of light artillery—a three-pounder and a six-pounder—and with the balance of his force.

15. The smaller gun was used two times; the threat of firing the larger cannon was enough to effect a surrender.

16. John Hinkston had first settled at the site of Ruddell's Station in 1775 but abandoned it in July the following year.

17. Trabue means, of course, that the majority petitioned the British officer to accept their capitulation.

18. This post, situated on Stoner Creek, fell on the twenty-sixth.

19. Logan, who was to be second in command, issued orders on July 17, 1780, that four out of every five men in each militia company in Kentucky County be chosen to serve. Colonel Clark set the place of rendezvous at the mouth of Licking River, where the force of nearly one thousand men crossed the Ohio on August 1.

20. William Trabue was one of some four hundred Virginia Continentals who became prisoners of war at the fall of Charlestown.

21. Charles Scott (1739?-1813), a native of Virginia, was promoted to the rank of brigadier general in the Continental Army in 1777. Sent by Washington to reinforce General Benjamin Lincoln, Scott was among the patriots captured at Charlestown, South Carolina, which fell on May 12, 1780, to the British army led by Sir Henry Clinton.

22. Daniel's mother owned eighteen slaves in 1783.

23. James Knox, a native of Augusta County, had been a leader of the Long Hunters in 1770-1771. During the Revolutionary War he commanded a unit of riflemen and served under General Daniel Morgan. On his latest trip into Kentucky, Knox had arrived at Logan's Fort on April 23.

24. Colonel Thomas Marshall, father of Chief Justice John Marshall, had been given leave from his Virginia artillery regiment in 1780 to visit Kentucky and locate land.

25. Crab Orchard was in the eighteenth century a large grove of crab-apple trees located near some big springs in the eastern valley of Dix River. This site, in present Lincoln County, had long been a favorite camping spot for hunters.

26. A folk word meaning "considerable" or "large."

27. This military action occurred later—on October 7, 1780—at Kings Mountain just inside the South Carolina border some thirty miles west of Charlotte. Leading a nine hundred-man force composed mainly of Loyalist militiamen, British Major Patrick Ferguson (1744-1780) set up camp on this elevated ridge, rising sixty feet above the surrounding area. There he was attacked in mid-afternoon by eighteen hundred patriots from the Virginia-Carolina frontier. Within an hour the Tories were completely destroyed—Ferguson lay dead and all his men had been killed or captured. Kings Mountain was a great hour for the patriot cause and marked the turning point of the war in the South.

28. Only seventy-five Loyalists were jailed at New London in the summer of 1780. They had been arrested by mounted infantrymen from Washington and Montgomery counties who swept over the western Virginia-Carolina borderland. Some of these men were court-martialed; others were tried by the Bedford County Court. The jailer had a full house for about a month, during which he was compelled to rent extra quarters and employ additional guards.

29. During 1780 twenty-seven men were charged in Bedford County Court with high treason or sedition. Eighteen persons were examined for the crime of high treason at New London. One man, who pleaded not guilty, was discharged because no witness appeared against him. The others were ordered to be tried before the General Court in Richmond. Nine persons were accused with violation of a law covering such acts as asserting the power of the British government, opposing the authority of the new Virginia state government, or

encouraging people not to enlist in the military service of the commonwealth. Two of these men were found not guilty; the rest were punished by fines and jail sentences. Bedford County (Va.) Court Order Book 6 (microfilm, Virginia State Library), pp. 287, 288-89, 290, 294, 295, 296, 298-99, 300, 301, 302, 303, 307, 311, 320; Hening, *Statutes*, 9: 168, 170-71.

30. The patriots captured at Charlestown numbered 2,571 regulars and about 1,000 militiamen and armed civilians—the greatest loss of Americans in any operation during the Revolution.

31. Earl Charles Cornwallis (1738-1805), a controversial leader during most of the American Revolution, was by April 1778 second in command to the British commander-in-chief in North America.

32. The spirit of disaffection was quite widespread in southwestern Virginia. "Many hundreds" of frontiersmen in Bedford, Henry, Montgomery, and Washington counties had actually enlisted in the British army and sworn allegiance to the king.

33. Sixteen of the Bedford men who were committed to the public jail at Richmond awaiting trial before the General Court were named in October 1780 in a legislative act which extended amnesty to them if they took an oath of allegiance to the new Virginia government. This pardon applied also to the disaffected in five other southwestern counties. Five months later some of the "Conspirators" in Bedford still refused to accept this clemency, because their lawyers had told them that they had committed no offense punishable under the law. In Bedford County some militiamen had been sentenced by court-martial to six-month tours of military duty. Most of these "Disaffected and Disobedient Wretches," having "Broke Jail" or escaped from their guards, banded together and caused considerable disturbance in the county. About forty of the Bedfordites who had enlisted in the summer of 1780 for eighteen-month periods of service deserted soon thereafter.

34. Horatio Gates (1728-1806) was appointed by the Continental Congress on July 13, 1780, to command the Southern Department.

35. After the British victory at Charlestown, Clinton hurried back to New York, leaving Cornwallis in command in the South.

36. Some seven hundred Virginia militiamen, commanded by General Edward Stevens, joined Gates's army on August 14 at Rugeley's Mill, South Carolina.

37. The Virginia regiments left Washington's army at Morristown, New Jersey, on December 9, 1779, under Brigadier General William Woodford, and arrived at Charlestown on April 6.

38. The siege of Charlestown began April 1 and continued until May 12, when Lincoln surrendered.

39. After the war Scott lived in Woodford County about a mile up the Kentucky River from Trabue's farm on Grier Creek.

40. Here Trabue uses an earlier spelling of the word *corpse*.

41. At Camden, South Carolina, on August 16, 1780, Gates suffered a complete defeat at the hands of a twenty-six-year-old British commander, Francis Rawdon-Hastings. As Charles Lee had warned, Gates's northern laurels now turned to southern willows.

42. Samuel Ewing, Sr., a resident of Montgomery County, was appointed an appraiser of an estate on August 5, 1779. His son Samuel, Jr., was sworn into office as a justice of the peace on the same day. It is impossible to determine whether Trabue visited the elder or the younger.

43. Cripple Creek, a western tributary of the New River, lies in the southern and southeastern parts of present Wythe and Smythe counties, respectively.

44. The reference here seems to be to Sir Henry Clinton (1738?-1795), British victor at Charlestown; thus, Trabue garbles his story. He probably did not mean James Clinton (1733-1812), the Continental general who commanded the Northern Department in 1780.

45. General William Campbell (1745-1781) of Washington County had acquired

considerable notoriety as an opponent of Toryism in southwestern Virginia. This fiercely patriotic frontiersman served as the commanding general of one of the three Virginia militia brigades in Lafayette's army.

46. The Block House, built around 1777 by John Anderson, marked the beginning of the Wilderness Road in the East. Being the last station before the Clinch Mountain, it was the place where travelers congregated to form parties headed for the West. Facing eastward, the post stood in a narrow valley (in present Scott County) two miles east of the ford over the North Fork of the Holston.

47. Here Trabue cancels the remaining twelve lines of this page of his manuscript and the first twenty-two lines of the next page. The succeeding portion of the narrative is a revision of the expunged part.

48. The touchhole was the vent in the breech of an eighteenth-century firearm through which the charge was ignited.

49. If the camp had been pitched at Cumberland Ford, this stream was Straight Creek, near present-day Pineville, Kentucky.

50. In his petition of December 1781 to the Virginia legislature James Trabue indicated that the papers relative to his public duty as a purchasing commissary had been seized by the Indians and not returned to him.

51. Alexander Noel had been captured by Indians on the Kentucky River in June 1780 and taken to Montreal.

52. The cartridge box was usually a leathern pouch containing a block of wood in which holes had been bored for holding cartridges.

53. The term Hessian identifies all foreign mercenaries who served the British king during the Revolution. It arose from the name of the tiny principality of Hesse-Cassel, which supplied more than half of the thirty thousand Germans sent to American battlefields.

54. Fort Ticonderoga, located on the west bank of Lake Champlain in northeastern New York, had changed hands twice during the war by the time of Gates's victory at Saratoga in 1777. After that disaster for the crown, the British garrison at the fort had been evacuated into Canada.

55. James's first pass was signed by Brigadier General Ethan Allen on October 19, 1780, at Castleton, Vermont. Subsequent passes and permits for rations indicate the following route homeward:

Bennington, [Vermont]	October [n.d.]
Albany	24
West Point	31
[New York City]	November 2
Trenton	5
Philadelphia	7
Alexandria, [Virginia]	14
Richmond	19

Passes, in James Trabue Heirs, Application, 1842, Land Bounty File, Rejected Claims, Folder 18, Box 52, Virginia State Library.

56. Here Trabue marks out the words "to Virginia."

57. Noel lived then at Bryan's Station about five miles northeast of Lexington.

58. A group of some sixteen men went to buy corn at the Falls of Ohio about June 1780.

59. Lee's Town was located on the east bank of the Kentucky River one mile below present Frankfort.

60. Five men were wounded.

61. Alexander Noel was living in 1803 on Russell Creek in Adair County, Kentucky, near the home of Trabue.

62. At this point in the manuscript the clause "he was wounded bad in one arm" originally appeared.

7. Militia Service in Old Virginia

1. This British force of twelve hundred men was commanded by Benedict Arnold. He sailed up the James and disembarked his men at Westover on the fourth. They marched the twenty-six miles to Richmond, camping overnight at Four Mile Creek and entering the town unopposed the next day.

2. In 1780 Richmond had replaced Williamsburg as the capital of the new state. Thomas Jefferson was serving his second one-year term as governor.

3. Manchester, formerly called Rocky Ridge, was incorporated as a town in 1769.

4. Governor Jefferson had called out a portion of the militia of certain counties on January 2 to counter the expected invasion. When the threat became more imminent, two days later he summoned all the militia of the adjacent counties, urging them to come in small groups without waiting for their companies to form.

5. On the fifth the militia in the Richmond area numbered two hundred—too few to be very effective against Arnold's forces. Five days later the patriot units north of the James had increased to about nine hundred men; "pretty considerable numbers" were located across the river.

6. Arnold offered to spare Richmond if his ships were unmolested while they came up from Westover and carried away the Virginians' tobacco. Jefferson refused, even though he could have done little to stop the vessels. It was then that much property, public and private, was destroyed in the capital. The enemy left on the sixth and embarked on the tenth at Westover for Portsmouth, where they spent the rest of the winter.

7. Robert Haskins (1732-1804), colonel in the militia, had taken Virginia's new oath of allegiance on August 1, 1777. He resigned this post sometime before April 6, 1781.

8. The governor recommended on January 29 that the Chesterfield men should be among the groups that were first discharged.

9. The British did not return to the vicinity of the capital until April. The reference here is probably to the expected advance of Lord Cornwallis upon Richmond. He had already chased the army of General Nathanael Greene out of North Carolina and over the Dan River into southern Virginia. Jefferson received intelligence to this effect on February 18 and promptly ordered the entire militia of five counties to join Greene's forces. He also called all militiamen in Chesterfield and Dinwiddie counties to gather at their respective rendezvous. Apparently Trabue's memory lets him mistakenly identify some events connected with Arnold's January incursion as having happened during this February tour of duty.

10. Trabue was perhaps among the 280 men whom the governor ordered on the nineteenth to assemble at Watkins' Mills in Chesterfield County.

11. By 1781 Virginia's ability to repel invasion had been greatly reduced by the following factors: a lessening of enthusiasm for liberty, inefficient state administrative procedures, constitutional restraints on gubernatorial action, and almost complete dependence on the militia for defense.

12. The reference here is to the destruction in January of the vital works near Westham, seven miles upstream from Richmond. They were Arnold's chief objectives and included an iron foundry, a gunpowder factory, and a boring mill.

13. Colonel William Davies of the Tenth Virginia Continental Regiment was the commanding officer of a replacement depot set up at Chesterfield Courthouse by the Continental Army in 1780.

14. Captain Richard Crump of Powhatan County was recommended to the militia rank of major on June 20, 1781, by the county court. Earlier that year he had been on duty for a few weeks in Chesterfield County.

15. At times during the British invasion of the James River area it was necessary to impress boats for the purpose of transporting troops across the stream.

16. Trabue was probably among the 164 men from Chesterfield County who were ordered on March 9 to go as reinforcements to the army of General John Peter Gabriel Muhlenberg (1746-1807), which had been stationed for some time in the Portsmouth area.

17. Edward Moseley was a militia captain in Chesterfield County.

18. The Dismal Swamp sits astride the Virginia-North Carolina border southwest of Norfolk and Portsmouth.

19. In the early months of 1781 General Muhlenberg, a former Lutheran pastor, was second in command in Virginia. Baron von Steuben, his superior, proposed to besiege Arnold's army at Portsmouth and thus prevent its incursion by land into the region below the James.

20. Whickering, a colloquialism for "neighing" or "whinnying."

21. Two men by the name of William Wooldridge are listed in the census of 1783 for Chesterfield County.

22. In 1781 a standing rule of the Virginia militia required that a wagon be sent with every seventy-five men.

23. Rockbridge and Augusta counties, lying west of the Blue Ridge, were on the frontier, from which it was the custom to recruit riflemen.

24. Virginia law allowed a militiaman to provide a substitute to serve in his stead, provided they were both from the same county. Also a man could volunteer to fill the place of a militiaman who had been called to duty.

25. This sentence originally began with the following expunged portion: "By this time Lord Corn wallis came from the south and Joined the other."

26. An enemy force of about twenty-five hundred embarked at Portsmouth on April 18 and sailed up the James, stopping here and there on missions of destruction.

27. The previous month Major General William Phillips (1731?-1781) had arrived in Virginia to supersede Arnold as commander of the British army there.

28. Brigadier General Benedict Arnold (1741-1801), the traitor and former Continental general, had been in command in Virginia from December 1780 until the following March.

29. Petersburg, located in Dinwiddie County, was an important center of tobacco trade. In his pension declaration Trabue recorded: "The enemy advanced and we retreated to Petersburg where we were reinforced by Baron Stuben, and where an engagement ensued." Adair County, Ky., Aug. 6, 1832, p. 4.

30. Appomattox River is a tributary of the James.

31. City Point is now known as Hopewell. The British disembarked there on April 24.

32. At Guilford Courthouse, North Carolina, Lord Cornwallis had won a Pyrrhic victory over Major General Nathanael Greene on March 15, 1781.

33. In addition to a knapsack of thick linen, each militiaman was expected to furnish his own gun, a bayonet and belt, a cartridge box, a wooden canteen with strap, a tomahawk, and a blanket.

34. Pocahontas Bridge spanned the Appomattox.

35. To Chesterfield and adjacent counties had gone out a plea for two hundred volunteer cavalrymen to augment the forces of von Steuben at Petersburg. These men were needed for a one-month tour to help prevent Phillips's army from joining Cornwallis in North Carolina.

36. Five days earlier the governor had ordered the entire militia of Chesterfield County to report immediately to Petersburg or Manchester.

37. Issuing rum to soldiers before they went into battle violated Virginia regulations for the use of spirits by troops. Following the Continental rule, the State Council had limited their use to men on long marches and on fatigue and wet-weather duty.

38. The size of each army was considerably smaller; Phillips's soldiers numbered about twenty-five hundred, while Muhlenberg commanded about one thousand militiamen.

39. Bakers Hill in present-day Colonial Heights.

40. A Hessian unit hit the flank of the Virginians' outpost line and drove it back to the

main defensive position which the patriots had set up on an elevation near the village of Blandford about a mile east of Petersburg.

41. With the support of artillery the main British force marched against the patriot position, while other units carried out a turning movement against Muhlenberg's right flank.

42. This retreat resulted from the turning movement executed by the British and their use of artillery.

43. The British moved cautiously, taking two hours to cover the first mile.

44. Ralph Faulkner.

45. Gabriel Vest.

46. Trabue greatly exaggerates British losses. Some sixty patriots were killed or wounded; the enemy probably lost about the same number of men.

47. It was the Virginians who retreated that day, leaving Petersburg to the mercy of the enemy.

48. William Boyce.

49. Courthouse is used here to indicate the county seat.

50. Lord Cornwallis did not join Philips's army at Petersburg until May 20, after a difficult march of 225 miles from Wilmington, North Carolina.

51. Lieutenant Colonel Banastre "Bloody" Tarleton (1754-1833), the leader of Cornwallis's light cavalry in the South, acquired a reputation for bold strikes against patriot forces and for ruthless treatment of civilians. His unit of horsemen was called the British Legion.

52. In 1783 Edward Moseley owned eighteen slaves.

53. Baron Friedrich Wilhelm Augustus von Steuben (1730-1794), the Prussian inspector general of the Continental Army, introduced a system of drilling.

54. The Falling Creek Church was perhaps the house of worship in Manchester Parish, which comprised the upper portion of Chesterfield County.

55. Meeting no resistance upon its arrival at the village, Phillips's main army promptly burned the barracks of the Continental replacement depot, the county's prisons for debtors and felons, and the interior of the courthouse. The public records were preserved, however, by the clerk's prior removal of them from his office.

56. The "Coal Pits" were situated about ten miles above Manchester.

57. This militia unit from Chesterfield County numbered 400 men according to a British report but only 250 according to a patriot story recorded by a Scottish doctor.

58. This plantation was situated about two miles southwest of Archibald Cary's grist mill on Falling Creek, a tributary of the James.

59. Colonel Tarleton and three hundred of his cavalry surprised the Virginians because their mounted sentinels stationed in advance of the pickets had been intercepted.

60. Lewis Sublett (1759-1830), a native of Chesterfield County, was the husband of Daniel's sister Mary.

61. Lafayette reported that the British killed six and captured about forty men but made no mention of the materiel.

62. Martin Railey.

63. Marie Gilbert du Motier, Marquis de Lafayette (1757-1834). An example of the contemporary American usage of Lafayette's name—such as Trabue here makes—is the naming of Fayette County, Virginia (now Kentucky), in 1780.

64. Anthony Wayne (1745-1796), an impetuous Pennsylvania tanner who had proved his military mettle early in the Revolution, had left York in the Quaker State on May 26 with some eight hundred men to be joined to Lafayette's forces.

65. Raccoon Ford on the Rapidan between Culpeper and Orange counties is located twenty-seven miles by a straight line above Fredericksburg. Lafayette moved southward over this ford on June 6 and Wayne crossed it two days later. Their juncture occurred on the tenth, probably on the South Anna River.

66. The earl was at Petersburg during May 20-24.

67. This meat was probably cured pork, a staple culinary item in Virginia. The poor quality of beef cattle and the absence of means for preserving freshly killed meat led to a widespread dependence upon pork cured by salting and smoking.

68. Cornwallis crossed the James to Westover on May 25 and ordered Tarleton to follow the next day.

8. Wartime Stress on Civilian Life

1. Robert Goode, the second largest slaveholder in the county, had succeeded on April 6, 1781, to the lieutenant colonelcy in the Chesterfield militia, after the resignation of Colonel Robert Haskins.

2. Thomas Jefferson, now nearing the end of his second one-year term as governor of Virginia, left Richmond on May 15; the legislature had adjourned to reconvene on the twenty-fourth in Charlottesville, the seat of Albemarle County.

3. This ferry ran from Manakin Town on the south bank in Powhatan County to the land of Stephen Woodson in Goochland County.

4. That day units of Cornwallis's army moved westward from their camp near Cook's Ford on the North Anna River. Well before daybreak a detachment of 180 dragoons and 70 mounted infantrymen rode out under the command of Tarleton on its famous twenty-four-hour, seventy-mile march to capture Jefferson and the legislators at Charlottesville. As Tarleton's route lay between the North Anna and the South Anna, he did not go as far down as Dandridge's.

Another outfit went out the day before. Cornwallis had ordered Lieutenant Colonel John Graves Simcoe with five hundred rangers to attack the patriot forces under von Steuben located to the southwest at the Point of Fork, where the Rivanna River joins the James. The unit then at Dandridge's was perhaps the van of Cornwallis's army, which was scheduled to move leisurely to the neighborhood of the Point of Fork. There the earl intended to reunite his larger force with the men under Tarleton and Simcoe.

5. Colonel Nathaniel Dandridge lived in Hanover County on the south bank of the South Anna River at the mouth of Goldmine Creek. His plantation, located at a prominent crossroads, was about twenty-three miles northwest of Richmond.

6. John Guerrant, Sr., (1733-1791) was the eldest son of Peter Guerrant and Magdelaine Trabue, a sister of Daniel's father. He was a justice of the peace in Goochland County at this time.

7. John Guerrant, Jr., took the oath as an ensign in the militia of Goochland County on February 15, 1781.

8. Cornwallis's main army, numbering over six thousand men, had left Cook's Ford very early that Sunday morning, moved southward on the route by Scotchtown, and crossed the South Anna River over Ground Squirrel Bridge. His encampment was strung out over several miles of the road south of the river.

9. The name of Tarleton conjured up considerable dread in the mind of the average Virginian in 1781; consequently, it was natural for Trabue to assume that the men who were then abroad were from the British Legion. This mode of thought may account for the fact that the narrator never mentions Simcoe and his rangers.

10. Benjamin Brown's Tavern stood at a prominent crossroads in the northwestern end of Hanover County between the North Anna and the Little rivers. The north-south route led from Anderson's Bridge astride the North Anna to Ground Squirrel Bridge over the South Anna. The intersecting road led westward to Louisa Courthouse.

11. These British horsemen were probably not Tarleton's men but Simcoe's. By early

Monday morning Tarleton's detachment had already arrived at Charlottesville; Simcoe's cavalry reached Point of Fork at noon the next day. In view of the fact that Simcoe's men wore green uniforms like those of Tarleton's Legion, it was difficult for Virginians to distinguish between the dragoons and the mounted rangers. This conjecture concerning the identity of these cavalrymen is grounded in the supposed accuracy of Trabue's memory that he left Chesterfield County on Sunday. If Daniel began his ride, however, on Saturday, he would have arrived at Brown's Ordinary early Sunday morning perhaps shortly after Tarleton's passage there, which occurred betwen 5:00 and 6:00 o'clock.

12. Cornwallis's cavalrymen were routinely instructed to destroy any accumulation of corn and other provisions at a private house, leaving only enough for the family's subsistence. This was to be done lest such abundant stores be converted to military use.

13. Whitby, the estate of Colonel Robert Goode, was located a few miles below Richmond.

14. In his pension declaration, Trabue recorded another mission: "Colo. Goode then petitioned me [to go] with a flag of truce to the enemy to See Some of our prisoners that had been taken at Sutberry's Old field as their friends wanted to let them have Some Money And Clothing, but he Said the flag would not be received if I were not an officer. And for the purpose of performing Said business I was commissioned a Captain by Thomas Jefferson, then Governor of Virginia, which I received with the flag from Goode And performed the business. This was the last Service I done in the Revolution; true it is I was at the Siege of York but was there only as a Suttler on my own business." Adair County, Ky., Aug. 6, 1832, p. 5.

15. The mission of Cornwallis north of the James was primarily to destroy military supplies and not to attack the army of Lafayette. Tarleton and Simcoe's cavalry were the instruments for inflicting fear and loss upon the civilian population.

16. One David Morrisett was listed as a taxpayer in Chesterfield County two years later. One John Thurman of Chesterfield County headed a family of eleven in 1783.

17. Edward Moseley.

18. The will of Virginians to continue their fight for liberty had been severely strained by 1781. A number of factors—including the lack of specie, the depreciation of paper currency, and heavy taxation—accounted for this decline of enthusiasm.

19. After Wayne's Pennsylvanians reached Lafayette on June 10, other detachments were added during the next nine days. General William Campbell of Washington County, Virginia, arrived from the frontier on the thirteenth with 600 riflemen. Baron von Steuben marched into the marquis's camp on the nineteenth with 425 Continentals. In addition some sixty volunteer dragoons had joined the Frenchman's forces.

20. The earl had entered Richmond on June 18 on his march down the James.

21. Lord Cornwallis evacuated the Virginia capital on the morning of the twenty-first.

22. Only Wayne's soldiers went through Richmond; this march took place on the twenty-second some twenty hours after the earl had left. The greater part of the marquis's army in a column accompanied by Lafayette was marching eastward on the north bank of the Chickahominy River.

23. These "Green bushes" may have been the "plumes" mentioned by Colonel St. George Tucker, who describes the Pennsylvania Line as "a splendid and formidable corps." Tucker to his wife, Bottom's Bridge, June 24, 1781, in Charles Washington Coleman, Jr., "The Southern Campaign, 1781: From Guilford Court House to the Siege of York," *Magazine of American History* 7 (Sept. 1881): 206 (hereafter cited as Coleman, "Southern Campaign").

24. The earl's leisurely movement down the James was not a retreat, as Lafayette well knew. The marquis was aware of the fact that both his transportation and his cavalry were too limited to allow him to press Cornwallis very closely. So he followed at a distance. The people in the Virginia countryside, seeing the British moving toward the Chesapeake,

believed that they were in retreat before the Americans; Lafayette promoted this idea in the public mind.

25. That day Wayne had marched his column twenty-two miles.

26. This was Bottom's Bridge over the Chickahominy River, which flows southeastwardly into the James.

27. June.

28. On the following day—June 23—the two columns of Lafayette's army were joined about two miles west of New Kent Courthouse.

29. The preceding twelve words are a substitution for the following expunged material: "Brother Stephen 14 or 15 years old had been helping me in selling spirits. Our mother could not well spair him and I gave him up. Brother Edward had been liveing in Pitsylvania with Joseph Minter, our brother in law, and he came to Chesterfield to see us and he agreed to go with me to camp. He told us."

30. Interpolated sentence.

31. The Rappahannock River lies north of the area where Lafayette's army was then located.

32. Elizabeth Hackney lived in 1783 in the Lower Precinct of Middlesex County.

33. The name Morgan does not appear in the state census of Middlesex County which was taken two years later.

34. This jut of land is called Stingray Point.

35. The Piankatank River lies south of the Rappahannock and also empties into the Chesapeake.

36. The position of this sentence, which is an interpolation, has been altered to allow in the following sentence the pronoun "it" to serve as the subject of the verb "landed."

37. Admiral François Joseph Paul, Comte de Grasse, responded to the pleas of Washington and the Comte de Rochambeau, commander of the French army in America.

38. Yorktown, situated on a thirty-five-foot bluff on the south side of the York River, was the seat of York County.

39. In fact Cornwallis did not begin to settle down at Yorktown until August 2 and de Grasse did not arrive off the Chesapeake until the twenty-sixth.

40. Cornwallis was encamped at Williamsburg from June 25 until July 4.

41. By the time Cornwallis reached Williamsburg, Lafayette's three Virginia militia brigades had actually shrunk to two, because many farmer-soldiers had gone home to harvest their grain.

42. Known as the Battle of Green Spring, this engagement occurred on the afternoon of July 6 in the woods and marsh between the mansion of the Green Spring Farm and the edge of the river directly opposite the northern end of Jamestown Island.

43. Exactly the opposite took place. A nine-hundred-man unit of Lafayette's army led by Anthony Wayne was surprised late in the afternoon by Cornwallis's entire force, which lay in wait for the Allies. Reacting admirably, Wayne attacked and for fifteen minutes held the enemy at bay. Lafayette was able to extract his army and effect an orderly retreat. By midnight he was back at Chickahominy Church, from which he had departed that morning. The action was clearly a defeat for the marquis.

44. Trabue errs about this detail. The earl crossed to the south bank of the James on July 7 and went down on that side of the river to Cobham and Suffolk and later to Portsmouth.

45. Skipping over two months of Lafayette's movements from the James as far north as the area between the Mattapony and the Pamunkey rivers, Trabue apparently records here the union of the forces of the marquis at Williamsburg on September 4. He was joined four days later by 3,100 marines disembarked at Jamestown from Admiral de Grasse's fleet. Camping in and around Williamsburg, this combined army made a grand appearance when it paraded up and down the Duke of Gloucester Street.

9. Yorktown and War's End

1. In August, on his authority as a Continental commander, Lafayette ordered out the militia in several Virginia counties.

2. The reference here is apparently to the movement of the American and French forces on the extremely hot day of September 28 from Williamsburg to their camp below Yorktown, a distance of about twelve miles. The British fortifications were now invested. This marked the first phase of the formal siege of Yorktown—the only one conducted during the Revolutionary War according to the rules of Marshal Sébastien de Vauban (1633-1707) and the last of its type in history.

3. On September 14 General Washington and a few aides reached Williamsburg, thus terminating his long march from New York begun August 19. Almost all of Rochambeau's troops and a detachment of twenty-five hundred from the Continental Army had arrived on the peninsula by the last day of September. Washington assumed command of the combined Continental and French armies.

4. Rochambeau's wagon train, which did not reach Williamsburg until October 6, brought with it eight hundred oxen from the North.

5. These inner lines of defense, set rather close to the town, included some sixty-five guns distributed among fourteen batteries and ten redoubts. This fortification was anchored on the river bank above and below Yorktown with redoubts, so as to enclose the village. The principal fort, called the "horn work," bestrode the Hampton Road. To the south of the town were located several outworks, guarding its approaches.

6. Pigeon Hill, part of the half-mile plain between the heads of Wormeleys and Yorktown creeks, was the site of three redoubts, which the British evacuated without contest on the night of September 29-30.

7. A gabion was fashioned by driving slender poles in the ground in a circle about two feet in diameter and weaving them compactly with smaller branches from trees. The open-ended, cylindrical basket thus formed was used in constructing breastworks. Fascines (bundles of sticks for making earthworks and filling trenches) and *saucissons* (long fascines) were also put together, but the context does not suggest that Trabue had these in mind.

8. Usually cast from bronze, the eighteenth-century mortar had a trajectory which caused the projectile to clear high obstacles and to descend upon the target from above.

9. This word replaces the expunged word *waggon*.

10. Entrenching tools uncovered at Yorktown include shovels, picks, and mattocks.

11. These preliminaries signaled that the time had come to open the first parallel, which conventional siegecraft specified should be dug six hundred yards from the enemy's fortification. Locating the route of this trench and marking it on the ground by the use of pine laths had been started the previous night (October 5-6), but a hard rain had stopped the work.

12. One soldier noted that three or more rows of gabions were used—set closely together along the front boundary of the trench.

13. Gloucester was situated on a point of land across the river from Yorktown. British occupation of the two villages had occurred simultaneously. Assisted by Virginia militia, French forces began a siege at Gloucester on September 27.

14. I.e., the one before Yorktown.

15. Only the right of the parallel ran to the river, because its left began at a redoubt on Pigeon Hill.

16. Trabue's estimate is an exaggeration—roughly double the length of the trench, which was 2,000 yards.

17. Only seven batteries with at least forty-six artillery pieces were built in connection with the first parallel.

18. This phonetic spelling of the word *bombs* represents its common pronunciation in Trabue's day.

19. The French began their bombardment of Yorktown at 3:00 P.M. on the ninth. Two hours later the first American guns were fired.

20. Trabue's use of the term *bombshells* in the early nineteenth century came at a time when the older word *bomb* was gradually being replaced by the word *shell*. This explosive type of projectile was highly effective for general bombardment and for the destruction of earthworks and other fortifications such as the British had erected at Yorktown.

21. This term replaces the expunged word *bottom*.

22. This eighteenth-century type of bomb was a cast-iron, hollow sphere, which was filled with powder only shortly before use. It had a projecting neck to accommodate a fuse—a wooden tube whose bore had a diamenter of one-fourth of an inch and into which was tamped a powder composition. In order to provide a larger surface for ignition, the head of the fuse was hollowed out; this area was filled with fine powder dampened with alcohol. The timing of the fuse was controlled either by sawing off its lower end to secure the correct length or by drilling a small hole at the right spot along the tube to allow the fire to flash out at the proper moment. At the time of firing, the fuse was forced into the neck of the bomb until only two-tenths of an inch was exposed. It was the burning of this fuse which so spectacularly illumined the bomb's nightly course across the sky.

23. That morning by daybreak the Allies put several twenty-four-pounders into operation—the French, four; the Americans, at least nine.

24. By October 7 two British cavalry units had killed at least twelve hundred horses because no feed was available.

25. Trabue's memory plays hob with him in connection with the method by which Cornwallis's proposal to surrender was delivered. Between 9:00 and 10:00 A.M. a red-coated drummer appeared on the parapet of the British horn work and beat a parley. At the same time an officer stepped from the fortification with a white handkerchief. The firing ceased; an American ran forward, blindfolded the Britisher, and conducted him to a house behind the lines. From there the letter he bore was sent by a rider to Washington.

26. This initial communication from Cornwallis in regard to his capitulation is in the George Washington Papers, Library of Congress.

27. After Washington received the first letter, the two generals exchanged correspondence that day and again the next. They agreed to open a treaty of capitulation.

28. On the eighteenth throughout most of the day and until nearly midnight, terms of surrender were negotiated by representatives of the two armies. The next day Washington altered the articles of capitulation as he saw fit and informed Cornwallis that he expected to have them signed by 11:00 that morning. The British army would march from the fort at 2:00 P.M. for the public ceremony of surrender.

29. The proceedings began at 2:00 P.M. as Washington had directed.

30. On the other hand, Colonel Henry "Light-Horse Harry" Lee was impressed that day by the "universal silence" that prevailed among "the vast concourse."

31. Probably an apocryphal story.

32. One-half of the British prisoners were destined for Winchester, the seat of Frederick County, Virginia; the other for Frederick Town in Maryland.

33. This word replaces the term *regular*.

34. Common; rife; prevalent.

35. John Trabue, eldest son of Jacob (an uncle of Daniel Trabue), was a resident of Chesterfield County. In February 1781 he became a lieutenant in the Continental service and later was awarded 2,666 2/3 acres of Kentucky land, the quantity to which an officer of his rank was entitled.

36. In view of the fact that Trabue left the Allied camp on October 21—the day of the

prisoners' departure from Yorktown—he may have visited the British fort late in the afternoon of the surrender rather than on the twentieth. The latter day was taken up by a trip to Williamsburg to purchase rum and by the sale of that commodity in the camp.

37. Trabue cancels this incorrect spelling of the word *abatis*, apparently realizing he had chosen the wrong term.

38. When "Secretary" Thomas Nelson abandoned his residence in Yorktown on October 10 and came into the Allied lines, he reported that Cornwallis was living underground in a grotto constructed at the lower end of the Virginian's garden.

39. Spanish dollars circulated extensively in eighteenth-century British America.

40. Sometime in October at Yorktown, Joseph Plumb Martin of the Corps of Sappers and Miners paid $1,200 in Continental paper (then worth $1 Spanish) for a quart of rum.

41. A French crown had the equivalent value of five shillings; hence, before the sutler advanced his price, he was obligated to return a shilling in change to each customer offering such a Gallic coin. The man who presented a Spanish dollar for a quart of rum got the better bargain because his money was worth only four shillings.

42. Trabue means that preparations were made to start for Winchester the next morning—the twenty-first.

43. By giving $10 for the gun, Trabue paid double the amount the rifleman had asked, because this number of Spanish dollars had the equivalent value of £2 (or 40s).

44. Escorted by General Robert Lawson of the Virginia militia, this line of about six thousand prisoners of war left Yorktown at 10:00 A.M. on Sunday, October 21.

45. At this place in the manuscript the following cancellation occurs: "When ever we stoped we would be selling our rum but not fast like we did."

46. The fourth article of the capitulation provided a basis for Virginians' legal claim to their escaped Negro slaves.

47. This estimate is excessively high. The Allied armies numbered approximately 20,000; Cornwallis's forces on land and water, probably over 10,000. The French fleet amounted to some 15,000. It is impossible to tally the Negroes, the Tories, and the spectators from the Virginia countryside.

48. Sir Peyton Skipwith owned at that time some 3,300 acres of land in Mecklenburg County, Virginia.

49. Day's apprehension was ill conceived because the articles of capitulation did not include such a provision. Rather they required that "any property obviously belonging to the inhabitants of these States, in the possession of the garrison, shall be subject to be reclaimed." Article IV, Articles of Capitulation, Oct. 19, 1781, in Henry Phelps Johnston, *The Yorktown Campaign and the Surrender of Cornwallis, 1781* (New York, 1881; reprint ed., New York, 1971), p. 188.

50. Skipwith's farm was located near the mouth of the Dan River, a tributary of the Roanoke in south central Virginia.

51. "Black and All Black" may have been among the fine horses which Tarleton captured in the southern Virginia Piedmont while on a mission to destroy public and private stores during fifteen sultry days of the previous July.

52. Such terror was due in part to the atrocities of the British, especially by Tarleton's cavalry.

53. Virginia enacted a law late in 1781 to adjust the payment of paper debts contracted during 1777-1781. This statute set a monthly scale of depreciation by which to calculate the value of such obligations in terms of gold or silver specie. The following shows the declining worth of Virginia and continental wartime currency for the latter eight months of 1781: May 150 to 1; June 250 to 1; July 400 to 1; August 500 to 1; September 600 to 1; October 700 to 1; November 800 to 1; December 1,000 to 1. Hening, *Statutes*, 10:471-73.

54. Mary Haskins Trabue was born April 11, 1761, in Chesterfield County, Virginia; died September 25, 1830, in Adair County, Kentucky.

55. Robert Trabue married Lucy Waggener in Adair County, Kentucky, on February 9, 1809.
56. The name Wilderness Road as the designation of the route into Kentucky through Cumberland Gap did not come into common usage until sometime after 1779.
57. Thomas Gist was a boatyard superintendent and an assistant commissary in the Illinois Department. He may have been the same Thomas Gist who was commissioned a militia captain in Green County, Kentucky, on August 28, 1799.
58. This was another designation for the Flat Lick.
59. Rockcastle River.
60. Skaggs Creek flows into Rockcastle River near Hazel Patch.
61. Woodford County was not established until three years later.
62. Such a procedure, carried out by men isolated from the protection afforded by government, was commonplace on the American frontier for nearly three centuries.
63. It seems that Daniel, who had been living in Powhatan County (perhaps at his grist mill), had moved back to his mother's house before this recent trek into Kentucky.

10. The Separate Baptists of Revolutionary Virginia

1. William Fleming of Powhatan County.
2. On September 16, 1784, Fleming had agreed to pay Trabue £420 for a water-powered grist mill and 176 acres of land on Swift Creek in Powhatan County.
3. At this place in the manuscript Trabue makes the following cancellation: "for a retail stoore or that."
4. Before its disestablishment in 1784 the Church of England was generally denominated in Virginia by the term Anglican rather than Episcopal.
5. William Webber (1747-1808) and Joseph Anthony, young unordained preachers who were members of Lower Spotsylvania Church, lived in Goochland County when they were invited by some people in the upper end of Chesterfield County to preach among them.
6. Archibald Cary (1721-1787), the senior justice of the peace in Chesterfield County, promoted in that jurisdiction the persecution against the Baptists. Later he served as chairman of the county committee in Chesterfield which encouraged resistance of Britain. He sat in the four revolutionary Virginia conventions in 1775-1776 as a representative of his county.
7. The warrant of arrest charged these two Baptists with "misbehavior by Itenerant preaching in this county being of that Sect of dissenters from the Church of England commonly called anabaptists." Even though they offered on January 4, 1771, to take the oath of allegiance and to subscribe to the test required of dissenting preachers by the English Toleration Act of 1689, the county court held that "their doing so in this Court will not authorise them to preach as the said act directs." Chesterfield County (Va.) Court Order Book 4 (microfilm, Virginia State Library), p. 489.
8. John Dupuy (1737/8-1837) was a son of John James Dupuy. At this time he lived in Cumberland (now Powhatan) County.
9. John Waller (1741-1802), the pastor of Lower Spotsylvania Baptist Church, was on his way to visit the two members of his congregation who were in the Chesterfield prison. Called "Swearing Jack," he had been notorious for his pofanity and gambling and had served on the grand jury which indicted Lewis Craig, the first Baptist preacher confined for preaching in the colony. In time Waller would spend 113 days in four different county jails for the same offense.
10. Thomas Wafford.
11. The prisoners were not released until March 1771. During their confinement they

preached through the prison bars. Many people heard them and some became converts, one of whom was Eleazer Clay, uncle of the future statesman Henry Clay.

12. Ofttimes eighteenth-century Baptists were derisively called Anabaptists—a polemical term applied to certain Protestants of the sixteenth century whose doctrines included believers' baptism, a gathered church, and the separation of church and state.

13. Matthew 18:7; Luke 17:1.

14. To stand while speaking and to take a scriptural text were symbols that constituted a technical definition of preaching.

15. A Baptist church was organized in Chesterfield County on August 23, 1773. These members of John James Trabue's family may have been baptized by that time.

16. Archibald Cary issued warrants for the arrest of at least five of the seven Baptist preachers who were committed to the Chesterfield prison.

17. The requirement by the county court of a recognizance bond was aimed at silencing these dissenters, because refraining from preaching in the county for a year was the condition of nonforfeiture. In view of the fact that Separate Baptists usually refused to give such a bond and chose rather to serve a jail sentence, the plan of the persecutors was thwarted. Thus it was almost impossible to stop their preaching, because upon imprisonment they could still make a pulpit of the jail window. By this way they secured from the common people not only sympathy for their plight but also a hearing for their doctrines.

18. Here Trabue cancels the following account of the arrest of an itinerant Baptist preacher:

> I was one time at a meeting when the sherriff came with a warrent, and it was understood that the sherriff had his instruction not to arrest the preacher untill he had took his text. Mister Easton got up to preach and he sung and prayed very leanthy and prayed very earnestly for the people and the persecutors of christ's gosple and exhorted and was much engaged before he took his text.
>
> And when he took his text, he [the sheriff] went up to Mr. Eastern and the warrent in his hand and said, "I have got a warrent against you."
>
> "For what?" said Mr. Eastern.
>
> "For your preaching in contrary to our order." Mr. Eastern went on preaching.
>
> One of the by standers said, "Let him a lone a while longer. I want to [hear] him some more."
>
> Mr. Eastern spoak so earnestly and feelingly that this was the persecution that the saviour had fore told of that he got the people—a number of them—to Crying, some women crying aloud.
>
> The sheriff stept up to him and said, "Come along with me." Mr. Eastern kept on speaking.
>
> The sherif reached out his hand to take hold of him, and his hand trembled as bad as if [he] had the palsy and pulled him a long. Mr. Eastern kept on a speaking until he got him out of the congregation. The people Did cry and pray for the lord to forgive them as they did not know what they weare a Doing.

After this arrest, probably on May 15, 1772, Augustine Eastin of Goochland was imprisoned in Chesterfield. Appearing before the county court on June 5, he was committed for having "practised preaching . . . as a Baptist not having a license." Chesterfield County (Va.) Court Order Book 5 (microfilm, Virginia State Library), p. 109. Eastin visited Kentucky as early as 1780.

19. When Morgan Edwards, a Philadelphia pastor, visited Virginia in 1772 to collect materials for his projected work on American Baptist history, he learned that Archibald Cary had surrounded the jail with a high wall to hinder Augustine Eastin from preaching through the bars. This obstruction was still in place a year later when John Weatherford

was imprisoned there. Crowds gathered at the wall to hear him and signaled their presence by a handkerchief tied to a pole.

20. The bounds or rules were a designated area of five to ten acres adjacent to the prison in which all inmates (except those committed for treason or a felony) who gave security were allowed to walk for the preservation of their health. For a period of time John Weatherford, committed on June 4, 1773, and Jeremiah Walker, on August 6, had been allowed the bounds at Chesterfield by the influence of Patrick Henry; however, on September 3 a court composed of only three justices revoked this privilege.

21. The circumstances by which these preachers left their Chesterfield cells were more varied than Trabue indicates. Joseph Anthony and William Webber, the first two, spurned the invitation of the jailer to escape; because they had been taken openly, they said, the officials of the court ought to dismiss them in the same way. This was finally done, apparently to stop the influence of Anthony's preaching. In 1773 John Weatherford was released by a court order secured by Patrick Henry. Near the same time Jeremiah Walker made so brilliant a plea before the court that he was discharged under the terms of the Toleration Act.

22. The arrest and imprisonment of their dissenting preachers promoted rather than retarded the Baptist cause in Virginia. This persecution, however, was a double-edged sword. It temporarily hampered the persecuted, but in the long sweep it permanently damaged the cause of the persecutors.

23. A colloquialism meaning to fail; to become exhausted or weary.

24. Trabue may describe himself as a deist in a very general way, meaning that he had scoffed at Christianity, organized religion, and the activities of preachers.

25. James Dupuy (1744/5-1837) was the youngest son of John James Dupuy. He was an early member of the Cumberland (later Powhatan) Church, which worshiped at the meetinghouse erected by his brother John. James and John Dupuy were part of an intimate group of seven converts who often got together to encourage one another in their newly found faith. In time all seven were ordained as Baptist ministers.

26. Benjamin Watkins (1755-1831), a prominent pastor among Virginia Baptists, had matured in his Christian experience as a member of the church at Dupuy's Meetinghouse.

27. Here the cancellation "forgive me" occurs.

28. Trabue's testimony indicates that he had been hearing preachers who stressed the sovereignty of God and the terrors of hellfire and eternal damnation.

29. Notice Trabue's emphasis on the role of the Scriptures in effecting and sustaining his period of anxiety.

30. One Richard Moseley was a resident of Chesterfield County in 1783.

31. Daniel's sensitivity to divine authority had produced a conviction of sin and a state of anxiety which continued five days and which ended in a religious conversion. This period of conviction was considered too brief by the Separates; two months would have been more desirable.

32. John Taylor (1752-1835), a native of Fauquier County, Virginia, moved to Kentucky in 1783. The following year he settled in Woodford County.

11. Postwar Conditions in Trans-Appalachia

1. James Locket, Jr., was a son of James Locket and Susanna Dupuy, a sister of Daniel's mother.

2. Redstone Old Fort was situated on the Monongahela River at present Brownsville, Pennsylvania. From its use in 1752 by the Ohio Company, it had been the port of embarkation west of the Allegheny Divide from which to descend to the Forks of the Ohio.

3. An early eighteenth-century Virginia statute set a penalty of five shillings for traveling on the Sabbath.

4. The term "find us" means "furnish us with provisions."

5. The boat that Trabue and his party bought was perhaps a Kentucky flatboat or "broadhorn," as it was commonly called. This craft, usually some fifteen feet wide and from forty to one hundred feet in length, was capable of carrying twenty to seventy tons.

6. Dead Man's Island was located only fifteen miles below Pittsburgh. Trabue's accident may have occurred at Gallipolis Island, three miles below the mouth of the Kanawha River.

7. Limestone, the present Maysville, seat of Mason County, was the first river port in Kentucky reached by travelers on their way down the Ohio. When the Trabue party arrived there it was only a small village of a few log cabins. Also known as the "Point," it was the chief landing place for people who were moving into the Bluegrass.

8. Grier Creek, located in Woodford County, flows westerly some seven miles into the Kentucky River.

9. Mrs. Richard Searcy was mortally wounded in the summer of 1787 as she returned home after spending the day at a neighbor's house.

10. Established by the Virginia legislature in 1785, this ferry spanned the Kentucky River from Stone Lick on William Steele's land in Fayette County to John Craig's in Lincoln County.

11. By 1789 Stucker had attained a captaincy in the militia of Fayette County.

12. The following sentence is lined out in the manuscript: "And as I lived on the out side and my family so exposed to Danger I Did not go out on."

13. This attack occurred on April 28, 1792, at Innis' Settlement.

14. John Major and Oliver Thomas Major were the husbands, respectively, of Daniel's sisters Judith and Susanna.

15. These men were brothers—Jesse and Hosea Cook.

16. John Finney.

17. At least three men by the name of Dement or Demint lived in Kentucky around 1789-1790.

18. Trabue errs in dating this event. The victory of General Anthony Wayne over the Indians occurred that year, but he did not reach a settlement with them until the next year.

19. Fort Greenville was established on a branch of the Miami River in October 1773 by Wayne as his winter quarters. By the Treaty of Greenville, signed on August 3, 1795, the Indians gave up almost all of present Ohio and a small portion of present Indiana. This agreement meant that the power of the natives of the Old Northwest had been crushed, their connection with Britain cut, and their lands opened to the westwardly advancing whites.

20. Early in 1795 Wayne invited the tribes of the Northwest to treat with him at Fort Greenville. By June braves from several nations began to assemble there. Others arrived the following month.

21. The musket, the most common weapon of the Revolutionary Era, was a smoothbore gun which could be rapidly loaded and discharged but whose accuracy was less than desirable.

22. To allay the apprehension of the visiting Indians, the officers of the post explained to them the army's regulations dealing with reveille, retreat, the observance of the Fourth of July, and various military formations.

23. Fort Jefferson, located south of modern Greenville, Ohio, was the second post constructed by St. Clair during his campaign of 1791.

24. Stephen Ruddell had been found at the Lake of the Woods by Stephen Shelton, who had been engaged for this purpose. Ruddell would not have returned unless the chiefs had required him to do so. General Wayne had written them that he would never leave the

Indians alone as long as any white captives remained with them. Even so, Ruddell refused to budge without his squaw. Abraham Ruddell, who later became a Baptist preacher, had been living at an Indian town far above Mackinaw but returned very willingly when Shelton came for him.

25. Captain Isaac Ruddell had remained in captivity from the fall of his station on June 24, 1780, until his parole at East Bay, Vermont, on November 3, 1782.

26. It is presumed that this person was from the Indian family into which Abraham had been adopted.

27. In 1780 Stephen was probably at least sixteen years old since he had enlisted in his father's militia company the previous year.

28. One observer recalled that after the father had given each of his sons a suit of clothes they were dressed again in their Indian garb within about two hours.

29. The following sentence is lined out in the manuscript: "Her countence altered."

30. The word *Merry* is expunged at this place in the manuscript.

31. General Josiah Harmar (1753-1813), a former officer in the Continental Army, had lost 183 men at the hands of the Indians in October 1790 on the headwaters of the Maumee River. General Arthur St. Clair (1737-1818), a Continental general who was born in Scotland, had been thoroughly beaten by the Miami Indians under Little Turtle on November 4, 1791.

32. At the Battle of Fallen Timbers on the Maumee River, Wayne delivered a crushing blow to the Ohio Indians on August 20, 1794. This encounter was the American response to the Indian victories wrung from Harmar and St. Clair. The battle occurred at a place of defense which the Indians chose where a tornado had left a tangle of trees in its wake. The Maumee originates in northeastern Indiana and flows through Ohio into the western end of Lake Erie at present Toledo. The site of battle was downstream from Fort Defiance, which Wayne had built at the mouth of the Auglaize River.

33. Fort Miami, erected by the British early in 1794 on the Maumee River below the mouth of the Auglaize, was intended to shield Detroit from Wayne's army. In view of the fact that the fort was well inside the territory conveyed to the United States by the Treaty of Paris (1783), Major William Campbell, the British commander, found himself on the horns of a dilemma. If he opened the fort to his Indian allies, he would risk beginning a war with the American states. If he kept the gates shut, he would give the lie to the English promise to aid the Indians.

34. Major Benjamin Price commanded a select battalion of about sixty mounted volunteers, which General Wayne used as a reconnaissance unit. Advancing five miles, the major received such intense fire from Indians hidden in the woods and tall grass that he retreated.

35. After Price retreated, Wayne formed his forces into two lines principally in a dense forest, which spread for miles on his left and for a considerable distance down the Maumee. The Indians grouped themselves into three lines, which extended almost two miles at right angles to the stream.

36. Not only did the British commander refuse to admit the fleeing Indians to the safety of his stockade, but also he failed to come to their aid.

37. The father relented and allowed Stephen to bring his squaw home. They were married in Kentucky much to the disgust of Stephen's younger brother George, who threatened to shoot his new sister-in-law. After about a year Stephen took his wife back into the Indian country, where he remained for some time. Eventually he returned home alone; he was living in Kentucky in 1806 when his father wrote his will, designating this son as an executor of his estate.

38. Trabue was not alone in holding this opinion, because several settlers had sworn to depositions a few years after the fort fell that Ruddell was "inimical to the United States."

39. Sandusky River.

40. The following clause is canceled in the manuscript: "but General Wayn Did Do as well as he could and at last made peace with them."

41. Colonel William Crawford (1732-1782) reluctantly headed an expedition against the Indians on the Sandusky River, north of the headwaters of the Scioto. During June 4-5, 1782, the patriot forces were outnumbered and routed at the Battle of Sandusky about three and a half miles northeast of modern Upper Sandusky, Ohio.

42. At least nine prisoners taken by the Indians during this expedition were killed by scalping. Three others—Colonel Crawford; his son-in-law, Major William Harrison; and his nephew William Crawford—were tortured to death by different means. The treatment of the colonel was especially brutal; he was stripped naked, fired at with some seventy charges of powder, wounded in each side of the head, prodded with burning hickory poles, scalped, sprinked with live coals and ashes, and finally roasted before a slow fire.

43. This man was John Slover, a guide for Crawford's expedition.

44. This term may refer to the region of the Monongahela River, which together with the Allegheny forms the Ohio, or to Monongalia County, Virginia (now West Virginia), lying on the southwestern border of Pennsylvania.

45. It seems that Trabue here fuses the story of George Rogers Clark's construction of Fort Jefferson in 1780 with that of his brief involvement in a plan to make a settlement in 1786 on Spanish territory at the mouth of the Yazoo River in the present state of Mississippi.

46. The Chickasaw Bluffs are located on the Mississippi River at the mouth of the Yazoo.

47. Squire Boone II (1744-1815), a younger brother of Daniel, was the first Baptist preacher to enter Kentucky. He had moved from the Kentucky River to Louisville in 1779.

48. Each identified member of this group nursed a grievance which perhaps prompted him to emigrate. Clark was disenchanted with the Virginia government because of its continued delay in settling the debts of his Illinois campaign. The Monongahela men were offended by the indifferent treatment they had received. Squire Boone was disgruntled over the loss of his lands.

49. Fort Jefferson, situated at Iron Banks (the nearest high ground below the mouth of the Ohio), was built in the spring of 1780 on orders from Governor Thomas Jefferson of Virginia.

50. The Chickasaw, incensed by the Virginians' intrusion and their failure to purchase the fort site, besieged the post in the summer of 1780. Artillery fire from the fort tilted the scales in favor of the whites, and after three days the Indians disappeared into the forest.

51. The presence of disease, the failure of Virginia's credit, the prospect of starvation, and the carousing of the officers spelled doom for the post. By May 1, 1781, the soldiers were destitute and on June 8 the fort was evacuated.

52. Natchez on the Mississippi River was held by Britain from the close of the Seven Years' War until 1779, when the Spanish moved up the river from New Orleans and took possession.

53. Trabue's original manuscript ends here. The remainder of his surviving work consists of accounts of two unrelated incidents, totaling twelve pages. The separate pagination of the first account indicates that neither was originally part of his narrative.

12. Violence on the Kentucky Frontier

1. An earlier numbering of the pages of this addendum shows that its first four are missing. Internal evidence in the remaining account points to the probability that in the lost

part Trabue had discussed the murder of his son. This addendum bears evidence that he had written it sometime, perhaps several years, earlier. When Lyman C. Draper first saw Trabue's work in November 1844 these four pages had already been lost. Draper MSS, 32S460. After Draper secured possession of the Trabue manuscript, he wrote that "the missing portions of the Harpe Narrative" could be supplied by Daniel's eldest son, Robert Trabue, who lived then at Mount Sterling, Illinois. Ibid., 57J149.

2. These adventurers were three McFarland brothers of Cumberland County— Alexander, John, and Daniel—and Robert White. Trabue encouraged and partially financed them to pursue Micaijah and Wiley Harpe, who had murdered his son and fled into western Kentucky. The McFarlands were appointed by Governor James Garrard on June 7, 1799, to take these outlaws into custody if they were found in an adjoining state. On April 22 the governor had offered a reward of three hundred dollars for the capture of each of the Harpe men.

3. This posse probably went down the Green River.

4. During the eighteenth century the Chickasaw Nation, one of the Five Civilized Tribes, lived in what is now western Tennessee and northern Mississippi.

5. The state legislature enacted this law on December 16, 1799.

6. Micaijah Harpe, a muscular man of some thirty years, stood about six feet tall and very erect. Such a physique had earned him the nickname "Big Harpe." His black hair was curly and short, falling down over his forehead and framing a full-fleshed face. The look on his countenance seemed to reveal a sinister and dejected spirit.

7. Commonly called "Little Harpe," the younger brother Wiley looked older, perhaps because his face was gaunt. He bore the same unhappy appearance.

8. The Harpes, entering Kentucky through Cumberland Gap in December 1798, had come from Tennessee, where they had lived for over a year near Knoxville. Two factors may have spurred them into their macabre career: rejection by their peers in North Carolina, where their father had reputedly been a Tory during the Revolutionary War; false arrest and imprisonment in Knoxville for an alleged offense.

9. Later when the Harpes were arrested in Kentucky they said that their family name was Roberts and that their wives were two sisters. Actually, Big Harpe's wife, Susanna, and his mistress, Elizabeth, were daughters of one Roberts who lived in Cumberland (now Russell) County. The third female in the party, the wife of Little Harpe, was the former Sarah Rice, whose father was a preacher near Knoxville.

10. The lacunae were caused by a diagonal tear of the page.

11. The murder of three men—a peddler and two Marylanders—had occurred in two isolated spots on the Wilderness Road near the Cumberland River. The missing portion of the text may refer to the first of these crimes, probably committed by the Harpes.

12. Named Thomas, this young man was a son of Benjamin Langford, a wealthy farmer of Pittsylvania County, Virginia.

13. Located on the Wilderness Road south of Hazel Patch, this house was the tavern of John Farris, Sr., where Langford had spent the night of December 11-12, 1798.

14. The press reported that two men found the body of Langford on December 14, after noticing some freshly mangled bits of a human skull by the roadside near Rockcastle River. After a search the corpse, hidden under pieces of decayed wood, was discovered beside a log some forty yards from the road. The Virginian had been killed two days earlier.

15. Joseph Ballenger, called "Devil Joe" by reason of his "reckless determination and courage," was a merchant at Stanford, the seat of Lincoln County.

16. Salt River is a tributary of the Ohio. The words "the Rolling fork of salt River" replace the canceled words "Green River."

17. The Harpes were captured on Christmas Day near Carpenter's Station, a settlement about two miles from the site of present Hustonville.

18. Imprisoned at Stanford, they were brought before the Lincoln County Court of

Quarter Sessions on January 4, 1799. The judges held that the evidence was sufficient to remand them to the Danville jail to await trial for murder before the District Court in April.

19. Ballenger again led a group of men in pursuit of the two Harpes, who had escaped from the Danville jail on March 16 and left behind their three women. Two of these women had already given birth to babies in the prison, and the third one would follow suit the next month. Governor James Garrard authorized Ballenger to chase these escapees, even into adjacent states.

20. The Rolling Fork of Salt River.

21. Danville had come into being around 1783 as the seat for the court of the new District of Kentucky.

22. Henry Skaggs was a leader of the famed Long Hunters, who roamed and hunted throughout Kentucky in 1770-1771. By 1789 he had settled down on the North Fork of Pitman Creek in Nelson (present Taylor) County.

23. James Blane, a justice of the peace, was elected the next month (May 1799) as the representative of Green County to the lower house of the legislature. Two months later he was commissioned a major in the Sixteenth Regiment of the militia. By the end of the year he would resign both the justiceship and the majority.

24. John, the second son of Daniel Trabue, was twelve years old when murdered. Probably early in April 1799 the Harpes killed John in Green (now Adair) County not far from his father's house, northwesterly of present Columbia. The lad had been sent on an errand to a grist mill and, returning home with a sack of flour and a bag of seed beans, was taken on the trail. His body was cut into pieces and thrown into a sinkhole, where the remains were found sometime before April 25.

25. The term *Knobs* was commonly used by early Kentuckians to indicate a group of separate knolls, although now it identifies a particular geographic region of central Kentucky. The area to which Trabue refers is currently designated by geographers as the Pennyroyal.

26. The East Fork of the Little Barren River, a southern tributary of the Green, is lcoated in the eastern section of present Metcalfe County.

27. Trabue does not record the fact that George Spears, a lieutenant in the Green County militia, with a small party pursued the two Harpes. The posse discovered the remains of their moccasin-making operation but did not overtake the murderers because they had too great a start.

28. The press reported this murder on April 25. Some of Stump's neighbors, suspected of the offense, had been falsely imprisoned. Later Micaijah Harpe confessed to this foul deed.

29. The route of the Harpes carried them down the Big Barren and Green rivers to the vicinity of Henderson.

30. Yellow Banks was the name given to the site of present Owensboro, Kentucky, by early boatmen of the Ohio. Trabue inadvertently used this name instead of Red Banks, the place on the Ohio where the town of Henderson was laid out in 1797.

31. The Harpes were prompted in part to hide away by Governor James Garrard's proclamation of April 22, which offered rewards of three hundred dollars each for the capture of the two desperadoes.

32. William Ballard was killed on July 24 near Knoxville.

33. Young Coffey met his death on the twenty-second about eight miles from Knoxville on Beaver Creek, the area where the Harpes had once lived. In 1802 Chesley Coffey was living on Russell Creek in Adair County, Kentucky.

34. The brothers were en route to Stocktons Valley in Kentucky.

35. The Harpe brothers came upon the Brasels on July 29. Four days earlier the Harpes had crossed the Clinch River at Davidson's Ferry, fifteen miles out of Knoxville.

36. James's throat had been slit and his body severely beaten. At this place in the text the words "the horse also was killed" are canceled.

37. Stocktons Valley, then in Cumberland County, now occupies the central portion of Clinton County.

38. John Tully, a holder of two hundred acres on Smith Creek in Cumberland County, had been slain by the Harpes on July 31.

39. At this point in the text the following words are lined out: "when James B. related his story to them."

40. The word *quickly* is canceled at this place in the manuscript.

41. The following sentence is lined out in the manuscript: "Also his horse was killed."

42. William Wood (1773-1851) lived in 1799 on Spring Creek on a two-hundred-acre tract. Nathaniel Stockton owned one hundred acres of land on Spring Creek in 1799.

43. The "Range" in Cumberland County was probably like the Barrens to the northwest. A Virginia traveler described the latter region in 1817: "Coarse grass, high and thick, with snaggy looking stunted saplings . . . rather thinly scattered, are almost the only growth of the uncultivated land." "Journal of Broaddus," Oct. 28, 1817, p. 412.

44. Here Trabue cancels the words "the same night about Dark."

45. Samuel Hopkins (1753-1819), agent for the Henderson Company, had come to Kentucky two years earlier from his native Virginia to survey on the Ohio the proposed town of Henderson, where he later practiced law. In December 1799 he was commssioned the major general for the militia division located in the western part of the state.

46. This deposition, notarized on August 5 by Trabue as a justice of the peace for Green County, appeared ten days later in the Lexington weekly newspaper. *Kentucky Gazette*, Aug. 15, 1799.

47. John Ellis was still a resident of Green County the next year.

48. The following clause is expunged at this place in the text: "the same night Mr. Woods was at my house."

49. Marrowbone Creek, about fifteen miles long, flows into the Cumberland River from the north. It is located principally in Cumberland County.

50. John Graves and his son of some twelve years had come from the Bluegrass that spring. The Harpes split the heads of these two with an ax and threw their bodies into a brush fence which surrounded their new cabin. This crime was detected some days later because of the unusual number of buzzards in the sky.

51. The time now was August 1799; the Harpes had first gone into western Kentucky in the spring of that year.

52. Moses Stegall lived in Henderson (now Webster) County, about five miles east of present Dixon.

53. William Love (1760-1799), the handsome surveyor of Livingston County, had come to see Stegall on a business matter. A native of Augusta County, Virginia, he had lived during the Revolutionary War in the New River country, from which his wanderlust had carried him into South Carolina and Kentucky.

54. This tragedy took place during the night of August 20-21.

55. This daring posse of seven hardy frontiersmen—Silas McBee, John Leeper, Moses Stegall, Matthew Christian, William Grissom, Neville Lindsey, and James Tompkins—pursued the Harpes southward up Pond River, which flows into the Green.

56. When captured the Harpes had a train of eight horses equipped with seven pairs of saddlebags.

57. This stream, located in Muhlenberg County, is one of the eastern tributaries of Pond River.

58. George Smith, Jr., was a brother of John "Raccoon" Smith, who became the famed Campbellite preacher of central Kentucky. He lived about two miles up Pond River.

59. Matthew Christian was a resident of Henderson County.

60. John Leeper, one of the pursuers, became celebrated as the man who captured Big Harpe. John had grown up in the Holston region and, after spending many years hunting and roaming in the wilds of Lincoln County and in the Nashville area, had finally put down roots at the Highland Lick settlement in western Kentucky. A typical woodsman, Leeper was a heavyset man, standing six feet tall and weighing 210 pounds. Trabue fails to identify John Leeper as a brother of Hugh, the wounded man whom he had rescued in 1778. John Leeper and his cohorts were not legally entitled to the governor's three-hundred-dollar reward because they were unable to deliver Micaijah to the Danville jailer. In December, however, by a legislative act, they were awarded the money.

61. Shortly thereafter Micaijah was pulled from his horse. Conscious of his imminent death, he confessed that he and his brother had killed some twenty persons. The murder of these innocent people, he declared, did not prick his conscience except in the case of his brother's child, whom he brained one night because the baby's crying kept him awake. Immediately after his death Stegall cut off Big Harpe's head. Leaving his sturdy torso to rot under an August sun at a site later called Harpe's Hill hard by Pond River in Muhlenberg County, the elated victors rode northward into Henderson (present Webster) County with their capital trophy. On the Henderson-Madisonville Road at the fork that led westerly to present Marion they displayed Big Harpe's head as a warning to evildoers.

62. An account of the arrest, imprisonment, trial, acquittal, and subsequent experiences of these three women is found in Lyman C. Draper, Interview with George Herndon, Logan County, Ky., June 23, 1844, Draper MSS, 30S186-93.

63. In light of the fact that this sentence ends at the bottom of a page and leaves the Harpe story unfinished, one or more pages of the manuscript are apparently missing.

64. These cabins were situated in Lincoln County twelve miles southwest of Logan's Fort.

65. William Montgomery, Sr., and his family had come into Kentucky from the Holston country late in the fall of 1779 and spent the succeeding winter at Logan's Fort.

66. Joseph Russell had accompanied the Montgomery family on their westering move. He was perhaps a son of Andrew Russell, Sr., of Augusta County, Virginia. Andrew's child Joseph was baptized on February 2, 1745/6, by John Craig, Presbyterian pastor of the Old Stone and Tinkling Spring congregations.

67. Three of Montgomery's sons were members of the militia company to which Trabue belonged.

68. William Montgomery, Jr., known as "Black Billy," served as a militiaman under Captain John Logan in 1780.

69. John Montgomery was also a member of John Logan's company.

70. Within very close range of each other, these cabins were located at the corners of a square. Montgomery may have planned to fill in the open lines of this square with palisades, thus forming a fort.

71. Benjamin Briggs told Lyman Draper that these Indians were Cherokee.

72. Thomas Montgomery was a member of the militia unit commanded by Captain John Logan in 1780.

73. The day before, Montgomery's wife, Jane, had gone to Logan's Fort to visit her daughter, Mrs. Benjamin Logan.

74. Trabue's narrative, written around 1827, is perhaps the oldest extant account of this Indian attack. Other sources have survived.

75. Jane Montgomery was eighteen years of age.

76. Here Trabue cancels the words "shot at two indeans."

77. The words "and a negro Girl" are lined out at this point.

78. Joseph Russell had married Molly, a daughter of William and Jane Montgomery.

79. Elizabeth Montgomery was two years younger than Jane.

80. When the Indian who chased Elizabeth failed to overtake her, his fellow braves laughingly said that he "couldn't catch a young squaw."

81. Another source places Flora with her mother at Logan's Fort.

82. Pettit's Station, settled by Benjamin Pettit, was located about three miles away in the direction of Logan's Fort.

83. William Casey (1756-1816), a native of Frederick County, Virginia, had been a private in the militia companies of Benjamin Logan and John Logan in St. Asaph's District. In 1789 he founded the first permanent settlement in present Adair County, Kentucky. Casey is noted as the maternal grandfather of Jane Lampton Clemens, mother of Mark Twain. In December 1792 Casey received a lieutenant colonelcy as the commandant of the militia regiment in Green County, Kentucky.

84. The Indians had covered their trail so carefully that its detection could have been made only by men on foot running ahead of the horsemen.

85. The point of encounter was on the ridge separating Green River and Licking River valleys.

86. Another source gives the age of Flora as twelve years.

87. Here Trabue cancels the word *Ravins*.

88. Thomas Montgomery, son of William Montgomery, Jr., had served for several years as deputy clerk of the Lincoln County Court.

89. This marriage took place during the winter of 1782-1783.

90. Note by Lyman C. Draper: From Mrs. Casey, Col. Trabue obtained this narrative, and wrote it down at the time. She Emigrated to Illinois, and then to Iowa, with her son Green Casey, and there both died, she some 4 or 5 years ago. She was one of the Excellent of the Earth—a pattern Christian.

Col. Casey was a man of Superior talents, and co[mman]ding appearance—5 feet 9 inches, heavily formed, weighing 200 lbs.—yet very active. Colonel of militia, representative, member of Ky. Convention, an assistant judge, very dignified on the bench. Many would resort to him to Settle disputes. Did not seek office, or he would have commanded almost any position. Of Superior judgment.

This note from James Trabue, now of St. Louis, Nov. 28, 1851. L.C. Draper.

91. This William Montgomery, a first cousin of his wife, was a son of John Montgomery and Martha Miller of Amherst County, Virginia. He died in Marion County, Missouri, on November 22, 1832.

92. Note by Lyman C. Draper: Memo.—Col. Daniel Trabue (says his son Daniel Trabue, mentioned on the preceding page) was many years a Justice of the Peace of Adair County, and two or three times Sheriff by successive rotations of Service in the Justices court. He was a merchant most of the time, and established a large mill; and, in the latter part of his life, engaged in the manufacture of iron. He was Colonel of the Militia. He was five feet 8 inches in height—stoutly made, weighing 160 pounds; dark hair, Eyes and complexion; and was for many years a leading member of the Baptist denomination.

His (oldest surviving?) son Robert Trabue, Mt. Sterling, Illinois, can Supply the missing portions of the Harpe narrative. L.C.D.

Bibliographical Essay

Daniel Trabue's Narrative covers the first 148 pages of Volume 57 of the J series (the George Rogers Clark Papers) of the Lyman Copeland Draper Collection of Manuscripts, owned by the State Historical Society of Wisconsin and totaling 487 volumes. The Narrative is designated by the symbol 57J1-148. Letters relating to the provenance and custody of Trabue's manuscript are found in other parts of Draper's monumental collection, namely 10J225, 227, 228; 57J148(a-b), 150-150(5); 3XX30(2). A paraphrase of the Trabue Narrative by Draper is in 32S395-473.

Contemporary materials relating to the career of Trabue are quite voluminous and widely scattered. Trabue's enterprises in postwar Virginia are recorded in Chesterfield County Deed Book 10, Court Order Book 6; Powhatan Deed Book 1. (Virginia county records mentioned in this bibliography are on microfilm at the Virginia State Library, Richmond.)

The militia service of Trabue in postwar Kentucky has been uncovered by using these records of the Office of the Governor, held by the Kentucky Historical Society, Frankfort: Executive Journals, 1796-1799, 1800-1804; reports and letters in Jackets 15, 16, 19, 24, 26, 27 of the Governors' Papers. G. Glenn Clift, *The "Corn Stalk" Militia of Kentucky, 1792-1811* (Frankfort, Ky., 1957) shows the organizational structure of military units.

His entrepreneurship in the Bluegrass country was studied by the use of Woodford County Deed Books B, C, C-2, County Court Order Books A, B (Microfilms, King Library, University of Kentucky). Woodford Tax Lists for 1794 were helpful. (Kentucky tax lists given in this essay are among the records of the Office of the Auditor, Kentucky Historical Society.) Interviews by John D. Shane (Draper MSS, 11CC) were also used.

The Skinhouse Branch story is well covered in Ruth Paull Burdette and Nancy Montgomery Berley, *The Long Hunters of Skin House Branch* (Columbia, Ky., 1970). Parts of the account are found in Reuben Gold Thwaites and Louise Phelps Kellogg, eds., *Documentary Record of Dunmore's War, 1774* (Madison, Wis., 1905); Lewis Collins, *History of Kentucky*, 2 vols; rev. ed. (Covington, Ky., 1874; reprint ed., Louisville, Ky., 1924); letters to Lyman C. Draper (Draper MSS, 5C).

Trabue's purchase of the land that includes the site of the Long Hunters' skin house and his settlement in Green County were reconstructed by using his letters in the Zachariah Johnston Papers

(Photocopies, Virginia State Library); an interview by Draper (Draper MSS, 9J); Virginia Land Grant Book No. 14 (Office of the Secretary of State, Frankfort); Green Deed Books 2, 7, County Court Minute Book 2, County Court Order Book 3; Willard Rouse Jillson, *Kentucky Land Grants* (Louisville, Ky., 1925) and *Old Kentucky Entries and Deeds* (Louisville, Ky., 1926); Joan E. Brookes-Smith, comp., *Master Index: Virginia Surveys and Grants, 1774-1791* (Frankfort, Ky., 1976); John Avroe Steele [Rollin M. Hurt], "Notes on Adair County," *Adair County News* (Columbia, Ky.), 1919; William B. Allen, *History of Kentucky* (Louisville, Ky., 1872). (Kentucky county records used for this study are in the respective clerks' offices, unless otherwise noted.)

The genealogy of the Trabue and related families is in Lillie DuPuy VanCulin Harper, ed., *Colonial Men and Times* (Philadelphia, 1916). The following Virginia county records revealed family connections: Chesterfield Deed Books 10, 11, 13, Will Book 3, Court Order Book 6; Cumberland Will Book 1; Goochland Court Order Book 14; Powhatan Will Book 1. These compilations of marriage records were used: Catherine Lindsay Knorr, comp., *Marriage Bonds and Ministers' Returns of Chesterfield County, Virginia, 1771-1815* (Pine Bluff, Ark., 1958); Ruth Paull Burdette, ed., *Marriage Records of Adair County, Kentucky, 1802-1840* (Burkesville, Ky., 1975). Two brief articles were helpful— Melville O. Briney, "James Trabue's Elegant Residence on Chestnut Street," *Louisville Times*, Sept. 24, 1953; J.D. Trabue, "The Haskins Family of Adair County, Kentucky," *Kentucky Ancestors* 8 (July 1972): 18-19.

The relationship of Trabue to the Green River and the Russell Creek Baptist associations was pursued chiefly by using their annually imprinted *Minutes*. John Wilson Townsend, ed., *Supplemental Check List of Kentucky Imprints, 1788-1820*, Historical Records Survey, *American Imprints Inventory*, no. 38 (Louisville, Ky., 1942; reprint ed., New York, 1964), preserves summaries of some associational minutes no longer available. I used photocopies of *Minutes* of the Russell Creek Association held by the following depositories for the years indicated: Southern Baptist Theological Seminary, Louisville, Ky., 1813, 1816; American Baptist Historical Society, Rochester, N.Y., 1822, 1827, 1828, 1830-1835; Southern Baptist Historical Society, Nashville, Tenn., 1895. The unique imprint *A Compendium of Church Discipline . . . to Which Are Prefixed the Constitution and Principles of Union of the Russell's Creek Association* (Bardstown, Ky., 1825) is owned by the Henry E. Huntington Library, San Marino, Calif. J.H. Spencer, *A History of Kentucky Baptists from 1769 to 1885*, 2 vols. (Cincinnati, 1885), is an invaluable survey.

My investigation of Trabue's role in the founding of Adair County and its seat at Columbia relied heavily on the following Adair records:

County Court Order Book A; Deed Books A, C; Tax Lists, 1802. A significant social document is the Columbia Board of Trustees, Book of Proceedings, 1811-1839 (Office of the County Clerk). The law creating the county is on pp. 68-71 of the Tenth General Assembly, *Acts* (Frankfort, Ky., 1802). Ruth Paull Burdette, *Early Columbia: The Beginnings of a Small Kentucky Town* ([Columbia, Ky., 1974]) is a carefully researched piece of local history.

The story of Trabue's entrepreneurial activities in Adair County is largely taken from these local records: Adair Circuit Court Order Books B-H; Adair Circuit Court Case Papers, File Boxes "Equity, Mar.-Sept. 1824," "Equity, June 1829-Mar. 1830," "Equity, Mar. 1830-June 1831"; Adair County Court Order Books A, B, D, E, Deed Books C-H, Y, Tax Lists, 1802-1810, 1814-1816, 1819, 1821, 1830; Russell Circuit Court Order Book 1; Russell Deed Book A; Green Deed Book 6, Tax Lists, 1799-1801. The Twenty-ninth through Thirty-second, Thirty-fourth General Asemblies, *Acts* (Frankfort, Ky., 1821-1826) were indispensable.

Daniel Trabue's efforts to secure federal pensions as a veteran of the Revolutionary War are detailed in his initial application, Adair County Court Order Book E, pp. 345-47, 355-57; his Pension File S14727, records of the Veterans' Administration, Record Group 15, National Archives; the application of the James Trabue Heirs, Rejected Claims, Land Bounty File, Box 52, Folder 18, Virginia State Library.

My study of the founding of the Columbia Baptist Church and Trabue's part in it was carried out by the use of H[erschel] C[lay] Baker, "Sketches of Adair County," *Adair County News* (Columbia, Ky.), 1918; James Garnett, [Jr.], *History of the Columbia Baptist Church* ([Columbia, Ky., 1927]); Church Minute Book 2 (Church Office); Adair County Court Order Book E, Tax Lists, 1827; Russell Creek Association, *Minutes,* 1827, 1828, 1830, 1831, 1834.

The balance of this bibliographical essay covers the materials used in annotating Trabue's Narrative.

The history of the Huguenot dispersal is well developed. John Baptist Wolf, *Louis XIV* (New York, 1968) is the best biography of the king who revoked the Edict of Nantes. Another significant study is Will Durant and Ariel Durant, *The Story of Civilization,* vol. 8: *The Age of Louis XIV* (New York, 1963). The most important collection of sources on Virginia Huguenots is Robert A. Brock, ed., *Documents . . . Relating to the Huguenot Emigration to Virginia and to the Settlement at Manakin-Town,* Virginia Historical Society, *Collections,* n.s., vol. 5 (Richmond, Va., 1886; reprint ed., Baltimore, 1966). I also used these archives: Virginia Land Office, County Abstracts No. 17 (Virginia State Library); Henry Read McIlwaine, ed., *Executive Journals of the Council of Colonial Virginia,* vol. 2 (Richmond, Va., 1927); Cecil Headlam, ed.,

BIBLIOGRAPHICAL ESSAY

Calendar of State Papers, Colonial Series: America and West Indies, 1700 (London, 1910). The tincturing of Virginia culture by the French Protestant colony is shown in James L. Bugg, Jr., "The French Huguenot Frontier Settlement of Manakin Town," *Virginia Magazine of History and Biography* 61 (Oct. 1953): 359-94.

There is a substantial volume of material dealing with the persecution of Separate Baptists in the Old Dominion. These basic studies were needful: Lewis Payton Little, *Imprisoned Preachers and Religious Liberty in Virginia* (Lynchburg, Va., 1938); Robert Baylor Semple, *A History of the Rise and Progress of the Baptists in Virginia*, ed. G.W. Beale, rev. ed. (Richmond, Va., 1894; reprint ed., Cottonport, La., 1972); Garnett Ryland, *The Baptists of Virginia, 1699-1926* (Richmond, Va., 1955). Wesley M. Gewehr, *The Great Awakening in Virginia, 1740-1790* (Durham, N.C., 1930; reprint ed., Gloucester, Mass., 1965), is a classic account that includes the Baptists. For the story of the disestablishment of Anglicanism in Virginia, see Hamilton James Eckenrode, *Separation of Church and State in Virginia* (Richmond, Va., 1910); William Taylor Thom, *The Struggle for Religious Freedom in Virginia: The Baptists* (Baltimore, 1900). A recent, incisive monograph is Thomas E. Buckley, *Church and State in Revolutionary Virginia, 1776-1787* (Charlottesville, Va., 1977). A history that stresses the role of Calvinistic evangelicals is Cedric B. Cowing, *The Great Awakening and the American Revolution* (Chicago, 1971). Chesterfield Court Order Books 4 and 5 were not overlooked. Rhys Isaac, "Evangelical Revolt: The Nature of the Baptists' Challenge to the Traditional Order in Virginia, 1765 to 1775," *William and Mary Quarterly*, 3rd ser., 31 (July 1974): 351-62, adds a new social dimension to the story.

The political status in Chesterfield County before the Revolution I found in a number of primary sources: Court Order Books 5, 6; John Pendleton Kennedy, ed., *Journals of the House of Burgesses of Virginia, 1773-1776* (Richmond, Va., 1905); *Journal . . . of the Convention Held at Richmond, in . . . March, 1775* (Williamsburg, Va., 1775); William J. Van Schreeven and Robert L. Scribner, eds., *Revolutionary Virginia: The Road to Independence*, vol. 1 (Charlottesville, Va., 1973). Francis Earle Lutz, *Chesterfield: An Old Virginia County* (Richmond, Va., 1954) is a valuable local history.

There is a sizable body of sources dealing with the early years of Revolutionary Virginia. Chief among the archival items I used were Henry Read McIlwaine, ed., *Official Letters of the Governors of the State of Virginia*, 3 vols. (Richmond, Va., 1926-1929); *The Proceedings of the Convention of Delegates for . . . Virginia, Held at Richmond Town, in . . . July, 1775* (Williamsburg, Va., [1775]); *The Proceedings of the Convention of Delegates, Held at the Town of Richmond, in . . .*

December, 1775 (Williamsburg, Va., [1776]); *The Proceedings of the Convention of Delegates, Held at the Capitol, in . . . May, 1776* (Williamsburg, Va., [1776]); Hamilton James Eckenrode, ed., *A Calendar of Legislative Petitions Arranged by Counties: Accomac-Bedford* (Richmond, Va., 1908); Julian P. Boyd, ed., *The Papers of Thomas Jefferson,* vols. 4-6 (Princeton, 1951-1952); Chesterfield Court Order Book 6; Bedford Court Order Book 6.

Hamilton James Eckenrode, *The Revolution in Virginia* (Boston, 1916) and Isaac Samuel Harrell, *Loyalism in Virginia* (Philadelphia, 1926) remain valuable. General reference works include John E. Selby, *A Chronology of Virginia and the War of Independence, 1763-1783* (Charlottesville, Va., 1973); Earl G. Swem and John W. Williams, eds., *A Register of the General Assembly of Virginia, 1776-1918 and of the Constitutional Conventions* (Richmond, Va., 1918).

These military reference works served good purposes: Mark Mayo Boatner III, *Encyclopedia of the American Revolution* (New York, 1966) and *Landmarks of the American Revolution* (Harrisburg, Pa., 1973); Christopher Ward, *The War of the Revolution,* ed. John Richard Alden (New York, 1952); Harold Leslie Peterson, *Arms and Armor in Colonial America, 1526-1783* (New York, 1956) and *The Book of the Continental Soldier* (Harrisburg, Pa., 1968).

To identify military men and other Virginians the following books were useful: Hamilton James Eckenrode, ed., *List of the Revolutionary Soldiers of Virginia* (Richmond, Va., 1912) and *Supplement* (Richmond, Va., 1913); John W. Gwathmey, ed., *Historical Register of Virginians in the Revolution* (Richmond, Va., 1938); *Heads of Families at the First Census of the United States in the Year 1790: Records of the State Enumerations, 1782-1785: Virginia* (Washington, D.C., 1908; reprint ed., Baltimore, 1952); J.T. McAllister, ed., *Virginia Militia in the Revolutionary War* (Hot Springs, Va., 1913); Lewis Preston Summers, *Annals of Southwest Virginia, 1769-1800* (Abingdon, Va., 1929; reprint ed., Baltimore, 1970) and *History of Southwest Virginia, 1746-1786, Washington County, 1777-1870* (Richmond, Va., 1903; reprint ed., Baltimore, 1966).

There exists quite a sizable quantity of materials pertaining to the Kentucky Road leading out of Virginia. Among the important works I used were "Journal of Doctor Thomas Walker, 1749/50," in J. Stoddard Johnston, ed., *First Explorations of Kentucky* (Louisville, Ky., 1898; reprint ed., [Berea, Ky., 1972]); Robert L. Kincaid, *The Wilderness Road* (Indianapolis, Ind., 1947; reprint ed., Harrogate, Tenn., 1955); William Allen Pusey, *The Wilderness Road to Kentucky* (New York, 1921); Thomas Speed, *The Wilderness Road* (Louisville, Ky., 1886); William E. Myer, *Indian Trails of the Southeast,* Bureau of American

Ethnology, *Forty-second Annual Report* (Washington, D.C., 1928; reprint ed., Nashville, Tenn., 1971); "The Journal of James Nourse, Jr., 1779-1780," ed. Neal Owen Hammon, *Filson Club History Quarterly* 47 (July 1973): 258-66; Neal Owen Hammon, "Boone's Trace through Laurel County," ibid. 42 (Jan. 1968): 21-25, and "The First Trip to Boonesborough," ibid. 45 (July 1971): 249-63, and "Early Roads into Kentucky," *Register of the Kentucky Historical Society* 68 (April 1970): 91-131.

Contemporary materials and studies dealing with Revolutionary Kentucky constitute a considerable library. Among the diaries of importance for my study were "The Journal of Colonel Henry Fleming," in Newton Dennison Mereness, ed., *Travels in the American Colonies* (New York, 1916); John D. Barnhart, ed., *Henry Hamilton and George Rogers Clark in the American Revolution, with the Unpublished Journal of Lieut. Gov. Henry Hamilton* (Crawfordsville, Ind., 1951); Journal, Richard Henderson, Draper MSS, 1CC21-102; "The Journal of General Daniel Smith, . . . August, 1779, to July, 1780," *Tennessee Historical Magazine* 1 (March 1915): 40-65. Various militia records are found in Draper MSS, 4B, 4C, 17J, 60J.

Interviews relating to wartime Kentucky, made by Lyman C. Draper, are in Draper MSS, 4C, 11C, 19C, 8-9J, 30J; interviews by John D. Shane, ibid., 11-13CC. Reminiscences of value are Milo Milcon Quaife, ed., *The Capture of Old Vincennes: The Original Narratives of George Rogers Clark and of His Opponent Gov. Henry Hamilton* (Indianapolis, 1927); "The Adventures of Col. Daniel Boon," in John Filson, *The Discovery, Settlement and Present State of Kentucke* (Wilmington, Del., 1784; reprint ed., New York, 1962); Timothy Flint, *Recollections of the Last Ten Years* (Boston, 1826; reprint ed., New York 1968); John Taylor, *A History of Ten Baptist Churches* (Frankfort, Ky., 1823; reprint ed., Cincinnati, 1968); Zachariah Holliday, Narrative, Adair County, Ky., Oct. 1844, Draper MSS, 9J206-35; Felix Walker, Narrative, ibid., 3B173-79; William Whitley, Narrative, ibid., 9CC17-60.

Biographies of prominent leaders in Revolutionary Kentucky are abundant. The best life of Boone is John Bakeless, *Daniel Boone* (New York, 1939; reprint ed., Harrisburg, Pa., 1965). Charles Gano Talbert, *Benjamin Logan: Kentucky Frontiersman* ([Lexington, Ky.], 1962) represents scholarly research. Other biographies I used were John Bakeless, *Background to Glory: The Life of George Rogers Clark* (Philadelphia, 1957); Temple Bodley, *George Rogers Clark* (Boston, 1926); Lyman Copeland Draper, "Life of Daniel Boone," Draper MSS, 4B; James Alton James, *Oliver Pollock* (New York, 1937); Edna Kenton, *Simon Kenton* (Garden City, N.Y., 1930); Kathryn Harrod Mason, *James Harrod of Kentucky* (Baton Rouge, 1951).

206 BIBLIOGRAPHICAL ESSAY

Studies on various topics helped to illuminate Kentucky during the war. Most pertinent in annotation were John James Audubon, *The Birds of America*, 7 vols. (New York, 1840; reprint ed., New York, 1966); Reuben T. Durrett, *The Centenary of Louisville* (Louisville, Ky., 1893); William Stewart Lester, *The Transylvania Colony* (Spencer, Ind., 1935); David M. Ludlum, *Early American Winters, 1604-1820* (Boston, 1966); Albert C. Manucy, *Artillery through the Ages* (Washington, D.C., 1949); Theodore Calvin Pease and Marguerite Jenison Pease, *George Rogers Clark and the Revolution in Illinois, 1763-1787* (Springfield, Ill., 1929); George W. Ranck, *Boonesborough* (Louisville, Ky., 1901; reprint ed., Berea, Ky., 1971); Jack M. Sosin, *The Revolutionary Frontier, 1763-1783* (New York, 1968); Samuel MacKay Wilson, *The First Land Court of Kentucky, 1779-1780* (Lexington, Ky., 1923).

The following general histories of early Kentucky were helpful: Mann Butler, *A History of the Commonwealth of Kentucky* (Louisville, Ky., 1834; reprint ed., Berea, Ky., 1968) and *Valley of the Ohio*, ed. G. Glenn Clift and Hambleton Tapp (Frankfort, Ky., 1971); Humphrey Marshall, *The History of Kentucky* (Frankfort, Ky., 1812; reprint ed., [Berea, Ky., 1971]). George Morgan Chinn, *Kentucky: Settlement and Statehood, 1750-1800* (Frankfort, Ky., 1975) is the initial part of a projected four-volume work. "The Certificate Book of the Virginia Land Commission of 1779-1780," *Register of the Kentucky Historical Society* 21, Supplement (Jan. 1923) was an important archival source for me.

In annotating Trabue's materials on the closing year of the Revolution in Virginia, including the siege of Yorktown, I used these journals: Jean-François-Louis, Comte de Clermont-Crèvecoeur, "Journal of the War in America," in Howard C. Rice, Jr., and Anne S.K. Brown, eds., *The American Campaigns of Rochambeau's Army, 1780, 1781, 1782, 1783*, 2 vols. (Princeton and Providence, 1972); Jean-Baptiste-Antoine de Verger, "Journal of the Most Important Events," ibid.; "Military Journal of Major Ebenezer Denny," Historical Society of Pennsylvania, *Memoirs* 7 (Philadelphia, 1860); *The Journal of Lieut. William Feltman, of the First Pennsylvania Regiment, 1781-82* (Philadelphia, 1853; reprint ed., New York, 1969); "News of the Yorktown Campaign: The Journal of Dr. Robert Honyman, April 17-November 25, 1781," ed. Richard K. MacMaster, *Virginia Magazine of History and Biography* 79 (Oct. 1971): 387-426; John Graves Simcoe, *Military Journal* (New York, 1844); James Thacher, *Military Journal of the American Revolution* (Hartford, Conn., 1862; reprint ed., New York, 1969); "St. George Tucker's Journal of the Siege of Yorktown, 1781," ed. Edward M. Riley, *William and Mary Quarterly*, 3rd ser., 5 (July 1948): 375-95; *The Diaries of George Washington, 1748-1799*, ed. John C. Fitzpatrick, vol. 2 (Boston, 1925).

These archival sources relate to the war's end in Virginia: *Journal of the House of Delegates . . . [1781]* (Richmond, Va., 1828); William P. Palmer et al., eds., *Calendar of Virginia State Papers*, vol. 8 (Richmond, Va., 1890); Chesterfield Deed Book 14.

Two narratives of military men were especially helpful—Joseph Plumb Martin, *Private Yankee Doodle*, ed. George F. Scheer (Boston, 1962); [Banastre] Tarleton, *A History of the Campaigns of 1780 and 1781 in the Southern Provinces of North America* (London, 1787).

Three special military studies were valuable—Burke Davis, *The Campaign That Won America: The Story of Yorktown* (New York, 1970); Henry Phelps Johnston, *The Yorktown Campaign and the Surrender of Cornwallis, 1781* (New York, 1881; reprint ed., New York, 1971); Robert C. Pugh, "The Revolutionary Militia in the Southern Campaign, 1780-1781," *William and Mary Quarterly*, 3rd ser., 14 (April 1957): 154-75.

The personal history of Revolutionary Virginia in 1781 is amply developed. The following biographies were of the greatest benefit to me: Robert Duncan Bass, *The Green Dragon: The Lives of Banastre Tarleton and Mary Robinson* (New York, 1957); Douglas Southall Freeman, *George Washington*, vol. 5 (New York, 1952); Louis Gottschalk, *Lafayette and the Close of the American Revolution* (Chicago, 1942); Dumas Malone, *Jefferson and His Time*, vol. 1 (Boston, 1948); John McAuley Palmer, *General von Steuben* (New Haven, Conn., 1937); Hugh F. Rankin, "Anthony Wayne: Military Romanticist," in George Athan Billias, ed., *George Washington's Generals* (New York, 1964); Willard M. Wallace, *Traitorous Hero: The Life and Fortunes of Benedict Arnold* (New York, 1954); Franklin B. Wickwire and Mary Wickwire, *Cornwallis: The American Adventure* (Boston, 1970).

To annotate Trabue's experience with General Anthony Wayne at Fort Greenville in the Old Northwest I used these special studies: Samuel F. Hunt, "The Treaty of Greenville," *Ohio State Archaeological and Historical Quarterly* 7 (1899): 218-40; Dwight L. Smith, "Wayne's Peace with the Indians of the Old Northwest, 1795," ibid. 59 (July 1950): 239-55; Thomas Alexander Boyd, *Mad Anthony Wayne* (New York, 1929); Alexander Scott Withers, *Chronicles of Border Warfare*, ed. Reuben Gold Thwaites (Cincinnati, 1895; reprint ed., Parsons, W. Va., 1961). Joseph Doddridge, *Notes on the Settlement and Indian Wars of the Western Parts of Virginia and Pennsylvania*, 3d ed. (Pittsburgh, 1912: reprint ed., Parsons, W. Va., 1960) is a unique frontier record by a contemporary. The following general works proved to be of value: Ray Allen Billington, *Westward Expansion*, 4th ed. (New York, 1974); Thomas Dionysius Clark, *Frontier America* (New York, 1959); Beverly W. Bond, Jr., *The Foundations of Ohio* (Columbus, Ohio, 1941). An interview by Lyman

C. Draper (Draper MSS, 9J) and one by John D. Shane (ibid., 11CC) were helpful.

For the story of the Harpe Gang the principal secondary source is Otto Arthur Rothert, *The Outlaws of Cave-in-Rock* (Cleveland, Ohio, 1924). W.D. Snively, Jr., and Louanna Furbee, *Satan's Ferryman: A True Tale of the Old Frontier* (New York, 1968); Robert L. Kincaid, *The Wilderness Road* (Indianapolis, Ind., 1947; reprint ed., Harrogate, Tenn., 1955) are important studies also. Newspaper accounts of the gang's crimes in 1799 are in *Kentucky Gazette* (Lexington); *Palladium: A Literary and Political Weekly Depository* (Frankfort, Ky.); *Mirror* (Washington, Ky.). Other contemporary materials used were Executive Journal, 1796-1799, records of the Office of the Governor (Kentucky Historical Society); Eighth-Ninth General Assemblies, *Acts*. Several interviews by Draper (Draper MSS, 30S, 2CC) and by Shane (ibid., 15CC) have survived. Vital local traditions are preserved by Judges Baker and Hurt in their county histories published serially in the *Adair County News*, mentioned above.

Index

Adair Circuit Court, 18, 20, 22, 26, 31
Adair County Court, 28, 29, 30, 33
Allen, Ethan, 179
Anabaptists, 128, 190
Anderson, Garland, 20, 30
Anderson, John, 179
Anderson, Sally Trabue (Mrs. Garland), 20, 22, 30, 31, 33
animals, domestic: cattle: death of, 75; destruction of, 61, 109, 110; use of, by militia, 81, 166. —dogs, 65, 71, 75, 77, 146-47. —hogs, 61, 62. —horses, 76, 93, 95, 102, 106, 126; one named Ball, 96-97; one named Black and All Black, 121-23, 188; drowned, 116-17, 187; lost, 81-82; owned by Indians, 57; pack, 75, 81; recovered, 174; stolen by Indians, 54-55, 61, 62, 91. —oxen, 47, 114, 186
animals, wild: bears: hunting for, 47-48, 75, 76-77, 85; weight of, 65. —beaver, 57, 63. —buffalo: hunting of, 56, 72-74, 77; killing of, with dogs, 48; supply of, 47; uses of, 74, 165. —deer, 8, 47, 72, 75, 76, 126. —elk, 8. —raccoon, 71-72. —turkey, 47, 71-72, 74, 136, 175. —wolves, 52, 65
Anthony, Joseph, 128, 161, 191
Antle, Jacob, 17, 18, 22
arms and armory: artillery, 97, 177, 186, 187; ax, 111; bayonet, 181; bomb (now shell), 115-16, 187; bow and arrow, 46, 61; cannon, 58-59, 80, 100, 101, 113, 114, 139; cartridge box, 179, 181; flint, 165; gunpowder, 50, 167; mortar, 114, 115, 186; musket, 139, 192; powder horn, 47; rifle, 86, 98, 138, 139, 148, 164, 179; shot bag, 47; tomahawk, 65, 88, 89, 181
Arnold, Benedict, 99, 180, 181

Bailey, William S., 17
Bakeless, John, 169
Ballard, William, 147, 196
Ballenger, Joseph, 146, 195, 196
Banks: Iron, 194; Red, 196; Yellow, 147, 196
Baptist associations: Elkhorn, 174; Green River, 11, 156; Russell Creek, 11, 15, 23, 24, 25, 26, 33, 157; Stockton's Valley, 11

Baptist churches: Columbia, 23, 24, 26; Cumberland, 191; Lower Spotsylvania, 189; Mount Gilead (formerly Russell's Creek), 10-11, 15-16, 24, 25, 26, 156, 158; Mount Pleasant, 23, 25, 158; Pitman's Creek, 25; Trammel's Creek, 11; Union (now Milltown), 24, 25; Zion, 23
Baptist preachers, 161, 173; imprisonment of, 41, 128, 129
Baptists, 41, 42; Regular, 161; Separate, 128-33, 161, 189-91
Barger, Mrs., 89
Battles: Blue Licks, 166; Camden, 178; Charlestown, 81, 82-83, 85, 177, 178; Fallen Timbers, 9, 193; Green Spring, 185; Guilford Courthouse, 99, 111-12; Kings Mountain, 82, 84, 177; Petersburg, 99-103, 181-82; Point Pleasant, 42, 162; Sandusky, 194; Sutberrys Old Field, 104, 105, 118, 182, 184; Yorktown, 6, 114-21, 186-88
Beard, John, Sr., 13
Beatty, Martin, 18
Benham, Robert T., 64-65
Bennett, Charles, 17, 18
Bird, Henry, 80-81, 177
Blane, James, 10, 147, 196
Block House, 85, 164, 179
bloomery, 22, 26
boats: broadhorn, 192; flatboat, 192; keelboat, 50, 56, 64, 145, 166
Boone, Daniel; actions of, during Boonesborough Siege, 58, 170; capture of, by the Shawnee, 165; court-martial of, 63-64, 172; escape of, from the Shawnee, 57; justice of the peace, 168; leader of salt makers, 47; location of trace by, 164; militia captain, 165; recovery of horses by, 168
Boone, Squire, II, 144, 170, 194
Boonesborough, 69, 165; arrival of Trabue at, 46-47, 68; commissary at, 50, 54; conditions at, 165, 169; description of, 165; expedition from, 165, 168; officers of, 63; reinforcement of, 170; residents of, 57; roads to, 164; siege of, 58-59, 60, 62, 63-64, 170-71

Bowman, John (county lieutenant, Kentucky), 53, 68, 166, 168, 174
Bowman, John (militiaman, Virginia), 105
Boyce, William, 102
Boyle, John, 173
Bramblit, Mr., 125-26
brandy, 80, 99, 103, 104, 105, 107, 108
Brassel, James, 147-49, 196-97
Brassel, Robert, 147-49, 196
Breathitt, John, 28
Bridge: Anderson's, 183; Bottom's, 110, 185; Ground Squirrel, 183; Pocahontas, 100, 101-2, 181; Trabue's, 8
Briggs, Benjamin, 167, 198
British Army, 95-104, 105, 109, 110; officers of, 57, 63, 64, 80, 83, 93, 96, 119, 123; prisoners, 173; size of, 188
British North America, population of, 162
Broaddus, Andrew, 15
Brodhead, Mr., 70
Brodhead, Daniel, 174
Brooks, Thomas, 47, 165
Brooks, William, 47, 165
Brown, Benjamin, 183
Buckner, Richar A., 32
Bullitt, Thomas, 169
Bunyan, John, 130
Burbridge, William, 23
Byrd, William, I, 160
Byrd, William, II, 40, 41, 160
Byrd, William, III, 173

Caldwell, Elizabeth Hodgen (Mrs. Robert H.), 25
Caldwell, Robert H., 25
Caldwell, William, 12, 21
Calhoon, John, 32
Calloway, Richard: actions of, during Boonesborough Siege, 58, 59; charges against Boone by, 63-64, 172; justice of the peace, 53, 168; legislator, 67-68, 173; opposition to Boone by, 57, 58
Campbell, Alexander, 23, 24, 26
Campbell, Arthur, 172
Campbell, William (British major), 193
Campbell, William (Virginian), 84, 178, 184
Campbellism, 23-25
canebrake, 49, 51, 53; description of, 166
Carleton, Guy, 172
Cary, Archibald, 128, 129, 189, 190
Casey, Green, 199
Casey, Jane Montgomery (Mrs. William), 152, 153, 198, 199
Casey, William, 12, 152, 153, 199
cavalry, British, 106, 107; Simcoe's Rangers, 183-84; Tarleton's Legion, 182, 183, 184, 188; Virginians' fear of, 183

Chesterfield prison, 41, 129, 161
Chickasaw Bluffs, 144, 194
Chiswell, John, 173
Christian, Matthew, 151, 197
Christian churches: Mount Gilead, 25; Mount Pleasant, 25
Christmas, 65-66, 169
Church of England, 41, 128, 160, 161, 189; mistreatment of pastors of, 163
Clark, George, 54, 55, 169
Clark, George Rogers: arrival of, at Louisville, 49, 55, 56, 166, 169; construction of Ft. Jefferson by, 194; Illinois campaign of, 44, 50, 53, 164, 167; justice of the peace, 168; Ohio campaign of, 81, 177; papers of, 4; settlement of, at Chickasaw Bluffs, 144
Clary, John, 66, 171, 173
Clay, Edwin C., 161
Clay, Eleazar, 161, 190
Clay, Henry, 158, 161, 190
Clay, Magdelaine Trabue (Mrs. Edwin C.), 41, 129, 161
Clemens, Jane Lampton (Mrs. John M.), 199
Clinton, Henry, 85, 177, 178
Clinton, James, 178
coal pits, 104, 182
Coburn, Samuel, 51, 52, 167
Coffey, Chesley, 147, 196
Collins, Josiah, 165
commissary, 30, 49-50, 80, 81, 159, 169, 174
Congregationalists, 39
Congress, U.S., 30, 31, 32
Conover, Jemima (Mrs. Peter T.), 23
Conover, Peter T., 23
Continental Army, 85, 118, 163, 179, 185, 186
Continental Congress, 162
Continental currency, 90, 110, 124, 188
Cook, Hosea, 138, 192
Cook, Jesse, 138, 192
Cornwallis, Charles, 119, 178, 188; arrival of, in Virginia, 103, 105; fortification of Yorktown by, 112-13, 114; military mission of, 184; proclamation of, 82; surrender of, at Yorktown, 117-18, 119, 124, 187; underground dwelling, 188; Virginia expedition of, 108, 110, 111
counties, Kentucky: Adair, 11, 12, 22, 27, 199; Barren, 30; Bath, 30; Bourbon, 171; Bullitt, 169; Christian, 150; Clay, 30, 33; Clinton, 197; Cumberland, 11, 17, 32, 197; Fayette, 6, 7, 70, 136, 182; Franklin, 30; Green, 8, 9, 10, 12, 25, 30, 33, 155; Henderson, 197, 198; Kentucky (extinct),

52, 165, 166, 167, 168, 171, 173; Knox, 165; Lincoln, 29, 167, 169; Livingston, 197; Magoffin, 172; Mason, 192; Mercer, 30, 169; Metcalfe, 196; Muhlenberg, 197, 198; Pulaski, 18; Russell, 17, 22, 27, 33; Scott, 13; Taylor, 196; Todd, 25; Webster, 197, 198; Woodford, 7, 9, 27, 127, 136, 189, 191
counties, Virginia: Albemarle, 164; Amelia, 79, 175, 176; Augusta, 98, 162, 177, 181, 197; Bedford, 69, 70, 82, 125, 164, 167, 177; Bland, 173; Botetourt, 167; Buckingham, 164; Caroline, 164; Charles City, 160; Charlotte, 164; Chesterfield, 1, 5-6, 28, 82, 100, 105, 127, 128, 161, 162, 163, 164, 180; Cumberland, 164; Dinwiddie, 180, 181; Essex, 90, 92; Fauquier, 191; Frederick, 199; Goochland, 106, 183; Halifax, 165; Hanover, 163, 183; Henrico, 160, 161; King George, 161; Mecklenburg, 188; Middlesex, 185; Monongalia (now West Virginia), 144, 194; Montgomery, 173, 177; Norfolk, 160; Pittsylvania, 185, 195; Powhatan, 6, 27, 160, 164, 183, 189; Prince William, 161; Rockbridge, 9, 17, 98, 121, 181; Tazewell, 173; Washington, 164, 172, 177; Westmoreland, 161; Wythe, 173; York, 185
Craig, John (Lincoln County, Kentucky), 192
Craig, John (Presbyterian pastor, Virginia), 198
Craig, John (Scott County, Kentucky), 13
Craig, Larkin F., 23, 157
Craig, Lewis, 189
Cravens, Elijah, 20, 21
Crawford, William (colonel), 142, 194
Crawford, William (nephew of colonel), 194
Creek: Bear Grass, 79, 176; Beaver, 196; Big, 11; Blackfish, 17; Cripple, 84, 178; Elkhorn, 174; Falling, 160; Four Mile, 180; Gilberts, 74, 127, 175; Goldmine, 183; Greasy, 22, 23, 26; Grier, 7, 8, 9, 136, 192; Knob Lick, 167; Marrowbone, 150, 197; Otter, 165; Paint Lick (Kentucky), 77, 176; Paint Lick (Ohio), 168; Pitman, 196; Russell, 8, 11, 12, 13, 20, 27, 196; Skaggs, 126, 189; Smith, 197; Spring, 197; Straight, 87, 179; Swift, 161, 189; Tomahawk, 1; Wormeleys, 186; Yellow (formerly Flat), 165; Yorktown, 186
crops: barley, 41. —corn: British confiscation of, 107; cultivation of, 48, 75, 77, 80, 124; harvesting of, 88; killing of, by frost, 41; purchase of, 166, 179,
scarcity of, 75; use of, as food, 60, 63, 66, 171. —grain, 185. —oats, 41. —rye, 41, 161. —tobacco, 40, 41, 95, 161, 181. —wheat, 41, 161
Crump, Richard, 95-96, 180
Cudjo's Cave, 164

Dale, Mr., 148
Dandridge, Nathaniel, 106, 183
Davies, Jeffery, 71, 75-76, 89, 174
Davies, William, 95, 180
Davis, Azariah, 166
Day, Mr., 121-23
Deist, Trabue as, 130
Dement, Mr., 139, 192
DeQuindre, Antoine Dagnieau, 59, 171
Detroit, Michigan: Boone at, 57, 63, 169; British post at, 55, 63; defense of, 193; military unit from, 80, 167; prisoners taken to, 89, 93
Dismal Swamp, 97, 181
doctrines, religious: baptism, 24, 133; conversion, 130-33; conviction of sin, 130, 131, 191; forgiveness of sin, 24; Holy Spirit, 24; predestination, 16; redemption, 24; repentance, 11
Don Quixote, quotation from, 165
Dorchester, James, 168
Downey, John, 85-88
Draper, Lyman Copeland, 1, 4, 195, 198
Dulain, Mr., 64
Dunmore, Earl of, 42, 43, 162, 163
Dupuy, Bartholomew (great-grandfather), 37, 38, 39, 159
Dupuy, Bartholomew (uncle), 75, 79, 135, 136, 175
Dupuy, James (uncle), 130, 131, 136, 191
Dupuy, John (uncle), 128, 129, 136, 176, 189, 191
Dupuy, John James (grandfather), 37, 43, 159, 163, 191
Dupuy, Susanne Lavillian (Mrs. Bartholomew) (great-grandmother), 37, 38, 39, 159
Dupuy, Susanne Lavillian (Mrs. John James) (grandmother), 159

Easter, 46, 47
Eastin, Augustine, 161, 190
Eckert, Allan W., 172
Edict: of Fontainebleau, 37, 159; of Nantes, 159
Edwards, Morgan, 190
Ellis, John, 149-50, 197
England, 39, 40, 79, 162
Epperson, Captain, 100-101
Erwin, Andrew, 18
Ewing, Andrew, 28

212 INDEX

Ewing, Samuel, Jr., 84, 178
Ewing, Samuel, Sr., 84, 178

Falling Creek Church, 104, 182
Falls: of the James River (*see* towns, Virginia: Richmond); of the Ohio River (*see* Louisville)
Farris, John, Sr., 195
Faulkner, Ralph, 100, 101, 111-12
Ferguson, Patrick, 82, 84, 177
Ferry: Ingles', 66, 164, 173; Manakin Town, 106, 183; Steele's, 137, 192
Field, John, 21
Field's Scrap Book on the History of the Great West, 4
Finney, John, 138-39
Fleming, William, 128, 175, 189
Flournoy, Jacob, 160
Floyd, John, 79, 165, 168, 176
food: bacon, 46, 79, 136. —bear meat: preservation of, 56, 65; supply of, 63. —beef, 166. —bread, 47, 71, 84, 136. —buffalo, 47, 72, 75, 166. —butter, 47, 88. —cider, 99. —coffee, 67, 73. —eggs, 67. —fish, 76, 98. —fruit, 47. —gingerbread, 100. —hominy, 66. —milk, 47, 67, 88. —mush, 67. —oysters, 98. —pork, 46, 166, 183. —potatoes, 88. —pumpkins, 60, 88. —raccoon, 71. —salt: making of, 47, 56, 63, 70-71, 73; price of, 175; purchase of, 112; scarcity of, 42-43, 163; use of, 65. —sausage, 67. —sugar, 56. —sweetbread, 107. —tea, 73. —turkey, 71-72. —vegetables, 47. —venison, 47. —white shad, 98
Ford: Cook's, 183; Cumberland, 164, 179; Raccoon, 105, 182
Fork: Caney, 8; Glens, 11; Hanging, 167; Pettits, 11; Rolling, 146, 174
Forks of the Ohio, 191
Fort: Chiswell, 164, 173; Defiance, 193; Duquesne, 173; Greenville, 192; Jefferson (Kentucky), 194; Jefferson (Ohio), 139, 192; Miami, 193; Pitt, 64, 69, 70, 127, 168, 173; Ticonderoga, 92, 179
fortifications: abatis, 119, 188; blockhouse, 61, 170, 171; fascine, 186; gabion, 114, 115, 186; horn work, 186; redoubt, 114, 186; *saucisson*, 186
Foster, James, 71, 73, 174
Foster, Martha Dupuy (Mrs. James), 174
France, 37, 39, 160
French, Mrs. Richard, 172
French Army, 121, 186
French Fleet, 185, 188
French refugees, land grants to, 160
frontier, 125, 142, 189; violence on, 146-53
Fuller, Andrew, 16

Gap: Blue Ridge, 164; Cumberland, 44, 125, 164, 167, 195; Moccasin, 164
Garrard, James, 10, 12, 195, 196
Gass, John, 171
Gates, Horatio, 82, 84, 85, 99, 178
George III, 3, 57, 82, 85, 105, 109
Gewehr, Wesley M., 161
Gist, Thomas, 125, 126, 189
Goode, Robert, 106, 108, 163, 183, 184
Grasse, Comte de, 112, 185
Graves, John, 150, 197
Gray, Jesse, 9
Great Britain, boycott of goods from, 162
Greene, Nathanael, 180, 181
Green River country, 9, 11, 168
Greenup, Christopher, 16
Grissom, William, 197
grist mill, 6, 128
Guerrant, John, Jr., 106, 183
Guerrant, John, Sr., 106, 183
Guerrant, Magdelaine Trabue (Mrs. Peter), 183
Guerrant, Peter, 183

Hackney, Elizabeth, 112, 185
Hamilton, Henry (Canada), 167, 169, 172
Hancock, William, 57, 169
Hand, Edward, 168
Hardin, Parker C., 21
Harmar, Josiah, 141, 193
Harpe, Micaijah, 10, 31, 146-51, 195-98
Harpe, Sarah Rice (Mrs. Wiley), 195, 198
Harpe, Susanna Roberts (Mrs. Micaijah), 195, 198
Harpe, Wiley, 10, 31, 146-51, 195-98
Harrison, William, 194
Harrod, Ann Coburn McDonald (Mrs. James), 55, 56, 167, 169
Harrod, James, 51, 55, 56, 166, 167, 173; justice of the peace, 168
Harrodsburg (fort), 55, 62; Clark's men at, 48; commissary at, 50; county court at, 167, 168; expeditions from, 70; location, 166; officers of, 63; residents of, 51, 53, 169
Haskins, Creed, 12
Haskins, Robert, 6, 9, 95, 124, 133, 161; militia colonel, 180
Hatcher, Samuel, 89
Henderson, Nathaniel, 168
Henry, Patrick, 164, 172, 191
Hessians, 91, 119, 179
Hill: Harpe's, 198; Pigeon, 114, 186
Hinkston, John, 80-81, 142, 177
Hite, Isaac, 168
Hodgen, Isaac, 15, 16, 24, 25
Hodgen, Phoebe Trabue (Mrs. Isaac), 9, 15

213 INDEX

Holder, Fanny Calloway (Mrs. John), 171
Holder, John, 59, 171
Holladay, John, 23
Holston River community, 8, 60, 61, 63, 164, 166, 170, 172
Hopkins, Samuel, 149-50, 197
Huguenots, 33, 159
Huling, Marcus, 18
Hurt, William, 27

Illinois, 18, 50, 145, 164
illnesses, frontier, 175; cholera, 30, 31; common, 175
Indian captivities, 69-70, 81, 89-94, 152-53
Indian chiefs: Blackfish, 169, 170, 171; Cornstalk, 162; Little Turtle, 193
Indians, 79; attack by, on Innis' Settlement, 136-38; attack by, on Logan's Fort, 61; attack by, on Montgomery cabins, 151-53; attack by, on Ruddell's station, 80-81, 89; attitude toward whites, 69-70, 143-44; death by, 51-52, 53, 64; defeat of, in Old Northwest, 192; encounter with, on Wilderness Road, 45-46, 86-88, 125-27; fear of attack by, 77-78, 92; prisoners taken by, 67-68; pursuit of escapees by, 93; recovery of horses from, 55; torture by, 194; towns of, 163
Indian tribes: Cherokee, 10, 44, 62, 164, 165, 171, 198; Chickasaw, 146, 147, 194, 195; Shawnee, 44, 57, 162, 165, 168, 169, 174
Ingles, William, 173
Innis' Settlement, 137, 192
invasion: British, of James River area, 180; Virginia's inability to repel, 180
Iroquois Confederation, 162
Island: Corn, 166; Dead Man's, 135, 192; Gallipolis, 192; Jamestown, 185

Jackson, Andrew, 32, 158
Jefferson, Thomas, 27, 105, 106, 180, 183, 184, 194
Johnson, Andrew, 168
Johnston, Zachariah, 9, 156
Jones, Mr., 76
Joux, Benjamin de, 160
July the Fourth, 3, 6, 124, 192

Kearns, Adam, Jr., 17, 18
Kennedy, John, 168
Kenton, Simon, 54, 55, 168, 170, 171
Kentucky: disappointment about, 71, 89, 98; frontier of, 142; Virginia legislators from, 67; word about, during Dunmore's War, 42
Kentucky County Court, 53, 167

Knobs, 147, 196
Knox, James, 81, 177
Knoxville, Tennessee, 147, 195

Lafayette, Marquis de, 114; dispatch carried to, 106; sutler's permit from, 107-8, 113; trailing of Cornwallis by, 110, 111, 113, 184-85; union of, with Wayne, 105; use of name of, 182
Lampton, Benjamin, 21
land office, establishment of, 173
land patents, 173
land warrents, 68, 80, 81, 89, 90, 173, 175
Langford, Benjamin, 195
Langford, Thomas, 146, 195
laws: Boston Port Act, 162; Fee Act (1745), 163; "Intolerable Acts," 162; Land Act (1779), 173, 174, 176; Replevin Act (1820), 157; Toleration Act (1689), 189, 191
Lawson, Robert, 188
Layl, Mr., 48-49
Layl, George, 166
lead, 173; mines, 68
Lee, Henry, 187
Leeper, Hugh, 53, 54, 168
Leeper, John, 151, 197, 198
Lewis, Andrew, 162
liberty, 42, 109, 184
Lick: Big (Lincoln County), 51; Big Flat (Roanoke), 164; Blue, 47, 63, 165, 168, 169; Bullitts, 56, 65, 70, 72-73, 169, 175; Flat (or Big) (Knox County), 125, 164, 165; Flat (Lincoln County), 167; Little Flat (Lincoln County), 53; Stone, 192
Lincoln, Benjamin, 177
Lincoln, Mary Todd (Mrs. Abraham), 168
Lindsay, Joseph, 49-50, 166
Lindsey, Neville, 197
Locket, James, Jr., 134-36, 191
Locket, James, Sr., 191
Locket, Susanna Dupuy (Mrs. James, Sr.), 191
Logan, Ann Montgomery (Mrs. Benjamin), 88, 167, 198
Logan, Benjamin, 88, 94; aid to the Montgomerys by, 152; commander at Logan's Fort, 48; justice of the peace, 168; militia captain, 166; Ohio campaign by, 89; opposition by, to Boone, 64; preparation for siege by, 59-60; search for horses by, 49; search for Indians, 51-53; wounding of, 62, 171
Logan, John, 68, 174, 198
Logan's Fort, 55, 65, 71, 88, 151; ammunition for, 68; Boone's court-martial at, 63; Clark's men at, 47, 48; commissary

at, 50; conditions at, 59-62; county court at, 52, 167; discontinuance of soldiery at, 70; horses stolen from, 54; location of, 165; residents of, 51 66, 80, 167; spring at, 59-60, 171; Trabue at, 8, 32
London, England, 42; population of, 162
Long Hunters, 8, 177, 196
Louis XIV, 159
Louis XVI, 166
Louisville (fort): arrival of Clark at, 49; ball at, 56; Christmas celebration at, 169; commissary at, 50; expeditions from, 44, 64, 73; location of, 164, 166; residents of, 33, 65; sale of corn at, 75; visits to, 79, 144
Love, William, 150, 169

McBee, Silas, 197
McClain, Joseph, 8
McColester, Mr., 139-40
McCoy, Mr., 51, 52
McFarland, Alexander, 146, 195
McFarland, Daniel, 146, 195
McFarland, John, 146, 195
McGary, Hugh, 55, 169
McIlwain, Moses, 69-70, 174
McKee, Alexander, 177
McKinney, Archibald, 54, 168
McRoberts, Archibald, 162
Major, John, 161, 192
Major, Judith Trabue (Mrs. John), 41, 137, 161, 192
Major, Oliver Thomas, 161, 192
Major, Susannah Trabue (Mrs. Oliver T.), 41, 137, 161, 192
Manefield, William, 66
Marshall, John, 177
Marshall, Thomas, 81, 177
Martin, John, 60, 171
Martin, Joseph Plumb, 188
Maxey, William, 71, 174
May, John, 80, 175
May, Richard, 51, 52, 166, 167, 173
meetinghouses, Baptist: Clear Creek, 133; Dupuy's, 76, 174, 175, 191
Merryman, Mr., 116-17
militia: enlistment of, 163; pension for officers and men of, 28; service by, 95-105, 110; substitutes in, 181; use of, 180, 181, 186; wagons in, 181
Minter, Jane Trabue (Mrs. Joseph), 41, 129, 161
Minter, Joseph, 161, 185
Montgomery, Alexander, 51, 54, 55, 167, 168
Montgomery, Elizabeth Montgomery (Mrs. William), 152, 153, 199

Montgomery, Flora, 152, 199
Montgomery, Jane (Mrs. William, Sr.), 152, 198
Montgomery, John (merchant), 21
Montgomery, John (son of William, Sr.), 151, 198
Montgomery, Nathan, 10
Montgomery, Thomas (son of William, Jr.), 153, 199
Montgomery, Thomas (son of William, Sr.), 151, 152, 198
Montgomery, William (son of John), 153, 199
Montgomery, William, Jr., 151-52, 153, 198, 199
Montgomery, William, Sr., 151, 198
Montreal, Canada, 89-94
Morgan, Mr., 112, 185
Morgan, Daniel, 177
Morrisett, D., 108-9
Morrisett, David, 184
Moseley, Blackman, 163
Moseley, Edward: militia service of, 96-99, 103, 105, 109-10, 181; owner of slaves, 104, 182; purchased land from, 6
Moseley, R., 132
Moseley, Richard, 191
Mount Gilead (community), 22, 30, 31
Mountains: Allegheny, 164; Appalachian, 6, 164; Blue Ridge, 173; Clinch, 164, 173, 179; Powell, 164
Muhlenberg, John Peter Gabriel, 97, 99, 181
Mungrel, Daniel, 65

Natchez, Mississippi, 144, 194
Negroes, 103-4, 110, 142; assistance of, to hunters, 71, 73, 75; assistance of, to militia men, 53, 68; fear of uprising by, 81; hiring of, by owners, 89; migration of, to Kentucky, 85, 124-25, 127, 134-35; work of, on plantations, 107, 111. See also slaves
Nelson, Thomas, 188
New Orleans, Louisiana, 50, 172, 194
New York, 92, 167; frontier of, 142
Nicholson, Francis, 160
Nickle, Jean, 169
Noel, Alexander, 90, 92-94, 179
North Carolina, 146, 173

occupations: blacksmith, 27; bricklayer, 90; distiller, 27; drover, 146; fur trader, 171; gristmiller, 6, 7-8, 13-14, 22-23, 27, 199; gunsmith, 164, 170; hunter, 146, 166; iron manufacturer, 22-23, 199; merchant, 16-17, 42, 119-20, 128, 162, 163, 199; millwright,

22; salt maker, 17-19; shoemaker, 27; slave overseer, 121-23; stonemason, 90; sutler, 107, 113; tanner, 27; tapster, 104; tavern keeper, 17, 93, 123
Ohio, 162
Ohio Company, 191
Old Dominion. *See* Virginia
Old Northwest, 192

parishes, Anglican: King William, 160; Manchester, 182
Patterson, James G., 18
Patterson, William, Sr., 18
Patterson, William S., 18
Patton, William, 59, 62, 171
Pennsylvania Dutch, 166; presence of, in Kentucky, 48-49, 53, 89, 137; Tories among, 84-85; work of, as sutler, 107-8
Pension Office, 28, 29, 32
Pettit, Benjamin, 60, 171, 199
Pettit's Fort, 152, 153
Phelps, T., 65, 73
Phelps, Thomas, 173
Phillips, Mr., 54
Phillips, Jacob, 119
Phillips, William, 99, 181
Piedmont, 5, 7, 9, 160
Pilgrim's Progress, The, 130
Pittman, Tabitha Minter (Mrs. William H.), 23
plantations: Babbs Old Field, 97; Belvidere, 160; Green Spring, 185; Sutberrys Old Field, 182; Westover, 160, 183; Whitby, 184
Poage, William, 52, 53, 168
Point: Bush, 112; Stingray, 112, 185
Pore, Nehemiah, 168, 171
Powell, Ambrose, 164
presidential election of 1832, 158
Price, Benjamin, 141, 193
puncheons, 169

Railey, Martin, 105
Redstone Old Fort, 134, 191
Reformed Church, 159, 160
Regular Baptists. *See* Baptists, Regular
revivals, religious, 10, 11, 128-29, 131, 132, 133
Rice, Luther, 16
riflemen, 98, 99, 121, 181, 184
River: Allegheny, 194; Appomattox, 100-101, 110, 181; Auglaize, 193; Barren, 147, 196; Chaplin, 71, 174; Chickahominy, 110, 185; Clinch, 66, 164, 173; Cumberland, 17, 19, 22, 81, 85, 89, 162; Dan, 121, 180, 188; Dix, 75, 165, 175; Garonne, 159; Green, 73, 75, 89, 146; 151, 195, 199; Holston, 44, 82, 85, 164, 179; James, 39, 41, 95, 97, 99, 106, 109, 111, 114, 160, 161; Kanawha, 135, 192; Kentucky, 47, 59, 69, 89, 136-37, 164, 192; Laurel, 164, 165; Licking, 63, 64, 80, 165, 172, 199; Little, 183; Little Barren, 11, 147, 196; Little Miami, 169; Little Otter, 174; Mattapony, 185; Maumee, 9, 141, 193; Miami, 192; Mississippi, 144, 145; Monongahela, 135, 144, 191, 194; New, 66, 68, 82, 84, 164, 178; North Anna, 183; Ohio, 7, 44, 55, 57, 63, 79, 135-36, 144, 168, 172; Pamunkey, 185; Piankatank, 112, 185; Pond, 197, 198; Potomac, 161; Powell, 164; Rapidan, 105; Rappahannock, 112, 163, 185; Rivanna, 183; Rockcastle, 126, 164, 165, 173, 189, 195; Salt, 146, 169, 174, 176, 195, 196; Sandusky, 142, 194; Savannah, 162, 164; Scioto, 54, 142, 162, 168, 194; South Anna, 182, 183; Stones, 147; Tennessee, 9, 164, 173; Wabash, 167; Yazoo, 194; York, 185
roads: Boone's Trace, 164; Burkesville, 33; Campbell's Ferry, 19; Great Valley (or Philadelphia Wagon), 164, 173; Greensburg, 14; Hampton, 186; Kentucky (or Wilderness), 44, 125, 146, 179, 189; Skaggs' Trace, 164; Warrior's Path (or Indian War), 44, 125, 164, 165
Roberts, Elizabeth, 195, 198
Robinson, John, 173
Rochambeau, Comte de, 185, 186
Rocheblave, Sieur de, 50, 166, 167
Rogers, David, 64, 172-73
Ruddell, Abraham, 139-40, 193
Ruddell, George, 193
Ruddell, Isaac, 53, 80, 139-42, 168, 193
Ruddell, Stephen, 139-42, 192-93
rum: dealer in, 93, 119-20; general use of, 56, 73, 125; price of, 188; sale of, 99, 108, 116; use of, by militia, 100, 103, 181; West India, 120
Russell, Andrew, Sr., 198
Russell, Flora, 152-53, 199
Russell, Joseph, 151, 153, 198
Russell, Molly Montgomery (Mrs. Joseph), 152, 198
Russell Circuit Court, 18

Sabbath breaking, 134, 192
St. Asaph's, 165, 171
St. Clair, Arthur, 141, 192, 193
salt springs, 165
salt works, 169
Scott, Dr., 79
Scott, Charles, 81, 84, 85, 177

216 INDEX

Scott, Joe, 142
Scott, John, 20, 22
Scott, Judith Dupuy, 22, 31
Scott, Judith Dupuy Trabue (Mrs. John), 20, 22, 31
Scott, Walter, 163
Searcy, Mrs. Richard, 137, 192
Separate Baptists. *See* Baptists, Separate
Shelby, Isaac, 17
Shelton, Stephen, 192-93
Sherwin, Samuel, 79, 80, 176
sieges: Boonesborough, 58-59, 63-64, 170-71; Ruddell's Station, 80-81, 89; Yorktown, 114-19, 186-88
Simcoe, John Graves, 183
Simmermon, Peter, 18
Skaggs, Henry, 146-47, 196
Skaggs, William, 156
Skinhouse Branch, 8, 9, 10, 11
Skipwith, Peyton, 121, 188
slaves, 177, 188
slaves, individual: Aggy, 20; Green, 20; Jo, 71; Matilda, 20; Pompey, 58, 170; Sela, 142; Shearwood, 20
Slover, John, 142-43, 194
Smith, Mr. 61
Smith, George, Jr., 150, 197
Smith, George Milpon: baptism by, 133; hunting trip of, 76-78; migration to Kentucky of, 75; parentage of, 175; service of, in militia, 96, 98, 99
Smith, George Stokes, 77, 79, 88; attendance of, at revival, 132; hunting trips of, 71, 73, 74, 76-77; migration to Kentucky of, 85; parentage of, 174; residence of, 127; return to Virginia of, 81-82, 89; service of, in militia, 96, 98, 99
Smith, John "Raccoon," 23, 25, 197
Smith, Judith Guerrant (Mrs. George M.), 175
Smith, Magdelaine Trabue Guerrant (Mrs. Thomas), 174
Smith, Thomas, 174, 175
Smith, William, 110, 118
Smith, William Bailey, 170
snow, 66, 67, 73, 74, 75, 175
South, "Old Mrs." (Mrs. John, Sr.), 59, 171
South, Samuel, 172
Spears, George, 196
specie, 120, 124, 188
spirits, 47, 110, 112, 113, 185
Stapp, William, 18
Station: Carpenter's, 195; Glover's, 9; Gray's, 9; Linn's, 79, 175; Martin's, 81, 159; Pettit's, 199; Ruddell's, 80-81, 89, 159, 166, 176; Wilson's, 80, 175

Steele, John D., 23, 24, 25, 26
Steele, William, 192
Stegall, Moses, 150, 197, 198
Steuben, Friedrich Wilhelm von, 103, 104, 181, 182, 184
Stevens, Edward, 178
Stockton, Nathaniel, 149, 197
Stratton, Captain, 111
Stucker, Jacob, 137, 192
Stump, Mr., 147, 196
Sublett, Lewis, 104, 108-9, 161, 182
Sublett, Mary Trabue (Mrs. Lewis), 20, 33, 41, 161
Sublett, Samuel, 20
Sullivan, Mr., 73
Summers, Elijah, 156
Sycamore Hollow, 165

Tanner, John, 161
Tarleton, Banastre, 124; arrival of, in Virginia, 103; derision of, 3; raids of, in Virginia, 104, 105, 106, 108; recovery of horse from, 121-23; reputation of, in South, 110, 182, 183
Tavern: Brown's, 106, 183; Farris', 195; Ingles', 66-67
Taylor, John, 133, 191
Tennessee, 11, 25, 146
Thurman, Mr., 108-9
Thurman, John, 184
Tidewater, 161
Tinsley, David, 161, 175-76
Todd, John, 53, 168
Todd, Levi, 53, 168
Todd, Robert, 168
Tompkins, Christopher, 30
Tompkins, James, 197
Tories, 113, 119, 121, 163, 177, 195
Toryism, 82, 84, 178-79
towns, Illinois: Kaskaskia, 50, 56, 145, 166, 167, 169; Mount Sterling, 33, 199
towns, Kentucky: Burkesville, 32; Columbia, 1, 12, 13, 19, 30, 33, 196; Covington, 172; Crab Orchard, 81, 126, 127, 177; Danville, 146, 150, 167, 196; Dixon, 197; Frankfort, 20, 70, 92, 137, 149; Glasgow, 30; Greensburg, 10, 13, 20, 22; Hazel Patch, 164, 189, 195; Henderson, 196, 197; Hustonville, 195; Lee's Town, 93, 179; Lexington, 7, 32, 33, 151; Limestone (now Maysville), 136, 192; Owensboro, 196; Pineville, 179; Shepherdsville, 169; Stanford, 19, 146, 165, 195
towns, Ohio: Chillicothe, 54, 55, 169; Greenville, 192; Springfield, 169; Toledo, 193; Upper Sandusky, 194; Xenia, 169

217 INDEX

towns, Pennsylvania: Brownsville, 191; Philadelphia, 84, 144, 173; Pittsburgh, 162, 192

towns, Virginia: Baker's Hill, 100; Botetourt Courthouse, 173; Caroline Courthouse, 163; Charlottesville, 106, 183; Chesterfield Courthouse, 103, 104, 109, 110, 180, 182; City Point (now Hopewell), 181; Cobham, 185; Cumberland Courthouse, 163; Gloucester, 115, 186; Jamestown, 113, 160; Lexington, 173; Louisa Courthouse, 183; Manakin Town, 39, 106, 160, 161, 183; Manchester (formerly Rocky Ridge), 95, 96, 180; New Kent Courthouse, 185; New London, 82, 177; Norfolk, 96, 181; Petersburg, 99, 103, 104, 105, 110, 113, 181; Portsmouth, 181, 185; Richmond, 39, 40, 84, 95-96, 105, 110, 118, 124, 128, 130, 160, 180; Scotchtown, 183; Staunton, 173; Suffolk, 185; Washington Courthouse, 173; Westham, 180; Williamsburg, 57, 67, 113, 119-20, 121, 163, 167, 173, 180; Winchester, 120, 124, 134, 173, 187, 188; Yorktown, 1, 6, 113, 185

Trabue, Anthony, Jr. (uncle), 41, 161

Trabue, Anthony, Sr. (grandfather), 37, 39, 41, 159, 160-61

Trabue, Anthony Edward (cousin), 161

Trabue, Chastain Haskins (nephew), 29

Trabue, Daniel (cousin), 67, 173

Trabue, Daniel, Jr. (son), 3, 4, 20, 26, 32, 33

Trabue, Daniel, Sr. (narrator): ancestry, 37-41; authorship of narrative, 1-3; Baptist associations, attendance at, 11, 15, 156; birth, 5, 37, 159; Boone's court-martial, presence at, 63-64; church membership, 10, 23; commissary in Kentucky, 49-50, 159; conversion, 130-33; death, 33; description, 199; dwelling house at Columbia, 19-22, 156; education, 41; enlistment in Clark's campaign, 44; entrepreneur, 27, 34; farmer, 16; founder of Columbia, Kentucky, 12-13; gristmiller, 6, 7-8, 13-14, 22-23, 26-27; "Hard Winter" of 1779-1780, activities during, 73-75; Harpe brothers, efforts to capture, 146, 149-50; horses, recovery of stolen, 54-55; horses, search for lost, 48-49; hunter in Kentucky, 47-48, 75-78; iron manufacturer, 22-23, 26-27; justice of the peace, 10, 12-13, 17, 28; Kentucky, first trip to (1778), 44-47; Kentucky, second trip to (1779), 68; Kentucky, third trip to (1780), 84-88; Kentucky, fourth trip to (1785), 6, 124-27; land warrants, entry for, 80; Logan's Fort, activities during siege of, 59-62; Louisville, visits to, 55-56, 79-80; marriage, 6, 124, 161; migration to Kentucky, 7, 134-36; militia service, 9, 10, 95-104, 106-8, 109-10, 137-44; murder of his son John, 10, 31, 147; retail storekeeper, 16-17; Revolutionary War pension, 28-33, 159; sale of mills, 17, 128; salt making expedition, 70-73; salt manufacturer, 17-19; settlement in Green County, 9-10; settlement in Woodford County, 7, 136; sheriff, 16, 28; surrender at Yorktown, view of, 117-18; sutler, 98-99, 103-4, 107-8, 110, 112-13, 114-15, 116, 119-20, 124; tavern keeper, 17; Tories, encounter with, 84-85; Virginia, first return to (1778), 65-68; Virginia, second return to (1780), 81-82; Virginia, third return to (1780), 5-6, 89; Virginia, fourth return to (1785), 127

Trabue, Edward (brother): marriage of, 161; migration to Kentucky, 8, 136; parentage of, 41; service of, in army, 81, 111-12; work of, as sutler, 112, 114, 116, 119-20, 185

Trabue, Elizabeth Haskins (Mrs. William) (sister-in-law), 9, 161

Trabue, Jacob (uncle), 41, 161, 173, 187

Trabue, James (brother). See Trabue, John James

Trabue, James (son), 3, 20, 26, 33, 199

Trabue, Jane Clay (Mrs. Edward) (sister-in-law), 161

Trabue, Jane E. Porter (Mrs. John James) (sister-in-law), 161

Trabue, Jane Haskins (Mrs. Stephen) (sister-in-law), 161

Trabue, John (brother), 41, 80, 81, 88-89, 129, 161, 174

Trabue, John (cousin), 118, 187

Trabue, John (son), 10, 31, 147, 196

Trabue, John James (brother), 75; cultivation of corn by, 48; entry of land warrants by, 80; Indian captivity of, 80-81, 89-94, 142, 159; marriage of, 161; parentage of, 41; return to Virginia of, 57, 70; service of, as commissary, 50, 54-55, 65, 68, 166, 176, 179; service of, in Dunmore's War, 42, 162; service of, in militia, 51-52; service of, under Clark, 44, 46-47, 164; trip to Kentucky by, 125-27

Trabue, John James (father), 5, 6, 43, 130, 159, 161, 163

Trabue, Lucy Waggener (Mrs. Robert) (daughter-in-law), 20, 189

Trabue, Macon (cousin), 161

Trabue, Magdelaine Flournoy (Mrs.

218 INDEX

Anthony, Sr.) (grandmother), 160
Trabue, Margaret Pearce (Mrs. John) (sister-in-law), 161
Trabue, Martha Haskins (Mrs. Edward) (sister-in-law), 161
Trabue, Mary Haskins (Mrs. Daniel, Sr.) (wife), 131; birth of, 188; church membership of, 23; conversion of, 133; death of, 22, 188; marriage of, 6, 124, 161
Trabue, Mary Jane Paxton (Mrs. Daniel, Jr.) (daughter-in-law), 20
Trabue, Nancy (niece), 9
Trabue, Olympia Dupuy (Mrs. John James) (mother), 55, 103, 130; conversion of, 129; marriage of, 41, 159; migration to Kentucky of, 8, 136; Negroes of, 81, 104; parentage of, 37; wartime conditions at home of, 105, 185
Trabue, Phoebe (sister), 41, 161
Trabue, Presley O. (son), 20, 22, 31
Trabue, Robert (son), 6, 16, 20, 33, 124, 189, 195, 199
Trabue, Robert Paxton (grandson), 3
Trabue, Samuel (brother), 6, 41, 161
Trabue, Stephen (brother), 105, 137; donation of church site by, 10; grandsons of, 29, 159; marriage of, 161; parentage of, 41; settlement in Kentucky of, 9; work of, as sutler, 104, 185
Trabue, Stephen FitzJames (grandnephew), 159
Trabue, William (brother), 105; attitude of, toward the war, 109; escape of, from the British, 82-84; parentage of, 41, 161; service of, in Continental Army, 43, 81, 163, 177; service of, in militia, 95-96, 109-10, 113, 116
Transylvania Company, 175, 197
treason, crime of high, 177-78
Treasury Department, U.S., 29, 33
Treaty: of Ghent, 27; of Greenville, 139-44, 192; of Paris (1783), 193
trees: ash, 8; beech, 8; buckeye, 8; cedar, 59; chestnut, 85; dogwood, 76; elm, slippery, 171; gum, sweet, 122; hickory, 42; hornbeam, 8; maple, sugar, 8; oak, 40; walnut, 8, 79
True, Thomas, 22
Tuckahoe, 72, 73, 175
Tucker, St. George, 184
Tully, John, 149
Twain, Mark, 21, 199

Valley: Powell, 44, 66, 125, 164; Stockton's, 149, 196, 197; of Virginia, 173; Yadkin, 173
Vardeman, Jeremiah, 66, 173
Vardeman, John, Jr., 66, 173
Vauban, Sébastien de, 186
Vermeil, Moyse, 161
Vest, Gabriel, 100-101, 105
Vincennes, Indiana, 50, 167
Virginia: Easter in, 47; economy of, 160; frontier of, 142, 162; salt from, 18; wartime conditions in, 43
Virginia Council, 160, 172
Virginia Land Commission, 176
Virginia Legislature, 67, 68, 70, 106, 162, 168, 173
Virginia revolutionary conventions, 162, 163

Wafford, Thomas, 128-29
Waggener, Elizabeth Carlile (Mrs. Herbert G., Jr.), 23
Waggener, Herbert Green, Jr., 23
Waggener, Herbert Green, Sr., 23
Walker, Mr., 51
Walker, James, Sr., 12
Walker Jeremiah, 161, 191
Walker Thomas, 164, 165
Waller, John, 128-29, 189
Ward, Mr., 85-88
War Department, U.S., 28, 29
War: Dunmore's, 42, 162, 169; French and Indian, 173, 194; Indian (1776-1777), 164
Washington, George, 43, 82, 85, 117, 118, 163, 186
Watkins, Benjamin, 131, 191
Watkins, John, 134-36
Watson, John, 64-65
Wayne, Anthony, 9, 105, 107, 139, 142, 182, 184, 185, 192-93
Weatherford, John, 161, 190-91
Webber, William, 128, 161, 189, 191
whiskey, 66, 107, 139-40
White, Ambrose, 69, 70, 174
White, John, 10, 11, 23
White, Robert, 195
Whitley, William, 9, 52, 167, 168
William III, 39, 160
Williams, Sherrod, 32
Wilson, Elizabeth Trabue (Mrs. Fenelon), 41, 161
Wilson, Fenelon, 161
Wilson, John S., 25
Wood, William, 149, 197
Woodford, William, 178
Wooldridge, Jessee, 22
Wooldridge, Josiah, 161
Wooldridge, Martha Trabue (Mrs. Josiah), 41, 161
Wooldridge, Robert, 102-3
Wooldridge, William, 97-98, 181
Worley, William, 17
writs: *ad quod damnum*, 8, *fieri facias*, 20, 21; *venditioni exponas*, 21